Reviews for Craving Part 2 Out Of Control

This is the second book I've read from this talented author Don Fullington, and I enjoyed it as much as, if not more than, the first. We get right into the action here, and there are plenty of crazy developments and shocking twists. I thought the whole storyline and character development to be very well done and thought out. I feel like this level of plot and characters complexity could have easily ended up badly, but instead it was handled with compassion and depth. Like the first book, the characters and the dialogue were really believable and authentic, and I appreciated the unexpected twists that really kept me hooked till the very last page. Recommend. (5 stars) Laura Clarke – Indie Book Reviewers

I enjoyed reading this continuation of the "Craving" books. It picks up right where the first leaves off, so they definitely need to be read in order (this is part 2). I like reading about characters with struggles and personal demons, and the decisions they make that impact their life… especially with what Noah goes through that was hard to watch. I found it to be emotionally gripping and held me captive throughout. This had more shocking twists and heightened tension. It was very well written set of books to get lost in. (5 stars) *Essie Harmon – Goodreads; Shelfari; Barnes & Noble; Indie Book Reviewers*

Solidly-paced, riveting and complex, "Craving-Out of Control" is exactly that…out of control. Characters in this one face crisis stage and it makes for some great literary drama that keeps you on pins and needles. A few tragic and unexpected turn of events keeps you reading late into the night with a compelling narrative tension that keeps it all moving forward smoothly. I like that it's not predictable or cliché at all. Recommended for fans of women's/lit fiction and drama. (4-5 stars) *Stacy Decker – Goodreads; Shelfari; Barnes & Noble; Indie Book Reviewers*

After finishing this 'duology' I almost feel like I've read 5 different books instead of just two (which really is just one long one split into two…) SO much happens, it would be impossible to sum up (I don't do that anyways). And based on just the description, I think I expected something different… I think I expected more of a romance, and while that element is definitely there, it takes a side seat to the bigger picture of the struggles of life and character transformations. I thought the conversations were great and really allowed me to connect with the characters. But I got my emotional payoff and think this was time well spent. Looking forward to reading more from Fullington in the future. (4 stars) *Jenna Brewster– Goodreads; Shelfari; Barnes & Noble; Indie Book Reviewers*

Oh wow, I loved this book (both of them actually) and read the whole thing in one night! Right from the beginning we are pulled right back into Noah and Nora's world as they leave Ireland and return to the States where drama awaits…. I love these characters that Don Fullington has created and the vivid way they come to life so that we really feel their struggles and fight their battles with them. From the "real events" and places and people that he uses to decorate the background of the story, everything just feels authentic and real. And I thought the way Mr. Fullington brought all the storylines together made for a very satisfying ending. Great read. Recommend. (5 stars). *Claire Middleton– Goodreads; Shelfari; Barnes & Noble; Indie Book Reviewers*

I really liked this book, and honestly the more time that passes, the more I think I like it… I finished these last week (this book and part 1, 'Uprising'), but it is really sticking with me for some reason, and I think I'll re-read it in the future. I read tons and tons of lit fiction, and this one stands out as having more "character" and "depth" than most I've read. It was totally unpredictable at several parts and not at all contrived. The writing is very good and natural sounding. I think this is a series definitely worth reading and I hope the author continues writing because he's very good! (4-5 stars). *Sam Ryan – Goodreads; Shelfari; Barnes & Noble; Indie Book Reviewers*

Don Fullington demonstrates a strong, and almost addicting narrative style and great attention to detail in "Craving: Out of Control" (part 2) that kept me eagerly turning the pages of my Kindle late into the evening, much more than the first, admittedly. The prose is powerful and vivid, and the characters really move the story forward in an entertaining and engaging manner, especially the supporting characters. I felt for Noah (and Nora) and there were several sad and surprising twists of fate… a really great story. Hope to see more from Mr. Fullington soon! (4 stars) *April Dawn – Goodreads; Shelfari; Barnes & Noble; Indie Book Reviewers*

These books were a great change of pace for me, as I normally gravitate towards more fantasy-style fiction, but this was one compelling tale that I couldn't put down! I did have to have some patience in the beginning until I felt that I was more caught up in the thrust of the story and all the pieces start falling into place. In that sense I thought that this was a stronger book than the first because we see more action and fallout from decisions. Happy that they were not cliché, cardboard cutouts of typical literature, but relatable and real. Easy to read and get lost in. Recommend. (4-5 stars). *Kaylee Stevens – Goodreads; Shelfari; Barnes & Noble; Indie Book Reviewers*

This book is meant to be read directly after the first as the events pick up from where the other leaves off. I must say that I liked that better about this one, that we are thrust right into the 'forward-action' now that all the backstory and plot set up is out of the way. This book seemed to have more deeper/darker twists that really pushed the characters to their limits (no spoilers). I read it as fast as I could, because I needed to see what would happen. The ending wraps up everything satisfactorily and all in all these were really good books. I'd like to read more from Don Fullington in the future. (4-5 stars) *Layla Messing– Goodreads; Shelfari; Barnes & Noble; Indie Book Reviewers*

CRAVING

a novel

Don Fullington

PART TWO—OUT OF CONTROL

Contentment Press*New York

Book template *Legend* by Joel Friedlander. Font designer Alexey Kryukov.

ISBN-13: 978-0692349700 (Contentment) ISBN-10: 0692349707

Library of Congress Control Number: 2014922251 Contentment Books, New York, New York

Contentment Books*New York
contentpubs@gmail.com

Printed in the United States of America

PART TWO rejoins Noah and Nora on

the turbulent flight from the solitude of

Ireland back into the frenetic spin of

New York society in the late 1960s.

The first and greatest victory is to conquer yourself.

The Laws of Plato

THREE

"ARE YOU TREMBLING?" Nora asked after they'd crossed the Atlantic and were cutting down over the Newfoundland seaboard. She had just awakened from a doze to find Noah gripping the seat arms as the pilot announced that passengers fasten their seatbelts.

"Oh its nothing. I just don't like turbulence."

"Ah it's only a bad patch of weather." But then she looked at him more closely. "Why you're perspiring like mad."

"It's alright," he said quickly wiping his forehead. It was true of the turbulence bothering him but this anxiety had brought on a wave of fear over their future that he'd kept well below the surface until now. As the aircraft proceeded down over the Maritime waters the weather from what the pilot now called a northeaster continued to worsen until the flight was finally diverted to a bumpy landing in Montreal. There they sat well into the night waiting for take-off clearance, as Noah continued to sweat and Nora tried to calm him.

When they finally arrived at JFK very early the next morning, over twelve hours later than expected, a taxi raced them to their apartment where Noah hastily showered and dressed for the office. After toast and coffee, he held and kissed Nora. "Sorry for the sloppy ending to our trip and even more so for the loss of last night's intended plans."

"Ah sure, we'll more than make up for those tonight."

"That's a promise. I love you so much." And off he went.

2

EXHAUSTED Noah arrived at Wilton and found Murphs anxiously waiting to whisk him away to a dingy coffee shop around the corner on University Place. "We have to talk," she said in a tone more urgent than he had ever heard her use.

"What's wrong?" he pleaded as a sickening wave already overtook him.

"I had to get you out of there before anyone arrived. So much has happened since you left. I didn't think you were coming back until next week, or I would have called you at home."

"Well that sounds pretty fatal."

"I don't know what it means. They seem to be making changes everywhere since Champion Communications took over. Most people feel Oliver's just using the opportunity to flex his power muscles in front of them. Anyway there's this girl, you know her. She used to be one of our southern stringers. Mae Dupree. Well no longer so. She's here now, and she's been doing society pieces as though she were you."

"Why? How did she get here?"

"I have no idea. I never expected *anything* like this. She came a few days after you left, and word went around that it would be amusing to have someone from the Deep South covering these scenes. A southern belle takes New York sort of thing."

"And?"

"Well it's terrible. Perfectly dreadful compared to your pieces. But it's so bad it's funny. With just a turn of phrase she's making everybody sound and look like they're part of the southern aristocracy. And then she's slipping in little faux pas. Slams and jeers, but staying just this side of character assassination. Why it's hilarious."

"How can that go down?" Noah snapped.

"I don't know except that her father's some big tycoon from Charleston who everybody's taken a cotton to. Pardon the humor."

"Montgomery Dupree? That's her father? My god. Shit. He's into everything. He couldn't be a bigger tycoon. Or more influential. No wonder she's here and can write whatever she wants."

"Noah, I'm afraid it gets worse."

"How could it?"

"It could. The day after you left, a gossip item appeared in the *Daily News* saying you were writing a novel based on your *New Yorker* short story."

"You are kidding. How did that happen?"

"And that you were gathering further material as you work on for *FCD*."

"What?"

"It went on to say that that's probably the only reason you continue to work here, since it's such a good source for you. A veritable society research depot."

"Holy god! But I've told no one."

"No one except—Jason Blackwell. They attributed it to him."

Noah gasped. "I'll kill him!"

BACK AT THE OFFICE amidst a wave of frenzy, Jack Warden rushed to his side. "Noah, it's great to have you back. How was your vacation?"

"I don't know. I don't even remember having one. Look Jack--"

"Well, it's just as well. Boy, are we under pressure. Jackie Kennedy is going to marry Onassis on Skorpios on October 20. We just got official word it's definite. And most likely Valentino's doing the dress. We want you to call everyone you know who's close to him. Gloria Guinness, Mrs. Wrightsman, Jacqueline de Ribes, Countess Crespi, Audrey Hepburn. They're all customers of his and they might know some of the details. We've got to get a sketch of that wedding dress as soon as possible. It's vital to Oliver and to the paper."

"Jack, back off. Don't you think I know this shit?" Noah snapped loudly startling the city editor. "What I want to know is what the hell has been going on here while I've been away?"

"Oh that's right," Jack said. "I want you to meet our new addition—Mae Dupree." And he motioned her over before Noah could stop him.

"Noah," gushed Mae as she rose from her already established nearby desk wearing a long-sleeved black cashmere a-la-*Bonnie-and-Clyde* sweater and a pink and black magnolia-strewn midi skirt. Engulfing her head including all her hair was a black felt hat with a wide down-turned encircling brim. A harbinger albeit ridiculous if there ever was one, Noah thought. Although short, she swept over in true beautiful people fashion, clutched his hand, gazed up at him and drawled: "I'm so happy you're back at last. Why I've been dying to work with you. You're my journalistic hero, you know."

"Oh really, you don't say?"

"Yes," she went on as she continued to squeeze his hand. "I think you're just matchless. Why they've been having me do these things while you were away. Things that only you could do. Why I was petrified, I tell you."

"Yes, I'm sure you were," Noah replied through a frozen smile as he dropped her hand. "Petrified that is. But I wouldn't fret too much about that if I were you. I'm sure you won't remain permanently calcified with such a sweet disposition."

"Noah!" Jack Warden snarled. But when Noah merely walked away, he turned to Mae. "Don't let him upset you, Mae. He's just in recovery from his vacation." Then he took after Noah. "Noah!" he called out over the newsroom clamour. "I want to talk to you."

Noah spun around and bellowed the newsroom into silence. "No Jack, I want to talk to you."

Jack looking shocked and suddenly meek said in a low tone: "Let's go into the conference room."

Once inside, Noah exploded: "What is this Jack? I go on vacation and come back to find someone else has taken my job?"

"Calm down. Just calm down. She hasn't taken your job. It's just that you know how Oliver is about change. It keeps things interesting. Lively. Fresh."

"Well she's *fresh* all right."

"Listen I have something to tell you. You cannot go around here pitching this haughty arrogance, ready to tell everyone to huff off. You know they've iced your column for the time being. So you won't be picking up on that right away."

"But what about all the ad revenue that the column was drawing?"

"Oh they haven't stopped the column. It's just that your name won't be on it anymore." Then he seemed delighted adding: "Oliver wants it called *FCD Spies*."

"So what you're telling me is that Mae and I are equals now?" he asked as he felt the blood drain from his face.

"That's the word that came down yesterday. They didn't offer a reason, although I could venture a guess after that item in the *Daily News*. But we haven't got time for this now with all this Kennedy-Onassis business."

As they walked out of the conference room in silence, Murphs motioned to Noah that he had a phone call. "Some furniture place. They called a few times while you were away and I picked up."

"Great," Noah replied sarcastically as he went toward his phone but then paused to ask Murphs: "Any calls from Doubleday in regard to what I told you before I left?"

"No and I was very careful to catch most of your calls." He shook his head and sighed as he picked up on his waiting call. "Yes, of course. I've been away, but I'll get you a payment sent out right off," he replied as he started to hyperventilate.

"Well it would be more than one payment we'd be needing," the voice answered back. "Actually it's four including this month's."

"No trouble. It's taken care of." And he was left with the sickeningly shabby feeling that he would have to stage larger robberies through his expense account. But that wouldn't be easy if he didn't have a column. "Oh what a great new beginning."

"I'M AFRAID THE ANSWER is still a no," the Wilton VP told Noah when he went to see him that afternoon. Noah, struck by the heat from the overly warm office and the panic within, instantly became aware of yet another of his body's sweat outbreaks.

"Well I don't know how you can say that," he snapped as he sat forward in his chair and tugged at his tie. "The last time we spoke of this, you told me that as soon as the Champ Com. merger took place you were certain I could just about name my own price."

He smiled and shook his head. "I'm just afraid you'll have to let the dust settle a little first."

"The dust settle a little—It's been several months since Champ Com. took over and grew stronger at the helm."

"Regardless, it's the policy of the moment to hold the raises."

"For some but not for others, I know for fact. And I'm the some. Why is that? I think I have a right to know. I do all this good work, and now I'm getting screwed because of it." The more Noah talked the more he raged. "I need money, too. The company's literally fucking me up."

"Really? It is? I'd look in the mirror if I were you," he replied looking askance. "Or maybe in the *Daily News*."

"That's rubbish. It's all a lie. There's no such book. Well I don't have to stand for this sort of behavior. It's pure shit the way I'm being treated. I'm going to Oliver Wilton. And if I don't get satisfaction there, I'll go to the Champ Com. people. To the top. I'll go to Stan Archer, that's what I'll do. That way I'll get my money and my column back. I mean I'm good. I know I am. I won't be passed over. They can't dispense with me."

"Oh?" he cocked his head and looked at Noah as he smoothed one of the lapels of his bespoke Paul Stuart suit. "There's that old cliché looming again. They don't know what they'd ever do without you. *But*—if they have to they'll think of something." Then pausing he looked into his eyes. "I wonder if they haven't started thinking already?"

HE COULD NOT have imagined a more destructive day, he told himself during his walk home that late afternoon. As he passed by the massive dark wooden doors of Luchows, the 19th century German gothic dinning and drinking emporium, he began to salivate over the vision of an icy Beefeater martini, and this after not having a drink in seemingly ages—not even in Ireland. As if magnetized back toward those doors, he had to fight to keep himself on his homeward path. But keep on, there would be peace at its end, peace in Nora's arms.

Hardly so. When he arrived at his doorstep, he found himself in the midst of a major commotion generated by a group of moving men hauling in furniture, including a baby grand piano, and hefting it up the stairs to the second floor. It seemed that while they were away the old tenants had moved out and the new ones had arrived.

"I'd guess it's almost finished," Nora shouted over the explosion of noise after he'd finally fought his way through the traffic and into their apartment. Then after he'd hugged and kissed her, he let his hands roam passionately over the silkiness of her dress. "Here I kept thinking once I got home we'd get it on and hop into the sack."

"I'd say with a fair amount of certainty if you were in that frame of mind nothing would be after stopping you."

"With all that racket, it would be like doing it in the middle of a construction pit." At that point, he glanced over at the dining table and let his arms slip from her. "What's that over there?"

"Oh I had to go up to the post office to collect it. It came while we were away," she replied uneasily. As he frowned and started for it, she grabbed hold of his arm. "Don't you let it be upsetting you now. Just keep in mind it could be the blessing in disguise."

They both knew it was a package containing the manuscript from William Morris. After Noah ripped it open, he barely glanced at the attached Jason letter of October 10, 1968. *This is not what the people at Random House had in mind when they suggested changes* etc. etc. etc. *I think they were thinking of something far more Updike-ian with young sexually adventurous suburbanites like in his Couples. Now that's a book. And you have to get with the speed of these times. Anyway, I'm far too close to have anything more to do with this project—as are you I feel* etc. etc. etc. *Siphon all your energy into the society project* blah blah blah. With that he pitched the whole mess into his desk basket and rubbed his hands up and down as a *fait accompli* gesture. "Updike-ian?!!"

"You haven't heard from Doubleday yet. I know you would have told me."

"Right."

"Well I think they're going to come through for you. Sure they have the best version. The great one."

"I think you're right. I really do. But why haven't I heard from them?"

"Ah you're forgetting we've been away for a long time. They might not even know we're back. But I did think you'd have rung them up today."

"Oh you don't know how horrible it was—the first day back."

"Well I'd chance it to call tomorrow. In the meantime it sounds as if all that roilin' noise is over. So--"

"Yeah," he grinned, lifted her in his arms and carried her to the bedroom. There he slipped the silky dress up over her head and found her fully naked.

"See I've only been mad with the longing for you all day."

When they were at the height of euphoric intensity and about to lose all control, another explosion of noise boomed down on them from above--this from the pummelling of piano keys failing miserably to release the score of *The Sound of Music*. "Oh this is great," Noah exclaimed with fury after all their passion was reduced to stunted orgasms. "Well now calm down," Nora anxiously insisted. "They can't get away with this. It is their first day. But I'll take care of it if it keeps up."

To escape the on-going assortment of noises they went down to the kitchen to have their dinner of shepherd's pie Nora had prepared from the ground lamb she had shopped for that morning at their west village butcher shop *Walter's*. It seemed to be a perfect calming agent. By the time they'd finished the racket above had ceased and since both were so jaded from loss of the previous night's sleep and Noah's added horrible office day that they took advantage of trying for a good night's sleep. Yet for Noah this lasted only a few short hours. Then he awakened from troubled dreams that soon combined with his disturbing true realities to augur great ill. He hadn't taken any Valium since days before they went to Ireland. But now he needed it. So he crept over in the gray darkness while Nora slept and quickly extracted the vile from the back bottom of his top dresser drawer. Then he went into the bathroom, took one, looked in the mirror saw the rising panic in his eyes and quickly took another.

3

THE NEXT MORNING when he appeared so removed and scarcely ate any breakfast she asked: "Didn't you sleep?"

"Not really," he sighed as he sat his nearly full cup of coffee back down on the table and stared out the kitchen window all the time suppressing his anger over succumbing to the pills.

Nora got up and came around to massage his shoulders. "I wish you didn't have to go. Just stay here and I could take care of you."

"I wish that were possible."

"Well do call that woman today. That could bring you great relief."

"Let's hope." He smiled a little as he got up, kissed her and prepared to leave. "Say a prayer."

"Ah Noah, you have to remember that line from Philippians we used to write back and forth to one another-- *I can do all things in him who strengthens me.*"

"*Omnia possum in eo qui me confortat,*" Noah replied. "I still remember."

After he was gone, she dressed and went off to Mass at Epiphany. There following the Eucharist she prayed silently for their dreams and their togetherness but especially for Noah's book. Then as if to enforce those thoughts, kneeling she whispered: "*SanctaMaria, spes nostra, sedes sapientiae, ora pro nobis. Sancta Maria, stella maris, filios tuos adiuva.*" But when she stood, she found she was shivering from the vision of Noah's distant look at the breakfast table and the thought that her prayers might be answered in the negative. Finally she uttered over and over again: "*Credo, sed adiuva incredulitatem meam.* I do believe; help my unbelief."

Later that morning she sat at her easel but instead of working she stared out at the cold autumn rain that started falling in sheets across the park. She began to wonder as she had from time to time in the past that if along with all his writing worries she could be doing something wrong. When she couldn't rid herself of the thought she wandered through the apartment to the storage closet in the bedroom. Almost unconsciously she pulled out one of the rolled up canvases that still remained from those she'd sent over from Dublin in what now seemed so long ago. It was an oil, one she had done of a jolly family gathering at Christmas. The family was in the background viewed through the sitting room window from the vantage of the lonely child in the frosty garden foreground. When was it she wondered that they had drawn a full circle around themselves leaving her on the outside as if she were no more than an ugly duckling. What was it they so disliked about her? And she began to weep as she realized now that it wasn't by accident she had gone to the closet and rediscovered this picture.

After that she tried to work but found it hopeless. To keep occupied she tidied up her working area and then went on to do the rest of the apartment. At one point as she pulled together clothes for the cleaners, she came across a late notice bill in one of Noah's suit coat pockets. It was for almost two thousand dollars, the remainder he still owed on the American antiques. She had never known their cost, but if he still owed this much it must have been a fortune. She looked at the bill again and realized that this was not the first late notice. Once she would have been only *ragin'* over his prodigality. He was having problems paying for much of the lot of it, and it would serve him right. But now she realized that this quite likely, along with his writing, was part of his problem. He was suffering with no way out. So what if she took some of the money she had saved and simply paid the bulk of it? She'd still have enough left for the house, and if she worked harder she could quickly recoup the loss. If I do this for him, he'll care for me all the more.

AS SOON AS NOAH arrived at the office that morning, he so wished he had found an excuse to stay home and as Nora suggested let her take care of him. Instantly Jack Warren went on the attack. "Oliver Wilton called from his Tuscan estate very early and went into a total fury because we have absolutely no news on Jackie's wedding dress. And I'm considering you to be responsible for this mess. You know we've only got so many days left. AND we'd better not be scooped by somebody else."

"Don't you dare have the consummate gall to talk to me in such a manner. Not that I have to explain anything to you, you schmuck."

"What did you call me?"

"Just what you think," Noah roared right back. "Now you listen to me. Yesterday was my first day back and I already have a good dozen of my spies in Italy and France eagerly working on this from every angle. And that's not to mention another whole array of spies here in New York. Furthermore I want to tell you something. I will not under any circumstance allow you to turn me into some sort of slave cowering at your every command just because my name has been removed from that column."

When Jack realized that everyone in the newsroom was rendered speechless, most likely with delight, he whispered: "We'll see what Oliver has to say about that," and quickly disappeared like the paper tiger he was.

"Don't worry, we'll get it together and you'll get the kudos. You know Mae is hopeless at these things," Murphs went on. "My source says Valentino is definitely the designer. But that's no news. Jackie's endeared to everything he does. But somehow he got the word from Valentino's closet consort Giammetti that it won't be a classic wedding dress."

"That's what I've heard too from the likes of Jayne Wrightsman," Carole Dawson called to tell Noah. She was already working the story even though he hadn't asked her. "I hear it's a pale lace bodice that sort of floats over a white pleated short skirt. It would be perfect for Skorpios I should think and most likely right in step with his hot new *Collezione Bianca* collection. But of course this could all be based on rumor. So you keep checking around as will I."

He'd no more than finished the call thinking he was on the right track than another call came. "Noah we're just wondering if you were able to follow up on your promise of yesterday." It was a woman from the furniture store letting no grass grow. "Oh yes, it's already taken care of," he snapped the lie and immediately hung up. What the hell am I going to do, I can't come up with all that? But then he remembered what Carole said about checking around. This would be the perfect opportunity to call some of his BP acquaintances, the ones who in the past used to readily propose having lunch. Naturally he would accept giving him the much needed reiteration of his expense account scam. But after a half-dozen tries all he came up with was a little more information on the wedding dress but no luncheon offers. That was certainly the result of his column being iced. Now he wouldn't dare chance pushing through totally false expenses.

As his anxiety heightened he began to bemoan that he hadn't pocketed a Valium before he left home. "Well all I can tell you is that she has read the book," Marie McCloud's secretary told him when he called Doubleday that afternoon. "She's at an out-of-town conference right now and then she's going on a vacation for three weeks."

"Well did she give you any indication of what she thought of it?"

"No. Not at all."

"So that may mean she was disappointed."

"Well I really can't say. But I'm certain she'll call you when she gets back."

THERE WERE THOSE ENORMOUS DARK WOOD DOORS--the ones he had escaped yesterday. Today he went on through them noting the stained glass windows then the huge rare antique framed olden mirrors. And there were the chandeliers under which Gibson girls and Diamond Jims once walked. Yes now he was in Luchow's alone at the end of another traumatic day. He rarely came here even though it was near the office. But yet here he was, standing at the smoky bar. And he'd already ordered himself a Beefeater martini. He felt a little quiver of fear and was really so morbid about his state of affairs that he figured this might help. He was right he told himself. Now with the first icy sip, the fear began to subside. He sighed. Oh that first martini, he almost said aloud. "Dry enough for you, sir?" the bartender asked. "Oh, it's dry enough. Start making me another, if you would."

"I THOUGHT YOU MIGHT be working late so I already ate. But are you sure you won't eat at least something?" she asked after they'd hugged and kissed. "I was even able to keep the steak rare for you." She could smell the bit of gin on him and after so long it saddened her.

"Nah," he said smiling and stroking her face. "I think I'll wait awhile."

"Did you call your woman today?"

"Yeah and she'd read the book but I didn't find anything out. She's away for three weeks."

"Well so it's not bad. It's not a no."

"I don't know. It's a screwy industry."

"You have to stay hopeful though. And keep on praying."

"Yeah."

"Well anyway I'll leave the range on warming. But I've got to get back to work." And she put on her smock and went to her palette. As she started mixing more paints, she glanced over at Noah staring at the TV, at Cronkite detailing the Nixon-Humphrey campaign. But she knew he wasn't seeing it. He was in another world inwardly conversing with himself. She knew that look. It made her spirit plunge. It also translated to her brushstrokes where faces once prelim-ed as serene, joyous or occupied with intent now became lined with despair or tightened with bitterness and worse swollen with rage. When this had happened before, the gallery directors had been pleased that the darker aspects were appearing more frequently adding even greater diversity to her work. But god she thought this was certainly not the way she wished to achieve it.

4

DURING THE NIGHTS OF THE NEXT TWO WEEKS while Nora worked home alone struggling to curb her loneliness, Noah was swept into a swirl of major opening nights and glittering benefits. But because of his creeping disillusionment, those nights brought no gratification. He just passed through them unfazed, even though he was subjected to far fewer snubbings. Now that his column had been iced he figured he was less of an immediate threat. At home his lovemaking suffered. There was no ardor, no humor, no devilish glints. It just happened and was over, leaving Nora to wonder if it had ever happened.

"The pictures came," she enthused one of those nights.

"What?" he asked vaguely as he shrugged off his trench coat and tossed it onto the coat tree.

"The pictures of the ground breaking," she continued to bubble trying to spark his spirit as they had sparked hers. "They came in the post today. Hughie took them. Look, isn't it grand?" she said handing them to him. "The beginning of our house."

"You mean *your* house." And her secret account loomed in his mind once more.

"No, I don't." She was stunned.

"Well, it's your money that's buying it."

"It's *our* house."

"What good is it going to be anyway? What am I going to do, move over there and go on the dole forevermore? Or better still, you could open a shop to sell your paintings and I—I could sell old manuscripts as quaint fireplace lighters."

"You should be so happy today over these snapshots. And all you can do is give out with that bleedin' nagging pessimism of yours. Just look at you. *I can't do this. I can't do that. What am I going to do?* Just do it and keep doing it. Feckin' well enjoy life until the tide turns. And another thing, you'd be way the better off if you were to take this wasted time and put it to your society novel. God you've got so much. "

"Yeah. All the stuff I can't even pay for."

"What do you mean? The furniture? Is that what's worrying you?"

"The furniture. Everything. You were right. I had no business doing all this. No talent. No business. It's going to come down on me like a load of crap. I could even lose my job over it. I bought it under the mantle of Wilton Press. Now I'll just have to try to sell it or beg a bank loan." He couldn't possibly tell her it would be the second bank loan.

"Noah, I have something to show you. I think it should make things better. Just wait here for a second." She smiled and went into the bedroom. When she returned, she presented him with the statement from the furniture shop.

"How did you get this?"

"I found it in one of your suit pockets when I was sending it off to the cleaners."

"And what's this?" he said inspecting it. "*Paid in full.* Is this some kind of joke?"

"No, it's not. I paid for it. I know how much it means to you. And I couldn't bear to see you going through this. I love you so much."

"Love?" he asked as he inspected the invoice while reality set in. "I know you meant well by it. But Jesus it hurts so much."

"What does?"

"I can't believe it. I just can't believe it," he went on as he paced about the room. Then as he dropped the bill on the dining table, tears flooded his eyes.

"Oh Noah don't."

But he kept on as if he were haunted. "I feel—ripped

apart. You're so good, I know—and I love you so much. But even though you didn't mean it, I feel betrayed. I needed to do this so badly for you. I just don't know how to stop these feelings." Then when he could contain himself no longer, he went to the door, flung it open and was gone in a flash, while her cries of *don't go* went in vain.

Out into the cold rainy night he moved coatless. Around the slippery slate sidewalk borders of the park, he continued with his only awareness being the skeletal tree branches whipped by the wind. Then without stopping or looking he crossed the street to the blare of horns and screeching brakes. Even though one car actually skidded and slammed his hip, he advanced unawares, drawn as if by another magnetic force into the Gramercy Park and to his once usual seat at its bar.

Nora was stunned from the shock. Instead of bringing them closer together, her action had achieved the opposite. How could he be so ungrateful? But in her heart she knew better. It had nothing to do with ungratefulness. No, it was something far graver that he was driven to escape. And once again she was left to face the image of the child out in the icy front garden at Christmas.

5

IT WAS EIGHT O'CLOCK ON THE MID-NOVEMBER NIGHT of her next showing at the Winsor de Caine. Already people were arriving when Nora noticed that one of her landscapes was hanging askew. It was the fault of the wall bracket she decided. Another was required to correct the imbalance. Much to the chagrin of the gallery's directors, she removed the painting, produced a bracket and proceeded to hammer it into the wall. "Go way out of that," she told the shocked men. "You couldn't bloody well leave it in that condition. It isn't right sure it's not. It has to be fixed." So fix it she did.

Noah, who had just arrived, stood a distance away watching her and fighting off a powerful force of tears. When she saw him she rushed over, horrified he was fluthered, and whispered: "Don't tell me you'll be after covering the showing and in this state."

"What state?" he asked, and she realized he was sober. "I'd be better off drunk than the way I am," he continued coldly paraphrasing her nanny. "But don't worry Nora, I'm not here to cover your opening. I'm not good enough for that anymore. Instead they're sending Mae Dupree along with a host of photographers. I'm sure as such you'll be much better attended."

"Why are you doing this? What's wrong?" she asked still in a whisper.

Once again he looked over at the painting she had re-hung and then turned back. "There's nothing you can't do, is there?"

She looked at him and wanted to say—*well I'm not doing such a grand job bringing us together, am I now?* But she resisted because she wanted to avoid one of their domestic scenes. Then they were separated as she was absorbed by the arriving enthusiasts. After that Noah slipped away into the nearest bar.

6

PERHAPS IT WAS THE HAND OF GOD or that of a pitying saint the likes of John the Evangelist or Francis de Sales that reached down to dispel the desperation of the situation a few days later.

"Marie McCloud is on the phone for you," Murphs interrupted Noah in the art department. "She said she's from Doubleday, and she'd like to talk to you right away. Do you want me to tell her you'll call back?"

"No. No. No." Noah went on gasping. Then he grabbed Murphs by the hand as he hurried back to his desk. "Pray. Pray. Pray as you've never prayed before."

"But I'm not very religious."

"It doesn't matter. Pray. It's the book."

"Oh my god," she gasped.

"Hello Marie," he began as cheerily as possible.

"Noah, *Pictures In The Rain* is a beautiful book. I'm sorry I took so long to get back to you. But I'm back. And we want this book on our list for next fall."

"You do? Ah—you do!" Startling was the word of the moment.

"Absolutely. So we want to get going on this right away. But is Jason Blackwell going to be your agent?"

"Well I don't want him to be. Especially after what he did to me in the *Daily News*. I don't know if you heard about that."

"I did. My secretary cut that item out and had it waiting for me when I returned. He certainly didn't behave appropriately. I can just imagine the damage. But let me tell you, we do have an agent we sometimes use in this kind of situation. I don't think he's the guy for you on a permanent basis. But I'll tell you this. He'll fight for the money when he knows we're interested."

"Well how much do you think an advance might be?" he dared pursue.

"I'll level with you. I don't usually speculate with writers about their advances because we have to negotiate with the agent. But this is a very special book. I think it has strong growth potential for years to come. So I'm going to tell you if you promise never ever to reveal this to a soul."

"Oh I can guarantee that. I don't want anyone to know."

"Okay. The average is around eight for a first timer. But I'd think you'd at least get ten. And I wouldn't be surprised if he didn't push higher. Maybe fifteen."

"Thousand?" he said and held his breath.

"Well yes."

With that he crossed himself as he looked over at Murphs, then made a big fist and punching skyward mouthed the word—YES.

"Oh my god, they're going to buy it," Murphs cheered after he'd hung up.

"Yeah!" And she went to hug him.

"Shh, shh, shh. I don't want anyone here to know," he said noticing that Mae was already craning her hatted head their way to see what the fuss was about. "I don't want any more problems here," he whispered. "I still need this job."

"Maybe not much longer," she cocked her head and ruefully whispered back.

"AH NORA, you have to go. Just this once. I've something to tell you."

"Oh Noah, what am I going to wear? Why couldn't you just tell me over the phone?"

"It's too good to do that. Just wear the sapphire dress with the lapis lazuli necklace I gave you. I have to work right up till it's time to go. I brought my tux in this morning so I'll dress for it here and we'll meet in front of the museum at 7:30."

"Oh Noah."

"YOU LOOK RAVISHING in chiffon," Noah delighted when she stepped from the taxi and he kissed her neck.

"Yeah, well I feel like a klutz as they'd say in this country. I got ready in such a hurry."

"Don't be absurd. You'll be a star. Just like you are at your showings. Besides you'll meet Tom Hoving again. He was thrilled with your work at the Winsor and now that he's the director here, he'll be reminded again. He could be very helpful."

Nora shook her head at the thoughts of his opportunism and took his arm as he swept her up the grand carpeted steps of the Metropolitan and into the great hall where the glittering beau monde mingled with their cocktails at the outset of a medieval evening thrown by the Joseph Lauders and Thomas Hoving for the railroad heiress Mrs. Frank J. Gould. It was impossible not to recognize the heiress in her white Givenchy wearing so many jewels it looked as if she'd dropped by Harry Winston's and left the store bereft--a bit dangerously outré in these times when the thoughts of everyone of this ilk was still trusted to be aimed toward charity.

While musicians wandered with their flutes, lutes and dulcimers playing the medieval music of courtly love, Noah retrieved two glasses of champagne from a roving barman. "I'd better tell you this news before I don't have the chance," he said as he noticed people from the art world waving to Nora.

"A toast is in order." As they clinked glasses, Nora thought he's really bubbling tonight but not from alcohol. God what a relief. Then he leaned over and whispered in her ear. "We sold the book today." When he pulled back to face her, she had gone stunned from the shock of his words. "What? Oh my god. I want to jump up and down, but I can't. Why did you want to come here to tell me this?"

"Well I only just found out. And I wanted it to be special. Since I had to cover this. It seemed perfect."

She felt a few tears come as she stroked his face. "God I'm so happy."

With that he suddenly went firm of voice. "I'm going to take a chunk of that money and *I'm* going to buy that house. Now you'd better blink away those tears, because if memory serves me that tall dark-haired gentleman striding this way is none other than Tom Hoving.

"Nora Mason," he enthused as he hugged her and kissed her on the cheek. "I so hoped you would come along with your husband when we sent our invitations to Wilton." Then turning to Noah and giving him a powerful handshake, he continued exuberantly: "What a fortunate man to have such a virtuoso as a wife. I was wiped out by the incredible range she achieves. So even on such a festive night, it brings me to the point of being utterly fearless about conducting some business. If I might I'd like to send a couple of our curators over to the Winsor to see if we share the same feelings. Then we'll select and bring a bunch of it to the Met. I'm very determined about this, you know. So of course I'll get my way." Noah couldn't help but feel a slight tinge of jealousy over this man who was only the same age as he and yet through tenacity had turned the Met into one of the city's most powerful institutions.

"Bring a *bunch* of it to the Met? I can't believe he's so down-to-earth," Nora said when he was gone.

"The same frisky man that they say once got thrown out of Phillips Exeter for punching his Latin teacher. See how important this evening suddenly became for you? And now it seems there's even more glory headed your way. I think that crowd of your followers is about to take you captive.

And they seemed to gather about like a fan club Noah thought as he made his way to his photographer feeling a brief dip in the exultation he'd had upon their arrival. While they discussed photo plans for the evening, Noah looked over in shock to see Gloria Hamilton Collins approaching from the distance in a clinging plunging white crepe de Chine gown. "How did that snake get in here? Don't do any shots. Try to ignore her." But still she slithered over.

"Noah Mason. My dashing almost paramour. Where have you been all this time?" And she clutched him and whispered: "Maybe we could pick up where we left off. I'm more voracious than ever, you know."

"No doubt," Noah snarled pulling away. "But I think you wore the wrong color dress with all your *nostalgie de la boue.*"

She looked at him as her dark eyes fired darts of ice. "I see cruelty has now become a part of your repertoire. Are you cruel to your lovely wife as well?"

"Perhaps you'd best slither on back to whoever is your victim for tonight."

Smirking she replied. "Cold or not. I'm not finished with you yet." And she did slither away.

"What was all that about?" the photographer asked

aghast.

"She's a delusional freak. That's not blue blood running through her veins. It's blue vitriol."

"What did you say to her in French? She looked as if she was going to kill you."

"I said she has a passion for mud. Pure depravity." Thank god Nora by now was completely surrounded by her art devotees. As such they formed a sort of moat that he hoped would keep Gloria far away. It was at this point that he spied Carole resplendent in her black Empire waist gown, the latest from Dior with two modest yet most impressive diamond barrettes clipped in her long black hair.

"Noah, I haven't seen you in months," she called as she hurried over to him with a glass of champagne in hand.

"Carole, you look marvelous." And they hugged and kissed. "Oh, I have the most wonderful news. I can't believe it. I sold my book today."

"Oh Noah, I'm thrilled." And she clutched him again. "But to whom?"

"To Doubleday. It won't be published until next fall. It takes forever in publishing. But you mustn't say a word. I don't want it to get back to Wilton and Oliver."

"Of course not and obviously I can see why. Certainly not with that Mae Dupree sashaying all over your territory. And your column gone yet. I called and left messages but you never replied. "

"Oh I kept hoping I was on the cusp of something before I

called you. But until today it kept shifting away as if it were an illusion."

"You should have called though. You know how important that is to me."

"I know. I'm sorry. Truly I am." Then he glanced across the hall. "Look at her over there. Isn't she only gorgeous." And he sighed.

"Of course she is. You would never love anyone else would you?"

"Never. Never have. Never will."

"I imagine she's helped you greatly through the rough spells."

"Of course she has. But it hasn't been easy."

"I think when I look at you now I can still sense the rumblings."

"Well they should go with the news of the book."

"*Will they?*--- I'm fearful for you Noah. I've been thinking about you so often of late and with your brilliance I wonder if you're not wrong to continue all of this."

"Wrong? But why would you say that, Carole? You know I've weathered it."

"Noah, look at me. I don't want to bring spoils to your greatest of evenings, but by now I think you must have collected enough of a social trove of material. Then especially with this great news of your book, I wonder if it's not time to reconsider things. I really should say this to you. You're perfect for all of this," she went on and gestured around the hall. "But the more I watch you and consider it all, you're really an incongruity. Perfect for the location but completely wrong for the people."

He frowned. "Nora would salute you for that."

Well she would be right. And I'm going to keep working on this. It's not easy to slip someone into a top post with a society writing background. But I'm going to be meeting with some of my *Time* magazine friends next week. And I'm going to bring out the big guns this time. Because I can you know."

"Do I really look that bad?"

"No. But some things you can't leave behind, if they keep happening to you. And I'm not just talking about a few things. It's the sum that can do it." At that point she glanced over at Gloria Hamilton Collins as if to punctuate. "Noah---don't let them steal your soul."

GOD SHE WAS SPOT ON about everything, except for the puzzlement over her last remark about leaving things behind, Noah told himself as he drifted off to sleep that night with Nora in his arms. But he had strength again, he would move on with or without Carole's influence. He needed no one now, he told himself. And that night he slept as deeply as he had in Donegal.

Yet how strange it would be that the events of the next day would turn yesterday slightly askew.

7

"COME IN TO ME NOAH. *Ah* hear there's a bit of a disturbance out in our newsroom centered around your sadness over your plight here," said Oliver when he called Noah into his office the next morning.

"Well sir I haven't been exactly happy of late."

"*Ah* told you not to call me sir. You *ah* too important here to be calling me such. We have to have a heart to heart." And Noah went over sat on the leather sofa across from Oliver's magnificent George IV writing table patterned after one in Windsor Castle, so rumored by top brass. "Now what is all this about?"

"Well Oliver I'll level with you. I can't understand why my column has been taken away and why Mae is seemingly taking over for me or at least much of my work. I was surprised you didn't give the Met assignment to her."

"*Ah* iced that column because *ah* wanted to scare some sense into you. To make you stop and think. *Ah* wanted to be sure that you weren't going to be spending all your time going down other avenues and giving *ahwa* paper short shrift. Stan Archer felt you could be slipping away from us as well."

"Oliver that story simply isn't true. It's just wishful thinking on Jason Blackwell's part."

"Nevertheless the temptation. But *ah* think by now we've had enough time to think. And *aham* about to reveal my plans. *Ah* want you to realize just how *impahtant* you are about to become here. *Ah* would like you to be what *ah* consider a major part of the foundation of Wilton. Now *ah* thought we would start by returning your column. But this time *ah* thought we might be a little more aggressive. We'll call it *Inside Out--As Noah Sees It*. That ought to rattle the timbers of *ahwa* readers for a time. *Ahh* want to stir the pot with them. After all *ah* know they've abused you in their own nasty little ways. So we're going to gang up on them. Fur flying and all."

Noah chuckled and shook his head. "Well that's all very amusing Oliver. The devil certainly won't be dead while you're alive."

"That's what makes a paper. Or *ahwa* paper *ah* should say."

"What I want to ask is if the rules of the game start to change again you let me know in advance. And I would like to know what role Mae Dupree will be playing in all this? And is her tycoon father to have any influence?"

"Absolutely not! Why Mae Dupree is only a mere diversion here. Albeit a very humorous one. She'll stay on, but she'll have nothing to do with your column. She'll be in charge of more frivolous things like listening in on whispered conversations in what they used to call ladies powder rooms. We'll toss a lot of it into our *Zoom In* column names and all. It'll make your *New Yorker* short story seem like tepid tea."

"Oh Oliver." And he laughed again. "You *are* the devil incarnate."

"Well I haven't grown a tail yet. But if *ah* do *ah* hope that part of me stays in the attic."

Noah roared laughing. "I doubt if it will. But all humor

aside. There's one other thing."

"Yes. If we keep going in the right direction, *ah* see you as a bedrock here."

"Well your top brass doesn't seem to think so. They told me I was all but finished."

"Top brass-. That's all they are. Brass! And the brass is getting more *tahnished* by the moment. Greener by the day as it were. As Stan Archer and Champ Com. see it and *ah* as well, of course, you are gold standard here."

"Well how could I ever know that Oliver when you're making me do things like covering my wife's art showing. I'll never get over that."

"Oh that was only a ruse, Noah. Though *ah* do admit *ah* was wrong about that even though *ah* was furious at the time. But *ah* do say *aham* sorry now."

"Well beyond that, I can't even get a raise."

"Oh that's to stop here and now. To show *ah* mean business *ah* would figure *pahaps* a one fifty a week increase. We can do it now with Champ Com."

"Yeah," Noah tossed his head to the side figuring he may as well go along with the game.

"Oh all right. Two hundred. How would that suit you?"

"Well I guess—fine."

"And there's more. *Ah* along with Stan Archer have decided we'd like to start up a new consumer publication probably called *The Connoisseur's Life*. We would have liked to use just the letter *C* but that might have brought up some rather vulgar connotations." And he laughed gutturally.

"I'd say it might."

"Anyway we would like to have you on board for all your invaluable insights. And *ah* would say you would only be brilliant. *Ah* would further say there's a hint of vice-presidency in all of this. You see *ah'll* be putting all my support and resources behind *Connoisseur,* and *FCD* of course, from now on. Stan and *ah* feel that my efforts would better be directed solely to those publications since they are the heart of Wilton. Let others take care of the rest of this empire. While it's still valuable of course, the value on these two properties is going to reach the heavens. Well we'll discuss all these details over lunch at the Yale Club. That is if you would *condescend."*

"Wow," said Noah restraining a gasp as he leaned back on the sofa.

"Wow indeed. Noah it's all in your hands. And by the way, *ah* want to offer my congratulations on your book."

"How did you know about that Oliver?"

"Ahh know about everything. And *ah* would also like to say, *ah* would only be thrilled if you would write that society tell-*awl* that would knock that crowd off their feet. That is of *cauze* if you don't forget about us while you're at work on it."

Noah shook his head. It was unbelievable.

HE WALKED HOME IN A TRANCE that afternoon after a long lunch at the Yale Club followed by a meeting in the grand lounge with Champ Com's Stan Archer who endorsed everything Oliver said about their plans for *their star*. This had all been punctuated by the Yale Club staff's kingly treatment of the new arrival.

So much had happened in those whirlwind two days. Should he tell Nora the latest? A panicky quiver raced through him as he climbed their steps. Kissing and hugging him as he came through the door, she exclaimed: "I haven't been able to think of anything else today but the news of your book. It's only magic."

"Yes it is. But there's even a bit more news today. And hesitantly he sat down in his wing chair, took a deep breath and told her. As he did he could see her eyes losing their jubilance so he stopped before revealing the business of the Yale Club and his likelihood of a vice-presidency."

"Is this going to change our plans?" she asked with a note of fear.

"No. Why would it?" he answered with certainty but wondered if it might not. "The house won't be ready until at least next summer. And I'm sure I'll have to be here to do some editing on the book for Doubleday in the next months. We may as well be making all that extra money."

"Yeah—Noah, I have to tell you right off, I don't trust that one Oliver. He's always shifting you about. I'd want to be knowing what's around the next bend."

"Well if they're going to be paying me this money—"

"You'd want to be spot on your guard, Noah. Don't be the deer caught in the headlights over this."

BUT WHY WOULD THAT BE THE CASE, he asked himself. Now that everything was on the advance why not let it play itself out. And this feeling was enhanced when the first of several pleasures came about as the social world began its reversal most likely out of abject cowardice due to rumor of Oliver's ire.

--Let's do lunch and soon. La Grenouille."

--We must get together for drinks. The Oak Room."

--We're having a small gathering at our weekend retreat in Amagansett. We'd love to have you and Nora join us."

Along with this came the next delight when the agent and Doubleday reached a twelve thousand dollar advance agreement. And mixed right in was more talk of vice-presidency at Wilton. How could he help but drift upwards into the clouds, though, except for the news of the advance, he fought, he thought, valiantly to keep Nora from the realization that he had reconnected with the rarefied world and its sense of extravagance.

It was during this time leading up to Christmas as he was included in the swirls of intimate social gatherings that he began drinking again on a rather continuing basis. But only in the evenings and only wines he ruled truly fine. And how wonderful they were--the rare aging Bordeaux, the succulent full-bodied Burgundies. Savoring them, he came to think of the divinity of wine. It more than masked all the egomania and let him bask in the surroundings once again.

Now that Nora's success was escalating by the day, she would have been more than welcome to partake in these gatherings. But for the most part she was able to avoid them and contentedly work away at her easel instead. While she did notice that he was indulging again, she remained silent holding to the consolation that he was remaining steadfast. What really concerned her was that the workload at Wilton was speeding up to the point where he had to cancel their plans for a Christmas holiday at Yearnington. Now with a fresh new column and along with daily time consuming development work for the new publication, she sensed him being swallowed.

It was two days before Christmas when Carole called him at Wilton. "Can you talk for a moment?" What was this all about, he wondered. "*Time* wants you. I pushed for it and I got it. There's several editorial positions they're considering for you and all with strong salaries." "Carole, that's wonderful. I can't thank you enough. But you know a lot has happened to me here since we last talked." And he went on in a low tone to tell her all the hectic news. "Yes but you'll still be caught up in Oliver's power mania and the egocentricity of that whole world. At *Time* I think you could pretty much name whatever you want right now and you'd be disentangled. Anyway they'll be calling you right after the holidays, so why don't you think it over?" "Oh I will, of course." "But Noah I have an idea, especially if you're under pressure at work. Why don't you and Nora go up to Newport over the holidays? You could go under the perfect guise of doing a wintertime feature. I don't think one has been done on the town in ages. I'll tell you what, stay at Quintessence. No one will be there except the staff. And you'll have the time to think all this over." "Well it certainly does sound appealing Carole." More like a rapturous dream, he thought. "But what of John? He may be there." "Hah! Not on your life. He signed that property and all that goes with it over to me within days after I confronted him with his dalliances." "Well all right."

8

NORA HAD ONLY a vague memory of Noah's long ago piece on Newport, so she was more than delighted at the thought of being away from what appeared to be another society avalanche in his life. When the gates opened automatically and they drove up the long winding drive, she was so startled she gasped. Noah just stared in awe. There it was in the late morning gray-going-pink mist in all its glory just as he had remembered it. He tried to thwart the glorious shiver of his wonder as if he were struggling hopelessly against a force that he now sensed was one of betrayal.

He stopped the car and from around the majestic fountain with its bronze statue of Bacchus came Benjamin, Carole's still sprightly though by now weathered butler-caretaker. He greeted them. "Noah, and I believe Nora. It is so truly wonderful to see you," he called through their open window. Noah stepped out and shook his hand. "Carole thinks so much of you and I can see why. I've been with this family—or a once family—for all these many years. When you first walked up the steps of Quintessence for that big party they had a few years ago, I thought god had miraculously delivered Peter back to them. And I think he may have, certainly for Carole, no doubt."

"Well she's dearly beloved. And she struggles above it all."

"Yes she does. Not just for herself, but for everyone she cares for."

Noah was almost afraid to look into Nora's eyes as she emerged from the car and extended her greeting to Benjamin. His feeling was one of complete transparency. He was certain uncontrollable enchantment not only shown from his face but that his whole body radiated it. As two, more youthful staff members suddenly appeared and swept their luggage into the mansion, Benjamin escorted them up the grandiose stone steps through the breathtaking entry hall and into one of the more modest library sitting rooms enhanced by a warming fire in the gray-green marble fireplace. There he had arranged for *some refreshments after their long journey*. Refreshments being tea served from a stunning antique silver service and hot scones, jams and clotted cream from a matching gleaming salver. The china looked to be either olden Spode or Limoges.

That afternoon with a wintry breeze at their backs they walked down the grounds to the sea as it whipped the rocky shore. When they turned back the giant deciduous trees which were mostly bare now allowed them a sweeping view of Quintessence. It was then that Nora said in an almost inaudible and expressionless voice: "It would outdo an Irish castle, so it would." And Noah knew in that moment what she felt and he knew that she knew what he felt. They walked back to the mansion in silence.

Through the remainder of their stay even though they talked, strolled about viewing the mansion's art, went boating on Easton Bay and traveled around Newport, an overriding silence prevailed. It was never more obvious than in the evenings when they dined in the opulence of the Quintessence dining room. Carole had apparently instructed Benjamin to reinstate the estate's chef for the duration of their stay. And he lavished them with superb French and Italian cuisine served of course with the finest array of wines from Carole's vintage cellar. Afterwards they'd sit by the various firesides sipping rare noble Sauternes and reading selections from the host of libraries. When they went to bed and made love, it was as if they were in two different worlds of which neither shared.

The purpose of the weekend had been to consider the *Time* proposal. But Noah decided there would be no consideration if he told Nora. She most likely would not forgive him if he didn't accept it. In her mind not doing so would prove to be his resurgence to all the glories this weekend had epitomized.

How had he made such a blunder instantly accepting Carole's offer to come here, he wondered as they drove away from the estate. But when he'd considered it, in his heart he thought Nora might actually have come around to favoring this atmosphere, especially without the presence of the beautiful people and with her acceptance into the art world. He had been wrong. Very wrong.

ONCE BACK IN NEW YORK and with a new year upon them, the speed of events enveloped them. Oliver was ablaze with more ideas for his new *Connoisseur* consumer magazine and had called for meetings with art and photo along with editorial so they could advance on mockups and it was vital that Noah be present for every moment of these meetings. Then there was a whole slew of winter charity events on the horizon that would have to figure prominently in his new column *Inside Out*. Next *Doubleday* called to schedule editing sessions. Suddenly the agent had to meet with him over details of his advance. And along with all this, *Time* wanted to arrange an interview *a.s.a.p.*

As for Nora, Winsor de Caine was pressuring her for more output. And with good reason. Thomas Hoving and the Met did come through as Noah forecasted—putting their money where their mouths were. They purchased three of her paintings based on what Hoving considered their spiritual importance. Then following suit the Whitney came forth and went for one of her larger Irish stormy seascape oils. While on the surface all seemed to be moving in a positive direction for the Masons, Nora couldn't rid herself of her Newport frame of mind. Before Christmas she had resumed believing that their Irish dream was moving closer to their touch by the day. But seeing him at Quintessence put the curse to her thoughts. How could he ever shake the wonder of indulgence, she kept asking herself to no avail.

9

IN MID-JANUARY he agreed to lunch at "21" with the *Time* honchos. A month ago their offers would have come as a blessing, a perfect resolution for the short term. But that was being distanced by the day. He left them saying he'd be thrilled to work for *Time* but with the addendum that he would have to give an honorable notice at Wilton and that he would have to be in touch before they could finalize. They seemed stunned but accepted his reasoning in good faith. After that he wandered over and down Fifth Avenue all the while thinking that he didn't feel any joy in this. Yes the money was there. They had reviewed his Wilton work and his previous *Herald Tribune* stuff and had raved so much he was certain he could ask for even far more than they had offered. But from a working point of view, they seemed to be suggesting a vague rather lifeless miscellany of work—art, social issues, culture, current trends, even business. Yes he could put his own special twist to it all. *Flourish* was the word they used. But it all sounded so drab, and he came right back to the thought of why wouldn't he stay at Wilton as it turned in his favor, stay there until they were ready to leave for Ireland which could still be a very long way off. So stay and get from them what he could. And especially a vp— ship. He wouldn't really have to tell Nora of the *Time* offer. He knew what was best and going to *Time* would be an upheaval. Yes, he was right.

"NORA, ITS CAROLE DAWSON. I can't tell you how thrilled I was to see that item in the art section of the *Times* about some of your paintings being purchased by the Metropolitan and the Whitney. It's just a delight."

"Oh I know it's only fantastic and thank you so much for calling."

"Well we'll have to have a bit of a celebratory evening for that and for Noah's novel. But listen, I've been trying to reach him at Wilton for several days now."

"Well he's not here at the moment, but is something wrong?" she asked sensing some urgency.

"Yes I'm concerned. You see the people at *Time* magazine are putting me in the awkward position of finding out just where they stand with their offer to Noah."

"I don't understand."

"Well they put forth a number of positions as you must know, and he seemed very enthusiastic. But they've heard nothing more from him. I don't know if he told you I was the one who pushed so forcefully with the corporates there."

"Oh well I imagine he's still mulling it all over," Nora replied quickly trying to cover her total innocence. "I'll have him call you as soon as he gets home and I'm sure he'll straighten it all out. But I can't thank you enough for your concern, and I certainly hope we haven't caused you any problems."

"No. No. It's just that I want to make certain Noah gets the most mileage out of this."

WHEN NOAH WALKED IN that evening, Nora was still in a state of vague shock. "What's wrong?" he asked immediately sensing her discomfort.

"I don't know," she sighed. "I guess I've just been thinking more and more of Ireland and wishing our house were done so that we could be on our way."

He hugged and kissed her and asked: "What's got you in this mood? You know they're working on it over there. You want them to do a decent job. And that takes time."

"Yes," she replied as she pulled away. "Well I've got to go down to the kitchen. The dinner's probably ready." When she reached the stairs, she called back matter-of-factly: "Carole called this afternoon. She's been trying to reach you at Wilton. You should call her."

"Did she say about what?" he asked rather hesitantly.

"Something about *Time* magazine and being in an awkward position. I didn't know anything about it, don't you know. Oh well," she sighed. And she went down the stairs.

Noah trying to suppress his sinking feeling went after her. "Look I know how you feel," he said as she went about setting the kitchen table for the lamb stew she had prepared.

"Do you? Because I don't know myself," she answered sharply.

"Well I didn't tell you because I don't know if it's right. I'm still considering it. And I didn't want to confuse and worry you."

"Oh I'm confused all right. I thought you were trying for something like that."

"Yes," he sighed. "I was. But I'm not sure of the whole thing as it's presented to me."

"Well is there less money involved?"

"No. They'd probably match that okay. But I'm not certain of the work. They're kind of vague about that."

"It sounded from Carole like you could touch down on a whole variety of things."

"And then the executives are—I don't know."

"What? Worse than Oliver Wilton?"

"Well to tell you the truth Oliver's not so bad any more. I hadn't wanted to get hopes up but along with the raises he's insisted on giving me, there's an almost certain chance that I'm going to be named a vice-president at Wilton."

"So you were just going to continue on and never tell me any of this?"

"Of course I would have told you, but I wanted it to be clear in my own mind what was best. And then something happened today that made me think again about the whole matter." Then he went to the fridge, took out a bottle of Molson's ale, snapped the cap and sat on one of the pine chairs taking a deep drink. "It came as a disappointment. The agent called and said that instead of getting a lump sum check, Doubleday is going to divide it into installments. The first installment which I'll get next week is only going to be two thousand. He said he didn't know why but that some publishers do that from time to time if they feel a budget crunch. I only hope they're not trying to mess with me. But he says he feels certain I'll get it all."

"Well most likely you will. Probably they also want to make certain you're going to meet your part of the bargain with the editing schedule."

"Maybe. But it's bumming me out. They seemed to be so damned excited about the whole thing. And now they're doing this. I desperately wanted all that money—or most of it so I could pay for our house. I mean two thousand won't cover it. And then I wanted to pay you back for that furniture. My raises wouldn't even do that for a long time."

"Will you stop all this about the money. There's no urgency."

"Oh yes there is. I should be the supplier. I have to be," he replied approaching a near frenzy.

"Stop. Use your energy to think about the *Time* offer. I really wonder if it's right to pass on it."

"I'll handle it, Nora. I'm not a deer in the headlights. I just don't want to end up the blundering fool."

THAT WAS AT THE BEGINNING OF THE WEEKEND. As it progressed he realized how edgy she was becoming. And he knew that by now she was constantly praying that he would go to *Time* until they could be out of there. It pained him so to feel this creeping aura of subdued sadness. It was as if he were persistently wounding her and no amount of wooing or lovemaking healed or even soothed. When by Sunday afternoon it became unbearable, he dipped into his hidden reserve of Valeys once again. On Monday, he called Dr. DiCarlo and made an appointment.

"All you writers are so traumatized," the doctor went on as he scratched his gray haired head and peered over his reading spectacles. "I see your blood pressure is up a bit. So I guess we could up the strength of the Valium a little. But we have to be careful not to go too far. The libido you know."

"Well do you think something else might be better?"

"We could try Librium. It's very similar, but for some it works better. Will I try you on that?"

"Well yes. Anything. I need to be calm again."

THANK GOD, HE FORGOT to tick the box for the number of refills, Noah thought as he glanced at the prescription when he was leaving. I can probably get at least eight out of this without asking any more favors of the druggist. So he marked it for eight, filled it and popped one. Then he walked about several extra streets pondering whether he should go ahead and take one of the *Time* offers, if no more than for Nora's sake. He had to really think about this it was that important.

By the time he reached the office, the Libey, as the druggist called Librium, had begun to impart the soothing quality of an elixir. No sooner was he inside than Oliver called him to his office.

"Sit down, Noah," he said pointing to his leather sofa. "*Ah* believe your thoughts are wandering once again."

"What do you mean, Oliver? I've been killing myself here—with two jobs yet."

"Well *ah* you going to go to work for *Time* as well. If you have so much spare time that is," he tittered but then shrugged and glowered.

"Oh they just called and made me an offer. I get those sort of offers every once in a while."

"*Called!*" he roared. "You and all the top people along with Otto Fuebringer over there lunching at '21'. That's some call Noah."

"Well I thought only a fool wouldn't listen to their offer."

"Oh Noah, we have to stop these shenanigans here and now. Why *ah* feel betrayed. *Ah* want you to be ours and only ours. Oh *ah* don't mind if you're writing these books in your downtime as I've said. To be truthful *aham* madly jealous of that talent. That's why *ah* went to Yale, you know. But that's neither here nor there. *Ah* want no more episodes like *Time*. Do *ah* make myself perfectly clear?"

"Well they did offer me a lot of money," Noah chanced.

"Oh *ah'll* give you more money just to keep you because you're worth it. How would another two suit you? And to sweeten it all the more *ah'll* go a bit further. Judging from all the brilliant mockups you've been doing for *Connoisseur* and the thrilling features you and your people have already compiled. *Ah'd* say we could roll in a couple of months. Now the mast head in that first issue will bear *yaw* name as a Wilton vice-president and editor in chief and as such who knows where that could take us."

"Well I guess you've made your point."

"And *ah* think this deserves another luncheon visit to the Yale Club."

"I'd say it would Oliver."

ONCE AGAIN NOAH DID THE YALE CLUB. But this time his mind was on two tracks. He'd have his book, his column and he'd be editorial director and vice-president of a brand new magazine all under his belt. Then there was the money. Oh god, the money. But the image of Nora was ever present. Moving forward on this would mean more social events, more work and less Nora. And once again there would be the growing appeal of the trappings of that world. Then he began to stress over how all this could put off Ireland. One thing was clear. He couldn't postpone the decision on *Time* as much as he would so like to do. But that would be horribly unfair to Carole who had been such a devoted sponsor. By the end of that afternoon, the good effects of the Librium had worn off and he found himself in the midst of a growing turmoil. Oh god, I'll have to pop another one of these, he thought and did.

THAT WAS ON THURSDAY. On Friday he called Carole from Wilton. "You won't offend me by not accepting. Just tell them the time isn't right, that you would quite dishonorably be letting Wilton down at a time they most need and depend on you for the birth of their new publication. Then stress that playing fair is only honorable and that above all you have to be honorable. But—I must say to you Noah, guard yourself through all of this." He shivered at the thought but then still went ahead and gave a pass to the *Time* offer expressing great regret. Afterward as he put the phone down he felt a brief gust of relief—that is until he turned and faced the glowing framed photo of Nora he kept on his desk. And then the guilt. And then the Librium again.

Frequently that weekend he struggled to make love to her as if it would erase all the qualms. Instead an overriding silence prevailed quite like the one at Quintessence. He was sure she knew his decision. On Sunday afternoon he reminded her that the next day he'd have to go to Washington to attend the Nixon inaugural balls. "You wouldn't like to come along would you? I could get the tickets."

"No," she replied glumly as they lay naked after a long orgasm-less bout.

"Just no?" he asked as he propped his head up to face her. "What's wrong?"

"Nothing." And she blithely shook her head.

"Well there must be something."

"What's the use of saying anything? You've already done the deed."

"I didn't think it would be so bad. I mean I really did give it a lot of thought."

"I'm sure you did."

And then they lapsed back into silence.

SO AFTER LESS than a passionate kiss that next morning, he went off to meet up with a gaggle of Wilton photographers. All the way down on the train to Washington while they chatted and jested among themselves, Noah stared out the window into the fog considering only the impending emptiness he felt he was occasioning once again back in Gramercy Park. That night as he covered the various balls, he drank lots of champagne trying to submerge these constantly encroaching thoughts. Everything will fall back into place, he told himself as later he woozily fell into bed at the Washington Hilton.

But things really didn't fall into place. The days to come speeded into frenzy. Oliver's obsession with *Connoisseur* hastened by the moment. Evenings, when Noah wasn't covering events for his *FCD* column, were suddenly usurped by lengthy staff meetings over the new publication which was now due to make its grand public entrance at the beginning of April. To Nora the distance between them grew until he had all but vanished. When he did return very late those evenings, he was so removed he may as well not have been there. To make matters worse, his time was so scarce that the Doubleday editor had to schedule Saturday mornings for their meetings. While they went well, in that they were making the book a finely tuned work, the joy he should have felt just wasn't there.

Through all this, Noah knew that he was relying too heavily on the libeys. Now they were doing more than just relieving the strain. They were numbing him. So he decided he'd try for a balance—a little alcohol one day, a couple of libeys the next. It would be a very dangerous tightrope walk.

10

AS DEMANDING AS OLIVER had been, he grew even more so over Noah's *FCD* column. "We *ah* calling it *Inside Out* and it means just that, Noah. We have to cut to the bone. *Ah* want you to keep doing your beautiful but ever so nasty glittery balls and charity events—but, and *ah* do mean but, we need to do some bone cutting on these people. Do you understand me?"

"Well I think I do."

"Better still, let's boil them in *aull*, Noah."

"Well that's fine if we have any oil to boil them in."

"Oh come now, we surely can stir up some extra venom if we put *auwah* minds to it. Let's do a number on Bill Paley. He deserves to have a little fuel spilled and kindled under him, after his years of mistreating poor Babe with all those womanizing *ahhfares*."

"Well what would you have in mind? I have no proof of anything recent."

"Doesn't matter. You must have heard a whiff of something here or there. Put it in."

"And have all the legal eagles at *CBS* swooping down on us."

"*Ah* don't fear that. We *ah* stronger—and far wiser than they'll ever be. Besides Bill deserves it in spades. *Ah* hear he was even trying to spark it again with Pamela after all these years."

"Well I don't think I believe that. Besides I think Pamela after all her rascally times has turned the corner and is true blue to Leland, especially now in his delicate condition."

"Well *ah* believe it! So take me as your unidentified source. And not just on this occasion. *Ah* want *moah* scandalous items on people of this ilk."

"Even if they're not true?"

"They *ah* true. "Who's to say they're not?" he fumed then coldly winked. "These items are what make a *papah* sizzle. It's what we should have been doing all along. But now especially, we want all the publicity we can get to herald in *ahwha* new arrival in a couple of months."

"Even if we're arrogant enough to print lies?"

"*Airagant* is a good word, Noah. You should court it more often."

"I think you're trying to resurrect Walter Winchell."

"Well that wouldn't be such a bad *ahdeah*. Anything to sell *ahwha* publications."

"WHAT IS HE UP TO?" Noah asked Murphs after he escaped. "He's positively obsessed these days.

"Well in my opinion, it's not just publicity for *Connoisseur* magazine. I've heard tell a little rumor that Bill Paley has been making overtures to Oliver's wife and that despite Babe--or maybe in spite of her--she might be more than a little interested. But you've no reason to be unnerved about it."

"Except loss of integrity."

"I DON'T KNOW WHAT TO DO ABOUT IT," Noah told the steel-haired lady in the art department. "There's this friend of mine who's freaking out. I mean it's really a bad scene. He's on a little booze, and now he's taking the libeys. But he's starting to come apart."

"You know Pete over at Crossway Drugs, don't you?"

"Of course."

"Well take your friend and put him in touch."

"What's his angle?"

"None whatsoever. He's totally cool with artists and writers and musicians. He likes to rap once he's sure he knows them. He'll sell you all the under counter stuff you want at cost."

"Really? But why?"

"Cause he likes you guys. Of course you can always favor him with a designer shirt occasionally. He loves them. Talk to someone upstairs at *Men's Connoisseur.* Then you can get them for him wholesale. That's what I do."

"DO YOU KNOW BAUDELAIRE'S WRITING?" Pete asked as he led Noah into the bleak back room of the pharmacy late that afternoon. He was lanky with long black hair in a bun and a straggly beard flecked with gray.

"Yes I used to all right," Noah answered taken a bit aback.

"The poet is like the prince of the clouds, who rides the tempest and scorns the archer."

Noah picked up the remainder. *"Exiled on the ground, amidst boos and insults, his giant wings prevent his walking.* Yeah. But I've been trying to avoid albatrosses. Once they're gone they keep coming right back."

"I always think of you writer guys sweating it out when I come across that," Pete went on in his gravelly voice. "Good stuff, poetry like that. I like to get lost in it. Believe it or not, it pulled me through the Mekong Delta. Every time something bad happened I just kept spouting away verses like that to the top of my lungs. Scared everyone to hell. So they tossed me in the loco wagon and sent me back here." And he laughed nervously. "So what's your trouble?"

"Well—There's this friend of mine and—"

"Whoa! I don't get into any scenes with friends. I gotta know exactly who I'm dealing with. I got my license to think about, especially after all I've been through. I mean you gotta know this. I been through a war whether they call it one or not. I saw limbs shot off. I shot some of 'em off. I mean—they made me torture some of those guys. Blow them apart little by little. Now I got my license to think about. I—" And he started trembling.

"Okay. All right. Okay," Noah blurted. "It's me. I mean I'm the friend, the one who's got the problem. But this is strictly off the record."

"You better believe it's strictly off the record. I gotta know that first thing."

"Don't worry about it. I always protect my sources."

"Okay. So what's the problem?"

Noah took a deep breath. Suddenly it was painful to speak of it. How had he slid so far as to be in this situation in this dingy room after all he thought he'd risen above? "Well I thought I had things pretty much in hand first with the valeys and then the libeys. They were helping me get ahead. But now with things so crazy with the work, they just seem to be numbing me out."

"Well they can after while, if you rely too heavily on them. Maybe you should see another doctor."

"No. That's not on. It doesn't get me anywhere."

"How about weeding out for a while? I got an excellent source."

"No I hate smoke of any kind. There's enough of it in the office."

"Well I can give you other stuff. I can feel comfortable with that. I pop these things myself. Well after Mekong," he confessed and trembled some more.

"See what I need is something that will bring me back to life and give me more stamina. But then something that will calm me at the end of a rough day."

"Yeah I know what you're looking for. I think maybe some bennies for the daytime and then to get a little laid back at night maybe some tooies or I could give you nemies. You could see which one works the best for you. I think they'll get you back together. But they won't do anything for your sex life, I caution."

FIRST DAY ON THE BENNIES, he typed up a storm in the office. "What's gotten into you?" Murphs called to him. "Stop working so hard. You're putting us all to shame."

By five o'clock that high faded and anxiety was taking a strong hold. It grew worse when Oliver, attempting to relieve another bitter streak, ranted that Noah litter his column with salacious commentary about Governor Rockefeller, along with lascivious salvos pitched at Doris Duke and yet another savage dig at Bill Paley and poor suffering Babe. Quick, take one of the tooies he told himself convinced that they would calm him. "Oh shit, no," he muttered to himself in the men's room as he searched his pockets. "I left the bloody things at home."

Before he could flee, Oliver called another special *Connoisseur* meeting that went on for two hours. While Noah managed very well, his system was crying out as he left the building. Had the bennies done this, left him so rock bottom?

"A very dry Beefeater martini, please. Straight up," he told the bartender at the Cedar. He couldn't just go home and wait for a pill to work. His nerves felt as if they were beginning to tear him to bits, and he certainly didn't want Nora to see him like this.

"Nice to see your face for a change," she said when he walked in the door and kissed her on the cheek. She didn't return it.

"Well things have been pretty rough as the *Connoisseur* deadline gets closer."

"I'm sure. But it certainly seems to be sharpening your pen when it comes to your column."

"Well I guess I kind of have to get around that."

"Oh of course," she replied firmly and then after a second or two added matter-of-factly: "For the money. Oh and by the way if you're interested, Hughie sent a few more pictures of the land and the little more work the builders had been able to do. The weather there's been bad you know."

"Oh that's terrible. I'm certainly disappointed."

"Sure."

"Well I am you know."

"Oh, I know."

AS IT WENT the weather didn't improve anywhere else in the days to come. While at the same time he was driven beyond endurance with the preps for *Connoisseur*, he grew ever more Oliver's fall guy through his column printing even more items that were often either dubious or stretched beyond the bounds of truth. Big time lawyers and legal firms were falling by the wayside, daring not to pursue matters too far for fear Oliver would release through Noah a true tidal wave much worse than the gossip surges already in print. As for Noah no one of any ilk would dare as in the past to even hint at a snub. Wilton Press, its circulation and advertising were now rising to the moon. How much higher could they go with the arrival of *Connoisseur*?

But higher soon proved not to be the course for Noah. Even though the bennies kept him wound up and zipping along, the pressures continued to build so that left him with the needful drink or two at an event or an after-work bar, the latter being necessary because the nemmies and the tooies dropped him too low in spirit and could have easily put him out of sync.

WHEN MARIE MCCLOUD called from Doubleday, his spirits did lift. She had gone over the latest revisions he had made on *Pictures* and she was thrilled with the results.

"It's really going to be a beautiful work," she insisted. "I think it's pretty well set now. But I'm not very happy about the way the accounts-and-contracts people here have treated you. You're agent said they're being very slow on the advance payments. But you'll be happy to know I've gone ahead and cleared that up. You'll get the full remainder by mail sometime next week."

Well that was another sign from god he thought as he hung up. *It's going to be a beautiful work.* And almost as swiftly, he felt the need for the pills, to lift. Now if he could just get through the next month to the *Connoisseur* publication date most certainly he'd be able to calm Oliver's penchant for radical column items in the dazzling light of the publicity that event would produce. Yes, he would be able to handle it all and delight with these thoughts with only a drink or two each night.

As was promised the check arrived five days later. Now he could pay in full for their house in Ireland, he delighted. He gave no thought as to when they actually would move there. But they would have it—and all sorts of wonderful things. The joy buoyed him all the way to Tiffany's where he set about selecting a pearl and baby sapphire necklace that he hoped would set things right with Nora once more.

SHE DIDN'T GASP or react with shock or even protest when he presented her with the Tiffany box later that day after he told her of the arrival of his advance check.

"It's an early Valentine gift," he added hopefully as she walked over to the living room window staring into the box. A heavy snow which radio reports were already referring to as a blizzard was all but obliterating the park. As she glanced out, she could barely define the statue of Edwin Booth. "The reason they're sapphires is because I thought they would set off the color of your eyes even more."

"Is that what you were thinking?" she asked in a distant vague tone.

"Well—yes," he said as his face went to a puzzled frown. "Aren't you going to try it on?" he asked as he followed her to the window, took the necklace from the box and fastened around her neck. "It looks pretty great to me. Greater than I'd imagined."

"It is beautiful," she said almost in a murmur as she continued to stare out into the distance of white. With a pang of regret, he knew instantly and quickly continued. "Oh and I put the rest of the money in the bank. That's going to more than cover the full cost of our house and much of the rest of the money you paid on that furniture bill. What a great feeling all that is."

"The house. That's nice. Nice that you thought of it."

Pushing it even further, he stressed: "Anymore news of it?"

"Yes, I heard from Hughie a week or so ago," she continued in the same distant monotone. "There's a good deal more work going on now that the weather's improved."

He seemed shocked. "You didn't tell me that. How come?"

"Well you were so busy. And besides I didn't think there was any big rush—or need anymore"

THAT WEEKEND, as the storm that would be named after the ineffectual mayor—the Lindsay Blizzard continued dumping its twenty inches of snow, Noah attempted to revive his lover's routine of an early morning rush, now trudge through calf-deep snow to the Gramercy Pastry for the brioche and the crème coffees. But the snuggling in bed, the whispers of love and the once-again return of the culmination in love making never rang true. Noah's image of their weekend in Quintessence where together they were separate persisted in lurching forth. He kept thinking if only they could struggle a little longer until everything took root, they would have their

Irish dream and that much more. If only she could see that. If only she could see all that awaited them after he'd gone this far. But his words of such were failing to come across to her so he stopped himself. Then it came to him how their attitudes had shifted, how once it was she who was extolling patience and now the reversal was true.

All that weekend when he started to talk, to put things into perspective, she wanted to scream because all she could sense was the erosion. What had happened since that exhilarating night at the Metropolitan two short months ago when everything at long last seemed to be advancing for them and together they were moving forward again? Yes it began at Quintessence as their car waited for the front gate to open on everything she had let herself think was slowly fading from his life.

11

EVEN VALENTINE'S DAY failed to lift the aura of emptiness that by now appeared to afflict them both. But at the beginning of the following week, something happened that jolted Noah producing a seizure of panic and sending him racing to Epiphany and pleading for god's help. *Please forgive me for not trying to do more to prevent this distance from overwhelming our lives,* he whispered as he knelt in a pew. *You may consider it to be all my fault and you may be embarking on what you think to be a just punishment. But I plead with you not to do it in this way.* And he fell silent with his head in his hands as he relived the phone conversation of that morning.

"Noah, I'm afraid I have some very disappointing news for you." It was Marie McCloud. Without her saying it, he recognized the voice even under its unusual strain.

"What's wrong?" he asked fearfully and held his breath.

"As of today, I'm no longer a chief fiction editor here."

"Why? You're so good—truly great."

"Oh the powers that be have come up with a whole new concept of what the fiction department should be. Or something to that effect. Anyway I don't fit that bill. So they want to move me to non-fiction. Well I'm not accepting that. I'm getting out of here."

"Can't you fight it?"

"No. Old blood can't fight new blood. But I don't want to panic you. I think your book is safe. Luckily we've done all the editing and the galleys are already being set. And thank god you got all your advance."

"But how could things have changed so fast? And where will you be going? I'm so sorry for you—and for me."

"I don't know. I didn't really have a hint of any of this until today. But again as I say I don't think they'd take your book out of the fall line. Even though the new editor in chief is a total devil, she does recognize good work. And yours is far better than good. It's brilliant."

But the doubt was there, and now he was on his knees. *Miserere nobis.*

ALL THE REST OF THE DAY through meeting after meeting, he quelled his panic in favor of *Connoisseur.* He had to do this. If he lost his book he'd have to remain on the Wilton front maybe even at a reduced status. But maybe Marie McCloud was right. Maybe it was *brilliant.* Maybe everyone at Doubleday would see that. Yet maybe they wouldn't. Maybe they wanted change so much that they would screw everyone on their fall line and dump *Pictures In The Rain.* Above all he couldn't tell Nora any of this. It would force his apprehension to a full-blown state and riddle him with embarrassment and pain.

SO AS THE DAYS PASSED and time was moving closer to the *Connoisseur* arrival, Noah while quite under control during the day began to slide in the evenings once he left Wilton or after some society event ended. To Nora this was different. Yes, there was the drink but only a small amount. Instead he seemed to drift off to another plain quite in control but given over to near silence. Well she could hardly blame him when she may have caused it with her own persistent drifting. But soon she sensed more. This was when she would catch him in brief beneath-the-surface moments.

"No! No! I don't want anything to eat," he spewed the words as if in a frenzy. "No you go ahead and eat. Busy day. I think I'll take a shower. Relax a little." At that he just disappeared. Half an hour later he returned to the living room, showered and in a robe. Then he sat by the fire as calm as calm could ever be. "Oh the fire is so lovely," he said slowly, quietly almost with a blank expression. How could he have transformed so swiftly. And then there was that stare as if the fire had absorbed his entire being. This was only one occasion, and there were more to come, enough so that secretly she called Dr. DiCarlo's office to book his first available appointment.

12

WHEN IT CAME, it was as if he had stepped on a land mine.

"I'm afraid it's over. Doubleday did the dirty today." The agent he'd only seen once flatly stated. "They dropped *Pictures* from their fall line."

"That's a definite?" Noah somehow managed as he glanced over at Murphs typing away at her desk and wished, so wished he could somehow make her aware before he totally cracked to bits.

"It's definite. And it's not just you. It's half the books for fall they're replacing over there."

"I can't talk right now," he barely whispered. "I just want to be off the phone."

"I can imagine. There was no other way but to tell you outright. But you'll have to listen to this. They want all of your advance back as well."

"You must be joking."

"No. You'll be getting a letter from them soon. But I can tell you right now, they won't get it. Not one cent. Since they're dispensing with me too, I'm going to fight it for you. I know how to play their game. But it will be a fight."

"Oh god, thank you. But I don't know what to say about all this."

"Just be as cool as you can. If someone as great and with as much business savvy as Marie McCloud has that much confidence in your book you're going to get it published. Now I'm not the one to handle it. You need someone who loves it with as much heart as Marie does. You'll get there. And I'll stay in touch about this advance business. But I want no compensation—not for this massacre."

"MURPHS I NEED TO TALK can you take a break?"

"What's wrong?" she asked as she swung away from her typewriter and then in a whisper said: "You're sheet white."

They headed down the street for the big wide circular bar at Longchamps. "Noah, did you just get an incurable cancer diagnosis?"

"Comparable." And he took a deep drink of one of the martinis they'd ordered from Victor. "Why do they make these things so effen' small?"

"Noah, what is it?"

"They dropped the book from the fall line." And he held his head up with one hand as if it might fall off.

"Oh shit," she sighed as she stroked its crown. After a time she sighed: "If it helps any, I feel my heart breaking too. Have you told Nora?"

"No," he gasped. "That would kill me—without question."

"God." And she shook her head. "It's such a beautiful book, Noah. I'm so happy you gave me a copy to read. I'm proud to know someone as gifted as you. And if I do say so, they're damn asshole fools up there at Doubleday."

"I would concur. And I had to tell someone. But enough of it now. How are you doing?" he asked as he patted her hand that rested by her untouched drink. "We haven't talked seriously in so long. You should have been working with me on *Connoisseur*. I wanted that."

"Under almost no circumstance. That's far too fanciful for me."

"But that doesn't answer my question."

She gripped the stem of her martini glass. "Well Jimmy—things aren't so good on that front anymore."

"Oh Murphs, what happened?"

"I guess it's been happening. I mean I'd been thinking all along he was so happy because of me and because of our love for one another. But no. Now he's got this thing that he's growing old too fast. I mean he's only thirty. But he keeps saying that that's bad in this city because you start aging so fast."

"Well what can he do about that?"

"You wouldn't believe what." Then she took a swallow of her martini as Noah motioned Victor for a second. "He wants to move to Maine and set up a law practice there. Maybe even open an animal shelter. I think he's turning into a late blooming flower child myself. I mean it's perfectly ridiculous. And can you imagine me living in Maine?"

"No I positively can't," he said shaking his head. "But I would assume he'd get over that. He's a man of the city."

"Well that's what I thought. That we were two of a kind. Orphans of the storm healing one another. You know his father left his family completely bereft while he fruitlessly chased after the scent of money. Even though I've always trusted him so, Jimmy seems to be racing off in another direction. Yesterday he went up there to look for a house. He keeps telling me *you'll adjust.* But not up there, my god. Still I wonder if I could live without him."

"Yes, but maybe if your love is so binding you could—"

"What and leave Bloomingdale's? I could never, ever. He knows how much I need such things, even with our love."

With that she set her martini aside, smiled and tossed her hair back over her shoulder. The sheen of its rich redness combined with her silky golden blouse worked to lift aside the vision of her gloom at least for the moment. "But look unfortunately I've got to get back to that story. I've been at such a low point for the last few weeks that I haven't been working as exuberantly as usual. I don't want to lose my job yet." As she stood, the two hugged one another then she took hold of his upper arms and squeezed them. "Don't you give up. But you have to tell Nora. You can't keep it a secret from the one who loves you so much. She'll help you through. I just know. But make that your last martini before you go to her."

"Sure." But he didn't sound very positive.

"Noah look at me. You're going to get through this— and somehow I am too. That's because we're Depression babies. We survive."

Noah laughed as he sat back on the stool once again this time alone with his martini. Thoughts came now, and it was impossible to block them. Soon they would turn into a cascade.

I can't tell her. Secret or not. God I may as well chop off my balls. One for pride, the other for ego. How can I keep all this together so she won't find out. And what of that advance money I may have to pay back yet? Shit. And what about the house? Are we really going to move over there? Even for a short time? If I had that book under my belt it would be something. I'd be over the threshold of another career. But without it I'd most likely have no leverage here at all. Shit. Here goes a third martini yet.

13

BY THE DAY of her appointment with Dr. DiCarlo, Nora was even more disturbed than she had been. Noah's moodiness had become alarming. When she would ask of it, he'd quickly reply with an—*I'm just tired, you know. Nothing more.*

"I'm certain I know what all that's about Nora. It's what most of us doctors here would call a typical New York anxiety attack," Dr. DiCarlo insisted when she gently broached the subject after he'd completed her general yearly checkup.

"Well I find it more disturbing than that."

"I had the idea of switching him to a different drug. So we decided to go with the Librium for a time."

"Oh yes the Librium," she said matter-of-factly in a desperate attempt to hide her lack of knowledge.

"And then we found that the Librium seemed to be doing so much more for him than the Valium ever did. But if it isn't working well enough you should convince him to come back to me. So we can turn it all off for him. He's a writer, you know."

"I suppose he shouldn't be drinking at all with them."

"Oh it's all right. A few drinks can calm those feelings all the more."

"Right. Right enough. Calm those feelings all the more."

She left from the doctor's west Eleventh Street office first numb then angry over his thoughts. *Turn it all off for him.* After that she found herself inside the first Catholic church she passed—the Church of Francis Xavier on West Sixteenth Street. But instead of imparting any vague sense of serenity, its darkly Baroque interior weighed on her depression and underscored the doctor's words. Tears that now accompanied her mood as she knelt in the pew must have been noticeable, for a young priest who happened to be passing by came over and asked if she was all right. "I don't know," she replied in a gasp and hurried out into the late morning fog.

That afternoon she went about searching the drawers of his bureau wondering where he was keeping these vile tablets that were draining the life from him. It didn't take long to find them. But it was what she found along with them in that drawer that not only terrified her but went on to push her into a raging fury. Next to the standard prescription-labeled vials of Valium and Librium were those with only a strip of white adhesive with words written on them with a byro—bennies, dexies and the letter D after them. Then near those were nemies, tooies each followed by a U. Almost without a thought, she went to one of their living area bookcases and took down a slang dictionary that he frequently used as reference when he was working on the development of his society novel. Downers. Uppers.

Secrets, she thought as she closed the book and sat on the sofa. How long had he been taking those things in hiding? How could he have done this to her? Betrayed and trashed their relationship in such an ugly way? Well I'm going to do something in secrecy, she thought. I'm going to withdraw some money and have it ready. With that she stormed out of the apartment, hurried over to their First National City Bank on Fifth Avenue and withdrew a thousand dollars.

AT THE OFFICE THAT DAY, Noah had growled at Oliver over his insistence on placing an even greater savage swipe at Bill Paley in *Inside Out.* "But Oliver, it looks to me like we're running a personal vendetta against him."

"Well if Mr. Paley behaves in such a scandalous *mannah,* don't you think *awha* readers want to know about it?"

'"Not if we're inventing such scandal for spite."

"What spite and what do you mean by the word personal?"

"Oh I can't interpret the hushed tones and raised eyebrows of others."

"*Aham* certain that we *ah* a little stressed over this fiction of yours taking so long to see the light. But in the meantime, *ah* would just like to see the Paley item in print tomorrow."

"HE KNOWS about the book."

"Well I'm sure he probably does," said Murphs after Noah came out of Oliver's office. "He knows about everything. But just ignore it."

"How? I knew if he found out he would use this to really push my buttons."

"Don't let him. He's just using his power jollies as an escape. You have to know your book is going to sell sometime soon. In the meantime you've got Nora and he's got no one after he's let his wife be swiped by men like Paley. And that's sad losing someone. Boy do I know how sad it is."

"What do you mean?" he asked as he noted the way her bright face suddenly dipped into solemnity. "Oh no. Jimmy?"

"Yeah. I'm not in his vision much nowadays. Maine gets his full attention."

Just as he was about to commiserate his phone rang. "They're giving me a very hard time." It was the agent just as Noah had half anticipated. "They want that money back. But I've told them in no uncertain terms they're not getting it."

"Yes their letter to me was very strong. But I thought you'd have better luck."

"What would really help now is if you knew a powerful lawyer who could send them a powerhouse letter."

"Well I really don't but—" And he thought of Carole. She certainly would. But god he'd have to tell her the dreadful news and that would sink him even more. "Well I do know of someone who would."

"The sooner the better. We want to appear relentless too."

Relentless, yeah he thought as he hung up.

"Bad news?" Murphs asked and he nodded with a sigh.

"I don't want you to do the dirty to me, Noah," she said after she came over and sat beside his desk.

"What do you mean by that?" he asked in stunned surprise.

"Don't you slip away from me, too. And don't you slip away from Nora." He just stared at her. "Oh I sense it. How nice guys can be divested—a little here and a little there. Then without even knowing it, they're divesting others and—Well you get the picture."

AT THIS POINT HE FELT he couldn't breathe. Fear which until now he somehow had managed to sustain was spinning him out of the control zone. He did make a men's room stall where dizzily leaning against the wall he fumbled through some tissues and coins in his right pants pocket until he was able to extract a nemie. Before he could mouth it, his trembling hand let go. The pill just missed the john and tumbled far back behind the tank. On his hands and knees across the reek of the urine splattered floor, he struggled to retrieve the capsule and pop it before it evaded him again.

After his dizziness lifted somewhat he went to the water fountain and then took an elevator to the twelfth floor and the small company terrace where he stood breathing the freezing early March air. Shivering there, he reluctantly decided that he would have to call Carole. He could not in any sense afford to lose that advance money. And second he would have to knuckle under to Oliver even if it meant losing some of his cherished honor.

"OH I'M SO DISAPPOINTED to hear this news. It's such a superb book. I even had another read of it."

"Well thank you. But at this point I feel like I'm running full speed backwards instead of ahead."

"Well you're not. And don't give in to that. I certainly know a good handful of top lawyers who'll knock their blocks off as far as the advance is concerned. And I think we might even be able to rub their noses in that contract and force publication, especially since Marie McCloud was once so firmly involved. But the danger there is if they weren't fully behind it and didn't publicize it, it might be worse than not getting it published at all. It could just go right down the drain. But let's move ahead one step at a time. I'll get your legal thing initiated this afternoon. And in the meantime you messenger me a copy of their letter to you. Then the next thing I'm going to do is work on getting you a caring agent you're so deserving of someone who'll see that book through to print. I'll be able to work on this a lot more in another few weeks. That'll be after John and I are finally able to dismember each other now that we have our court date. Then thank god that situation will be over for good, and he'll be put in his proper place."

"Oh Carole don't be thinking of any of this until after that. I hadn't realized it was all coming to a head. I'm so sorry."

"Well don't be. You know how important it is for me to seek justice for you. I wouldn't have it any other way. And you and Nora remember that."

"Oh yes. We will." And he shivered all the more.

HE WAS STILL SHIVERING when he ducked into The Cedar which was thankfully empty at this hour. There he glimpsed a bottle of Jameson. "Better give me a double straight up considering I'm freezing," he pronounced without hesitation as the skinny young guy prepared his set up.

Noah hadn't a clue how long he sat there sipping and staring into the void of his own creation. He really didn't want to think. It was enough knowing the nemie had taken a somewhat calming hold and that the whiskey was keeping him from sliding under.

He arrived home that evening a little groggier. Since there was no sign of Nora, he suspected she was still involved with her planned gallery meeting. So after he lit a fire, he went about shuffling through pages of his society manuscript in progress. This way he figured she wouldn't notice he'd been into the Jamey.

"The sound of silence," she said when she came in later and found him nodding in his wing chair with pages draped across his chest and stomach. He jumped up in a daze just barely salvaging his work from scattering into the fire. Then he managed to kiss her on the cheek but she pulled away. "Just sit back in your chair and don't bother yourself," she snipped sullenly.

"What?" he asked in shock as he tossed the pages onto his desk.

"Why do you act surprised? More or less you've been behaving like this for days."

"Well I didn't think you were—"

"What? So angry until now? Well I'll tell you," she snapped staring directly at him. "After all, I know the reason for your silence now."

"What are you talking about?"

"I went to see Dr. DiCarlo today."

"Well—what—what's wrong with you?"

"You. Don't you know?"

"No—I don't know."

"The Valium. The Librium."

"He told you about that?" he asked aghast.

"I asked him what in bloody hell was going on and yes he told me."

"Well it's only temporary until I get through this *Connoisseur* stuff. It'll be over soon."

"And so will everything else, won't it? You'll just glide right over it all with those bloody yokes and all the other junk you've been taking from only god knows where."

"How do you know all this stuff?" he winced.

"Ah don't be makin' me out to be the feckin' fool Noah. There's no place left to hide."

"I think you're all but losing it Nora," Noah struggled as the insufferable piano from above struck its first evening cords. "If I need a little something to get me through these truly arduous days why would you care?"

"Well you know something. I don't," she roared at him. "You just keep gliding right along leaving everything else behind. All our hopes and dreams. As long as the money is there as it is now, you can just bypass any guilt you might have and keep right on going on the glory road."

"What in god's name is possessing you to say I don't care about our dreams. You've locked yourself in these rooms with your art far too long. That's what I think."

"Oh you do, do you. Well I'll tell you what I think. I think now that you've got your book and all this other stuff going with that Wilton crowd that you have absolutely no intention of moving to Ireland. You couldn't give a tinker's damn about that grand fine house that's being built. No. Your mind, oh more than your mind, your heart and your very soul are on the likes of *Quintessence* and they have been since the very day those gates opened once again for you. Remember I was there. I saw it all in an instant." And with that she burst into tears as the piano increased to such intensity that it rattled the chandelier.

"God damn it," Noah roared as he pounded on the dining table. "You saw how passionate I was about that land and the house in Ireland."

"When you came to the conclusion you were losing everything else. But not any more"

With that Noah stormed over to the liquor table and broke open a fresh bottle of the Jameson. "Oh that's just grand that is," she cried out. "Another great aid for your escape."

"Don't you talk to me this way," he roared. "You've no right after the way I've been slaving for us." And he tossed back a half a crystal tumbler of the brew. Then shaking the empty glass at her, he snapped in fury. "You know something, as much as I yearned for that house and that beautiful land, hearing you like this I wonder if I do want it anymore."

"Oh I wouldn't trouble myself with wondering. You know the answer to that. You're letting it all but drain away with your opulent zealousness. And you know something else, you're letting our love drain away right along with it."

"You don't mean that." Tears sprung to his eyes from the impact.

"Oh dear god I wish I didn't."

He shook his head in disgust and as he wiped the tears away instinctively countered. "Well I'm not going to listen to this idle chatter."

"And that's all it is to you—idle. Well I should have known."

He poured himself another half tumbler and downed it while she stared at him releasing all the bitterness she had been harboring even from herself for so long.

"Pity," he said after a moment, gesturing his glass toward the ceiling. "I used to love listening to that Mozart piano concerto that they're absolutely destroying. Such beauty to be turned into such spoils. It fuckin' well isn't fair. Damn you all." Then wiping his tears, he slammed the whiskey bottle down and smashed the glass on the floor. Afterwards he charged over to the hall tree snatched it up, raced back to his Empire dining table climbed aboard and nearly missing the chandelier began in jousting fashion stabbing the ceiling all to Nora's horror.

"You fuck ass bastards, you bloody fuck ass bastards," he bellowed his lungs out. Then tossing the hall tree aside he jumped to the floor and still roaring grabbed the whiskey bottle again: "I'm going up there and kill them."

In horror and rage, Nora stormed after him and snatched the bottle away threatening him with it. "Stop it, or I'll bloody well flatten ya," she roared.

"Get out of my way!" And he struggled to tear her arm from his shoulder.

"You'll have to kill me first," she bellowed on, looking him straight in the eyes. But what she saw there terrified her. There wasn't just rage; there was madness the likes of which she had never witnessed. As he continued fighting her, she crowned him. He collapsed to the floor, and once she realized his vital signs were all right she left him there.

AS BITTER AS SHE WAS her conscience prevented her from sleeping. So frequently through the night she went back to check on him. Each time she found him tossing about on the bare wood snoring his head off. Finally a sliver of pity managed to battle its way through her anger and she tossed a blanket over his agitated body.

When he awakened in the dazzling brightness of the next morning, he was horrified to find himself on the floor. As he scrambled to his feet flashes of the previous night rushed his mind—the bitter quarreling, the discordant piano, the drinking, the hall tree, the crack up. From the painful lump on his head and the nearly empty whiskey bottle, he gathered she had leveled him.

God it is Saturday isn't it? Fuckin' sure hope it is. I couldn't face Oliver or any shittin' events today. He staggered across the floor to the windows overlooking the park. *How could I have let this fuckin' happen. I've kept it altogether until now.* He rushed about the apartment. The bed was made and she was nowhere to be found. *God she must be raging. Quick I'll build up the fire so she'll be more forgiving when she returns.* As he did so, his pounding head worsened. *God I've got to take something,* he muttered aloud. Then he really panicked and his heart stopped as he rushed toward the bedroom. *Could she have tossed out my pill trove.* He yanked open the drawer and fished to the bottom of his underwear. Those were gone alright. Shit. But then he stopped himself as he remembered some better ammunition. Pete had given him an envelope of morphs *for really bad days* which he kept hidden under his sweaters in his bottom bureau drawer. He'd never taken one before but he figured this had to be the right day. So he popped it and jumped into the shower.

This lessened his headache considerably. But as soon as he realized Nora hadn't returned a new surge of fear arose. A walk about the park in the frosty air only served to undo the good of the shower. It was late afternoon when he returned to the darkened apartment. Turning on the lights summoned a wave of determination. He would go to the kitchen and prepare one of her favorites a *coq au vin* for when she did return. When he opened the fridge, he was stunned. There in the butcher wrapped brown paper was a rarity she must have remembered he was *only wild for* —a Muscovy duck. She must have purchased it earlier in the week from Walter's. That would have been before her discoveries. That would have been when she hadn't given up hope of still rallying them once again.

This thought was unbearable so he pulled another morph from his pocket and popped it before he set about preparing the duck. While he mixed a variety of dried and fresh fruits and chopped onion with port, he thought he heard sounds of her return from above. I won't rush up there he thought. Give her time to settle and the morph to work. After he'd shoveled the fruit mixture into the duck's cavity and waited for the oven to reach the proper temperature, he figured he was ready to face her.

When he reached the living room he could hear her in the bedroom so he threw a couple of logs on the waning fire and decided to sit in the wing chair and wait for her. It was some time later after the fire had begun to blaze again that he heard her steps approach. As mellow as he'd become by now, a shiver of fright coursed through him. At that point she came right up in front of the fire to face him and deliver the *coup de grace*. In one hand she carried a suitcase and in the other a small cardboard box. "What!" he gasped as he sat bolt upright.

"I'm leaving for Ireland this evening."

"Ah Nora, you're not," he snapped as he jumped to his feet.

"Sit down," she ordered as she fought away the vision of his shock and pain. He obeyed and with all the sternness she could muster she went on. "While you're still in your senses this day, I want you to have a clear vision of what I'm about." With that she pitched the cardboard box filled with all the tablets and capsules she had released from their containers into the fire.

"Jesus Nora, you could kill me doing that at a time like this," he gasped.

"Oh that you're already doing yourself, I'd say. You and your suppliers."

He collapsed back into the chair breathless. "I didn't mean—I didn't want to hurt—well it was just to get me through."

"Sure. To take everything we had and shite all over it. Well you've still got all of those over there," she went on gesturing to the marble bar table of bottles. "But I'll take no more of it." And with that she went to the door suitcase in hand.

"Nora. Nora! Don't. Do not go," he pleaded as he followed her with tears flooding his eyes. "I'll stop it. I will. I'll change everything."

She opened the door and then turned back to him. "To what?" As she went down the front steps hailing a passing taxi, he called: "Well when will you be back?"

Opening the taxi door, she swung her case in on the seat and climbed in after it replying: "I haven't a clue. But quite truthfully I don't think you'll even notice."

"Nora. Nora!" he roared as the taxi sped away. She could hear his tortured voice and she began to shake as fear quickly superseded all else.

14

ECHOES OF HIS CALL pursued her all the way to Kennedy where in the ruckus pre-departure she began quaking. It must have been obvious, for once she boarded the plane a stewardess who had been eyeing her came over and asked of her condition. "Ah sure I'm fine," she barely managed. "I just go a bit anxious when I fly."

"Ah love there's no need for a fright. We've only perfect weather conditions all the way to Shannon tonight. And with no one there beside you, you should be able to snatch a good bit of sleep."

Once in her seat, she hugged her body in an attempt to control the trembling. As soon as the engines started, Noah's voice returned only this time a great wave of guilt supplanted her fright. And the pain from this grew in time to such intensity that she desperately wanted to flee. But now it was too late. The plane was turning onto the runway. As it sped for takeoff she could hear the whisper of her words. *Agnus Dei, qui tollis peccata mundi: miserere nobis. Agnus Dei, qui tollis peccata mundi: miserere nobis.* She repeated it over and over. Then finally with the liftoff: *Agnus Dei, qui tollis peccata mundi, dona* Noah *pacem.*

She didn't eat, nor did she sleep. But intermixed with her grave regrets she continued praying her way across the Atlantic. Waiting during the Shannon layover in the still darkness before dawn and with the icy turf-scented dampness rushing the plane's open door, she for the first time realized. *I've gone all this way with me mind in the past and not a thought of what's to come.* When she had made her booking, she automatically said Dublin. Now confronting this, she knew there was no way she could go on to face the whole bloody lot of her family. Not this soon. But still she had time to whisk herself from the plane to the nearest phone box. Fortunately she remembered when she left her job at Aer Lingus the staff had given her parting gifts. Along with the free flights there was a certificate that she'd absentmindedly stuffed in her handbag, for a week's stay at the Dublin Royal Hibernian on Dawson Street. It was meant to be a romantic gift for the two of them. But now she would collect it alone.

THE HOURS OF PAIN that gripped him following the sadness of her departure he'd managed to numb with the pills in an envelope under his sweaters that she hadn't discovered. Since there were only a few left and with Crossland closed until Monday, he had to space them carefully for the remainder of that cruel weekend. The occasional Beefeater martini helped sedate the barren stretches. Late on Sunday afternoon he managed the block and a half to Mass at Epiphany. In a vacant lonely pew his soul cried out to god: *I do believe; help my unbelief!* He stayed there long after the Mass waiting for a signal, an assurance before closing time.

NORA'S ACCOMMODATION in the early 19th century hotel on Dawson Street was an entire suite, one that Noah most definitely would have favored. As such it was an instant irritant and even more so when the porter addressed the rich floral arrangement on the antique Georgian tea table with its complementary bottles of champagne, aged sherry and port. Once he departed the rooms drained to an emptiness that grew more hopeless by the seconds. Immediately she drew the heavy velvet draperies and in the prevailing darkness removed her clothes and crawled between the sheets and the eiderdown to summon the sleep she had lost on the plane. But the bedding offered her no warmth and even though her mind refused to cease recreating moments of their lovemaking, she remained chilled to the bone and unable to sleep. Still she stayed in the darkened rooms as if they offered some sort of refuge. Only once, on that Sunday did she take brief leave and cross through the misty streets over to nearby Johnston's Court and the ancient marbleized Carmelite church of St. Teresa where neither its beauty nor her prayers did little to ease her pain.

Finally on Monday morning after she'd taken a small amount of food for the first time, she left the hotel and made her way up Dawson Street. At the top, she crossed the road entered Stephen's Green then followed the path around until she came to the familiar pavilion overlooking the tree-shaded pond. She remembered how as a girl she had come here with her favorite uncle Freddy, the only person in the family who had really cared for her. His wife and children had been killed in a devastating fire in their flat in Dolphin's Barn when she was but a baby. So as the years passed she went on to share an unspoken loneliness with him. During this time she came to realize how worthy of life this man made her feel as they spent long weekend afternoons here feeding the bits of stale pan to the ducks while he vividly conjured, and for her ears only, the stirring sagas and tragedies of Celtic mythology. It was then that her mind first seized the opportunity to form richly colored, highly detailed painterly images. Now she wondered how her childhood might have changed had this continued. But when she was only twelve the poor man died of a stroke.

As she stood in the pavilion reflecting on this, a voice called out: "Why I can only think it's magic. Nora Clifford. I couldn't believe my own eyes. It is you." It was a voice from long ago that brought with it remnants of all but forgotten bitterness. It was that of Ruth Mary McGuire her one time schoolmate approaching.

"Black magic," Nora instantly responded with an iciness to match the morning air. But paying no mind, lanky Ruth, now dressed in a haughty full-length fox fur threw her arms around her forcing the now trendy two-cheek continental kiss as Nora recoiled in horror.

"Home on visit, is it?" she prodded raising her snoot in what Nora considered to be an obvious attempt to overcome her contempt. "I heard you were married back in the states some time ago."

"Did you now."

"You know, I'm going to be crossing the big pond myself for a fortnight's holidays next month. Funnily enough, I've been meaning to ring your ma to get your address and phone number so I have."

"And why would you want to be doing that now?"

This time Ruth obviously taken aback, stopped and shook her head. "Why surely you remember we used to be the closest of friends. You even had it that I was your only friend."

"*Had it*—would be accurate rightly so. But you see that was before you were after butchering such foolhardiness."

"Ah surely you've come a long way from that lot by now. You couldn't still be moonin' over that Bryan Murphy one. Why sure he was a *louser* from the get go, and I a foolish slip of a girl for letting myself steal him away from you."

"Ruth Mary, I am not about to be entertaining you with the likes of a discourse," Nora admonished with the fiercest glare she could manage. "But I will say this and only this. A betrayal is a betrayal. And from the cut of you, I can see you still wouldn't be past such a sin."

"Well!" huffed Ruth. "I can see you're as sanctimonious as ever. If I were you, I'd be only desperate with the fear that poor fella of yours might be rompin' off with another while you're here and no bother on him. Would you not consider the consequences for the love of god?"

"I'd consider consequences right enough if you don't swing yourself about in that fancy coat and march off down the path, because truth be known Ruth Mary—I can't wait to see the back of you."

With that Ruth Mary stormed from the pavilion leaving Nora quavering in the shifting icy sun as she leaned against the railing. How had she been so brutal to that one over such a long ago folly, she began prodding in her thoughts. After all she had been my closest friend—my only friend all those later girlish years. Yes *only* was right considering the distance of my family and the terrible loss of my beloved uncle. But it *was* true, there was that lovely young fella at the time. That Bryan Murphy who only moments ago that haughty one had vulgarized as a *louser*. How nasty could that be? He was a fine cut of a lad, lonely and innocent and gentle with fierce green eyes that were at the same time so kind and yes loving. I remember that now and how on the day when we walked on the pier at Dun Laoghaire he had taken me hand and whispered with such a nervous voice that he loved me. Then his eyes blanched with the tears, and I could feel me heart for the first time ever leppin' within me as he gave me my first soft kiss on the cheek. Ah sure it wasn't long after, that Ruth Mary was to banjax the lad's innocence only plying his mind with the lies and vulgarities that I had taken up with another on the side. I'd say mostly to this day that out of the terrible hurt she inflicted, he took up with her while she only preened and pranced and blathered it all about Dublin. Oh how only terrible those days that were to come. All to the worse, when after a time I saw him at a distance walking alone through the Green on a misty gray morning and he with the saddest look I could ever have imagined. But I walked on, without his notice, the opposite way only crying me heart out. Oh for sure, it wasn't long after that that he disappeared. He'd hired on as a shipmate and sailed off to Australia—or so they said. And I was left to wonder, still do, if he hadn't gone off with his heart in bits over me. Why didn't I face him with the truth that day in the Green, instead of hurrying from his pain? "God forgive me," she whispered into a stronger icy breeze that now crossed the pond sending the ducks paddling for shelter. The things we do and the things we don't do in this world. And yes her thoughts continued to provoke. "Forgive us our trespasses as we forgive those--" But what if I were to forgive Noah, would that offer a balm or a greater grief?

15

ON MONDAY Noah was at Crossland when it opened feeding Pete a concocted story about a flood in his apartment that had ruined all his ammunition. Replenished he was off to Wilton with the determination to carry on as though nothing had happened.

"How's it going?" Murphs asked as she looked up from her desk.

"Fine," he said with a smile. The two bennies had already set to work and Murphs was the perfect person to test if he was able to mask his heartbreak.

"Sorry, I don't have some decaf for you. I think you could use a good hot cup."

"Why do you say that?"

"Because you're too happy to be happy."

"No. I'm much better. I'm getting over things. I'll be even better once *Connoisseur* is launched next week."

"Well that certainly doesn't end my concern."

"No more than it ends mine about you."

BY NOON he felt as if he were headed in the opposite direction. Spiritless he realized he had to sparkle once more for the next event so he popped another bennie praying it would kick in quickly. It did but unfortunately the earlier bennies seemed to rebound along with it. Lunch at the St. Regis Roof was one of a series of charity events benefiting literacy organizations. By the time Noah arrived he was flying like Superman but with no control over the speed. Before anyone became aware, he had no choice but to do the unthinkable and toss back a couple of martinis. They did help in braking him. Everything was going to be all right. He was able to talk to the photographer, he was able to take notes, chat with the notables before the lunch. All was fortunate. Then he spied Carole Dawson approaching him before she took her seat at the dais. "I think I started a war with the Doubleday people," she whispered. "But never fear I've two legal eagles right behind me fighting for you. Still I can tell you we'd be a lot further along if this court case of mine weren't taking so long."

"How's it going?" he asked but suddenly he felt himself going.

"Fine. You can be sure of that. No matter how long this takes I'll come out way ahead." But her words were fading away. The sweat was rushing from his pours. He had to get out of there.

"Noah, are you all right?"

"I'm fine. I just remembered I-I have to go and phone in some of my—my story." And shakily he made for the door. In his blurred spotty vision the men's room seemed to be empty, he could barely turn on the cold faucet but managed and then struggled to push up his shirt cuffs still his suit sleeves were preventing most of it.

"I do that mister," a voice coming from nowhere and was insisting as he grabbed his arms and pulled off his suit jacket. After that he unbuttoned his shirt sleeves and pulled them up then plunged his hands and forearms under the icy water. The shock revived him for the moment. "You bad. You dopper?" Noah vaguely heard as the man held him. "I know kind like that from Mexico." Then he was soaking a hand towel and slapping it against his neck then his forehead. That took away the spots in front of his eyes and lifted more of his faintness. "You look after me, I get you to taxi." Now he was aware of a tall-middle aged man in a maroon uniform with stern eyes that called the shots. Somehow they made it down in the elevator with Noah breathing deeply and palming the guy a few twenties. Then he and the Mexican managed the steps to a taxi that began to blur "Go lay on back seat. Blood come back that way. Driver, look good after man in back. He look good after you." And so the taxi sped off under the murky sky with Noah lying in prone position all the way back to Wilton.

The Mexican was right. This had helped. He made it all the way to fifth floor editorial with no bother, then into the men's room to pull himself at least somewhat together. Afterward he gulped a vast quantity of water along with a bennie at the fountain. On the way back to his desk, the horror jolted him. He had popped the wrong pill.

"What happened? You look so pale." Murphs asked as she discretely came over and sat beside him.

"Jesus, I don't know what to do," he said in a whisper shaking his head. "I had some drinks at that luncheon and they started to get to me. So I thought I'd hit it with a bennie. But I just popped a nemmie by mistake."

"I don't know what all that means. But it sounds pretty dark and scary to me."

"Uppers and downers. I took a downer instead of an upper. And I'm on deadline with this column story and another *Connoisseur* meeting after that."

"Well that's not all you're on deadline with."

"What do you mean?"

"Oliver and Stan Archer from Champ Com. are making one of their frequent rounds."

"Oh god, what am I going to do? What about my fuckin' story?"

"Well whatever you're going to do you better start doing it fast because here they come now. Are these your notes?" And she snatched his notepad from him.

"Yes."

"I'll work on them for a while. You go hide somewhere until you feel—and look better." And she pushed him away in the nick of time. Hoping it wasn't noticeable, he struggled as he faded and ended up on the fourth floor in the morgue. "Terrific," he muttered then he hid between two sets of floor-to-ceiling dusty shelves housing old clippings. As the spots in front of his vision grew bigger once again, he slid downward into unconsciousness.

"HOW DID YOU READ MY NOTES?" he asked after he snuck back down to Murphs late that afternoon but fortunately a good hour before the *Connoisseur* meeting.

"I can read anyone's notes. I'm the world's worse scribbler. But your photo man Pierre was a great help. He's the best."

"God this copy is terrific." Noah said as he skimmed it.

"Well it wasn't easy compared to you. You could write it in your sleep."

"I almost had to. You saved my life."

"Well I was concerned enough. And so was Carole Dawson. I took your call and told her there were a number of us here with a stomach bug. I think she bought it. But Noah why? Something must be blowing your mind. And don't just blame it all on Doubleday."

He sighed, shook his head and bent closer. In a whisper, he answered: "Would Nora having left me be enough of a reason?"

"What?" she gasped, somehow managing a whisper as well. "When? Where?"

"A few days ago. She went to Ireland."

"Over the drugs?"

"Ah Jez," he sighed and looking around saw that most of the people in their area had gone spoke more freely. "Yes it's that along with *Connoisseur* and a whole bunch of other things including all the other stuff that this place represents and takes away. Then there's that little house in Ireland that I keep pushing further and further into the distance."

"Oh Noah, she loves you so much. How could you have let this happen?"

"It just does. Things start out fine and then they pull apart and go in opposite directions. I don't know why. Isn't that what's happening to you and Jimmy."

"Noah, you listen to me." And she tapped her hand on his desk. "I don't know of anyone in this city who has more than you and Nora together. Don't you see that?"

"But you—you see what happens."

"Leave me out of the equation. From the first day I saw the two of you together—wow. I knew when you were alone you couldn't keep your hands off one another. And it wasn't just sex. You adored each other. And it was a forever thing. And now you're saying stuff somehow got pulled apart. I can't buy that. Jimmy and I never have had anything as fantastic and I was so happy for you—that you did. Now you're going to stop all of this nonsense and get it back together."

"I know. I have to try."

"Have to try! You damn well will."

AFTER TWO MORE DAYS OF SUFFERING Dublin with her unbearable ache for Noah intensifying, she began to find the Royal Hibernian more intolerable than she could ever have imagined. And all this time she agonized over what she might do, where she might go and had arrived at the fearful conclusion that she couldn't manage anywhere without him the way he was when they first fell in love. Even at its worst on a day of gales and lashing rains when she had tried to escape by going to the National Gallery, heartache followed her and loomed doubly worse when all the art expressing doomed love seemed to command her attention, especially Fredric Burton's intense Pre-Raphaelite watercolor *Meeting On The Turret Stairs.*

When she finally fled the Gallery that mid-March afternoon, the rain had ceased and because the sun was in full warming bloom she let herself be drawn into a brisk walk hoping it would consume some of her grief. But she'd only begun when her mind reversed itself to Burton's turret stairs watercolor and the fated passion of Hellelil and Hilderbrand. When she tried to shoo it away, she couldn't prevent the tragic vision of the Celtic lovers Diarmaid and Grainne from taking its place. Even the rich brightness of the Green worked against her as music from Wagner's opera *Tristan and Isolde* came to play over her mind with its final *Liebestod* love-death aria. It guided her across the way to South King Street and the Gaiety Theatre where she had seen the opera performed a good few years ago. And sure there was something else about this theatre that had drawn her back to stare at it. Now it was as if time had switched further back to the Fifties and a haunting voice rose from the exterior. It was because the thoughts of her beloved uncle had resurfaced that first morning in the Green, she immediately recognized the voice of the Australian soprano Joan Hammond singing the aria from Puccini's *Gianni Schicchi—O My Beloved Father*. That voice along with the symphonic power of the orchestra and the thundering ovation upon its completion possessed her once again. She could see herself in the center front row of the grand upper circle—she and her uncle dressed in the only suit he had ever owned and almost never wore. He was an opera lover who could scarcely afford the bits for even the poorest seats. Yet on this night and obviously for her benefit he had scrapped together the necessary pounds for two of the finest seats. After the applause ceased, Miss Hammond proceeded with an encore in Italian—*O Mio Babbino Caro* that was even more electrifying. When she looked over at her uncle, tears were streaming down his cheeks. It was then that she reached over and stroked his strong carpenter's hand and realized that he was not only overwhelmed by the plaintive tone of the aria but was combining it with the terrible never ending pain of his own miserable life making it doubly worse. Later when they were filing out of the theatre, he took hold of her shoulder and whispered: "Nora, I'd want to be after telling you I'd have had everything taken from me if it weren't for you. I wouldn't even know there would be another world to come if--" And either he had stopped or his voice had trailed off into the crowd. No matter how much she prodded her mind after that evening, she couldn't sort out the meaning of those last words. She did think of asking him from time to time but always stopped herself feeling it might just encourage more sadness. Maybe later, she kept telling herself. But within a year he was dead, and she was left abysmally lonely once again.

After that, she let herself drift down through the Grafton Street bustle of which she was scarcely aware to Johnston's Court and once again Saint Teresa's Carmelite Church. Except for a scattering, it was empty this time so she sat and tried so desperately to unlock her mind to give free reign to the church's peace and its two-hundred year old marble and stained glass beauty. She had no idea of her lingering time. But at some point she found herself kneeling in prayer. Beside those for Noah, she prayed for her uncle who now felt so close it was as if he were sitting in the pew next to her. Oh now I think

I know what he meant, her mind leapt. It was heaven and god, that's what it was. He was saying that through all his grief I had guided him onward. Thanks be to god, she told herself as she left the church. Some good had happened of that emotional afternoon.

BUT WITH THE POSSIBILITY of anguishing through another sleepless night at the Hibernian, she decided that any situation would be better and told herself that perhaps she had been wrong about her family, that possibly there could be some compassion there. Well no matter how small the chance, it was worth the chancing.

"Nora, since you walked through the door of this house today, you've said so little of Noah," mammy said late that first night after they'd pulled up the sitting room chairs to a roaring fire and were sipping the Hennessy her ma had stowed away for special occasions. "When you did your words were as scarce as those of a Trappist monk. But I didn't want to speak of this before the da was asleep."

"I haven't spoken a word to anyone, nor in any way do I want the family to know." And she sighed as she decided to risk telling her. "He doesn't seem to care anymore. Least ways not the way he used to."

"Well what would you be after saying to me? Is he beatin' you? Is there another woman shagging him?"

"Mammy! No! I think he still loves me right enough. But by now he's taken to going mad when he's fluthered."

"Oh is that so?" Already Nora could feel the coldness edging into her mam's tone.

"Yes. Even now with a book that he's written and sold, he's so caught into that the bleedin' success and money business. That's when he goes on the tare." And she began shifting about nervously as though she might just jump and run.

"Well now let me tether you here for a time, Nora Ellen," mammy insisted. "Does he still have his job at the newspaper place?"

"Oh for sure he does. But you couldn't tell me for one minute that it's good for him. There's something so devious about it."

"What would that be? Making a living?" she snapped.

"Oh no mammy. You don't know how corrupting it can be. That society rubbish he has always to be writing. It's only blather, and it just takes away all that's so fine about him."

"Does it now?"

"Well yes," she insisted in an almost desperate plea for understanding. "And you know what would concern me the most? *Gravely concern* me now. I've been after finding him taking these tablets."

"What tablets?"

"These tranquilizers, barbiturates and those amphetamines. They have slang for that junk in America.

Uppers and downers. Speed they call some of them. That's because—"

"They make you high. For the love of god Nora Ellen where do you think I was born in a *clutchie's* byre? And would *grave concern* be the new phraseology in America today?"

"What are you after saying to me mammy?"

"Well, I'll tell you straight out. And there's to be no palaver about it. I think you've fallin' short of the full shillin', mind ya."

"Ah mammy, how could you be saying such a thing? You don't know what it's like—"

"Oh I don't do I? I don't know what it's like to see men drunk, to see them fade and disappear from the grand fine cut of brutes they once were. Well I'll tell you what's truly sad and you should know it from the days you were here. Half the ones in this part of Dublin are fluthered all the time. Why they don't even have the work to go to anymore. They're on the dole. Spendin' that money on the drink, then roarin' at their wives, beatin' them, and punishin' their children."

"Well I remember a good lot of that right enough. But I could never live it."

"So have you gone and blinded yourself then? You don't know the good fortune you've got. Your da was a clever able man in his day, a darlin' one all the same. But even with the good work he had, he was only drunk with the hunger to be trawlin' in all the more for the family. He had such hopes and plans. But I'll tell you even the strongest man who looks to the stars might find that there's dark nights in the lot of it. And I'd say that that would be doubly true in America. Sure it would be the truth anywhere that a man like that gets fluthered now and then seeing he can't quite catch hold of all he wants. It's only right minded that he should, don't you know. And you fussin' there that he isn't making the sheep's eyes at you anymore."

"Ah mammy, the sheep's eyes! Will ya give over for the love of god? Would you not try to understand at least a word of what I'm saying? It's the whole life that he's after taken to. I can't live with the likes of that. Seeing the one I all but worship only dissolving to bits before me eyes."

"God in heaven, I thought you had more pluck about you than that. *Whingin'* about and *crowin'* away. *I can't live with the likes of that.* How could you be one of the Cliffords and not have the wits you were born with. It's the way the world is. And don't you think you can be after changing things. It wasn't given to you alone, you know. Now I'll tell you this, and only this. Go back to that lovely fella who only adores ya, no matter what his problems might be, and look after him."

"But if I were to do that I think he'd only be making a turn for the worse."

"I won't be plaumausing you. I'll tell you Mrs. It's your job to be maneuvering him away from that road. That's what's intended. If you don't do that, and do that right off before your bread is baked, I'd say you'd lose him in a city as looney as that New York is."

"But if he's only bound to be lost, what can I do?

"Ah Nora Ellen! The longer *ya* live the shorter *ya* grow."

Once again Nora was going to protest, to defend in hopes of being offered some care or at the very least some consolation. But she stopped herself, for she realized that all that was ever to come was a greater slagging. And once again it came hurtling back at her, the vision of the child in the garden on Christmas morning.

"HEY, IT'S NOAH," he whispered rather breathlessly early the next evening, praying he had given her enough time to reverse herself.

"Yes," she replied coldly in a hushed tone from the privacy of the hall phone.

"Well I—I just wanted to say how I'm going half crazy missing you."

"Really? I'm surprised."

"Yeah. Whether it's worth anything or not."

"I don't know that it is."

"Do you think that you might come back—soon?"

"I don't know. But I wouldn't be after putting the word *soon* into it."

"Ah Nora. I can't stop thinking about you."

"Sure that must be quite a feat with your brain as poisoned as it is these days."

"That'll all stop if you come back. I'm bloody useless without you."

"And you're none the better with me. Look Noah, you've messed me about long enough. I can stick no more."

"What are you going to do then?"

"I'll tend to that at a future time, thank you very much. If I were to be in your shoes, I'd be worrying about what you were going to do. But I expect I know the answer to that already. Just more of the same old. You know I can't bear to be talking to you any longer. It's just too painful." Then she broke the connection.

16

NOW THERE WERE FOUR FORCES working against him—his book in the gutter again, the advance money that still might have to be repaid, the fear that Oliver could use this information as a leverage and now and far worse the possibility that Nora would never return. Oh god the thought of the later sent him trembling and soon something terrifying was splitting inside him. It was right there that he summoned the determination he now so desperately needed. He would take account of every move he made so there would be no more mistakes. One bennie in the morning after breakfast, one nemmie at night before bed and only small amounts of wine or champagne at events. This had to be if he were to move forward again. If he could lick all of this and get Nora back. But hadn't he been here before?

THE BIG NIGHT in honor of the birth of *The Connoisseur's World* at the lavish Four Seasons was suddenly upon them. With its horticultural decor of live trees and floral beds which had recently been switched from darker winter themes to the blooming brightness of spring that April, it's vast pool room was the perfect setting for one of the most touted events of the season. It was to be one that Nora no doubt would have referred to as a come-all-ya. Several hundred people had been invited and were congregating as the shimmering dark golden glitter of the brass chains and modern art overhangs highlighted them. And all were showering praise on the Wilton staff's table-book sized new magazine, which could only be called stunning with its lavish color photography printed on premium-coated offset paper and with writing that rivaled the finest literary publications.

Noah dressed in his dapper tux and holding true to his inner voice was busily greeting the many while Peter Duchin and his small orchestra quietly underlined the event with romantic interludes. Occasionally he would sip a champagne, but only occasionally. Then to his amazement a microphone was produced beside the pool and Oliver suddenly appeared before it to make an announcement.

"Ah would only like to express a few words tonight. Ah know how much delight you have expressed to me over ah new stah—Connoisseur. Ah have to say to you that much of this fine achievement is due to ah super writer, editor-publisher and now vice-president—Noah Mason." Applause burst forth with Stan Archer and the Champ Com. heading it. Then Oliver continued. *" Yes. We have the finest talent we could ask for in ah midst and ah'd just like to put forth that those few who may not have appreciated him in past performance should caution yahselves in the future to honor him for his fine achievements. Thank you Noah. And ah thank you all for being here tonight."*

And now there was an explosion of applause. Noah couldn't shed the shock of Oliver's words much less the scare when Oliver asked him to speak a few words. When that moment was over, Noah couldn't remember what he'd said. All he knew was that for the next hour he was hugged, kissed and received so many powerful grips that his hands were rendered numb. Even those who still held grudges suddenly shed them. Now for at least ninety percent of the affluent world, he *was* once again their star. It was as if a fever of exuberance had suddenly taken over the room one that completely erased the past. The only one that it seemed not to have touched was himself. For just below the surface and born with an intense pain, an overwhelming anxiety was overtaking him.

By now he had forgotten about the Dom Perignon and all the drinks that were wafting by on waiters trays. Even the most delectable hors d'oeuvres he'd ever seen didn't attract him.

"Well I see you're alone with all your splendor," a voice among the last of the well-wishers greeted him worsening his condition.

"Oh what business is that of yours, Gloria?" Noah asked coldly as he pulled away from her clutch.

"Well I wouldn't want to see you all alone on your night of nights—and other nights as well so word goes round."

"But why would you want to tear yourself away from those muscle men you snuck in here."

"Oh they're my protectorate. I can dismiss them at a moments notice."

"Well I want you to dismiss yourself as well and be on your merry way. And if you try anything—*protectorate* or not—I can assure you that I will lift you into my arms and heave you into that pool, because quite frankly Gloria I think you need a good bath."

IT WAS SOME HOURS LATER that he arrived at Gramercy Park. He prided himself in so determinedly keeping his powerful anxiety beneath the surface until now when facing the empty apartment it overflowed. Nemmie he thought and then quickly took one. But after twenty minutes it wasn't doing anything. At that point he spied the bottle of Beefeater atop the marble liquor table across the room. He hadn't thought of it or touched it for days. No alcohol from that table since Nora left. Oh go ahead, the other voice inside him said. Break the rule this once after the golden night you've had. You deserve it. So he listened.

17

"AH NOAH, SHE'S ALREADY GONE," mammy said when he phoned Dublin after his shower. "Sure she's on the Aer Lingus flight to New York this afternoon."

"Oh she is, is she?" he replied with such great relief. "Well I've been on assignment. I'd have no way of knowing."

"She left for the airport at half ten so I'd chance she'd be half way there by now."

"Oh I'll be off to meet her then."

"Sure I'd say you should. That would be grand. I only wished you'd come here with her. She seemed to take it as a bit of a loss all the same."

He knew from her tone that Nora must have told her things about them. But he told himself he had to put such thoughts aside as he phoned Aer Lingus and found that the flight would arrive at four thirty. Then he quickly called their occasional cleaning lady to come and do a swift morning job on the absent-minded mess he'd created living alone. After that he felt the first wave of pleasure since way before she left. But soon this was accompanied by a shock of fear. Was he ready? Could he truly hold himself together? God I've got to get rid of those, he said aloud as he began snatching the drugs from the fireplace mantle. I'll cut back. I'll ease out of them until they're all gone and that will be the end of it. So he pulled out one of the lighter bookcases between the living room and the dining room, hid them on the floor and then shifted it back. Maybe he should rid himself of all the liquor bottles on the marble stand. But no that might be going too far.

Still he feared deep in his gut that he was not ready. He told himself that maybe he could overcome some of this when he had lunch with Carole.

But when Carol called him at the office later that morning her voice was distant. It was as if he were talking to someone else. "How are you?"

"Oh I think I'm fine now. But I'll tell you all about it over lunch. It'll have to be an early one though."

"Well I do have to tell you the good news that came this morning. We've saved your advance for certain. But I've also some bad news. I'm afraid we won't be having lunch Noah. It's why I wasn't at the *Connoisseur* party last night."

"Oh I did miss you. What's wrong?"

"John had a heart attack in the courtroom yesterday afternoon. It was a massive one, and he died within five minutes."

"Oh my god."

"Well even though we'd grown to hate one another, it was horrific all the same."

"I can just imagine. Are you all right?"

"Well still stunned. He was from Newport you know. But most of the close members of his family have passed away or by now grown apart. So I've made arrangements for the body to be flown to Providence and then taken to the family's gravesite in Newport. There'll be a brief service there and that will be it."

"I'll have to make plans to come up."

"No you will not. Absolutely no. I want this over as soon as possible with no one. I greatly appreciate your concern though. But I will ask you to make me a promise. I would be far more upset than I am now if I thought you were still the way you were when I saw you at the St. Regis that day. You must tell me you won't let me fail on my second chance."

"You won't you know," he answered realizing she was referring to her son. "You're so good to be concerned, but just now things are looking so much brighter once again," he said with enough assurance to convince her and he hoped even himself.

18

"HOW DID YOU KNOW I was on this flight?" she asked with considerable irritation when he greeted her at the International Arrivals gate. She had not expected him nor did she want him there. She had hoped to slip into the city and establish herself first, this as a means of control over what the future might bring.

"It was a fluke. I couldn't last any longer without hearing from you. So I picked up the phone and your mother told me you were already on the flight. So here I am as if by fate." He took her suitcase, sat it down and began to put his arms around her to kiss her.

She immediately pushed him away. "I meant what I told you when you rang up. It's just too painful to be around you." And seeing him, she realized she meant it. The darkening around the eyes, the facial hollowness that had taken over in the weeks before she left were still there betraying him.

"Well why are you here then?"

"My work is here and I'm behind."

"What does that mean—*I'm too painful?*"

"Look Noah, I've booked a room at the Gramercy Park. I'll come round and collect some of my basics and work as much as I can there until I find an apartment."

"Find an apartment. But you have an apartment. This is crazy. I know I was wrong. I was way off base. Intolerable, I know that—"

"Noah, I'm not going to stand in the middle of this bloomin' big hall arguing with you in front of half the bloody world." With that she snatched up her case and headed for the door leaving him stunned. When he caught hold of himself, he chased after her as wishful patterns of their first meeting at

International Arrivals flashed through his mind. He hailed a cab and called out to her. "At least let us ride to the city together."

She yielded.

On their way, he continued. "I know you were right to go off. To give me the full jolt I needed."

"Well I have to tell you, you don't look all that much the better for having gotten it."

"That's because I never got over the pain of missing you. But I have stopped myself."

"For how long?" She knew it sounded nasty and felt a tinge of regret.

"I've got a whole new pattern going now. I've pulled myself out of the quicksand." He prayed she'd believe him more than he believed himself.

"Have you now?" she asked looking directly at him. "Well I have my doubts. How do you pull yourself out of that lot when it's already over your head? And you with no help."

"Ah I did have help."

"What? Who?" she asked startled of his answer.

"You."

"You chancer. I don't believe a word of it."

"Would you not give the chancer a chance?"

"Ah you've been given your chances." And she shook her head. "But I'd have to hand it to you, Noah. You still haven't lost your way about dancing with the words. And you certainly did a grand job with those in your new magazine.

They had copies of it displayed foremost over there in Eason's magazine section. You did do beautiful work on it. Oh and I'm after forgetting to tell you there was a piece in the arts section of the *Irish Times* about *Connoisseur* and you being responsible for this great new American magazine. I'm only ragin' that me ma snatched it away from me as I was going out the door and then they were all out of copies at the airport by the time I got there. But it was grand to see you dancin' with the words all the same."

And he laughed the way he'd laughed all those many years ago and that struck her and started something in her. Then he smiled ruefully. "Other than you I guess that's all I've got left."

"Other than me? You do presume there mister."

"Ah Nora."

"No. No ah Nora." And she was fighting herself.

"Well, would you not give it a night or two?"

"I'm afraid," she answered fighting a few tears. "It's as simple as that. I'm afraid for my sanity. You mess with me too much, you do."

"I won't. I won't. I promise," he insisted looking directly at her. "Besides I've already tidied the apartment. So there is no mess. And there's flowers. I-I mean I got flowers."

Then she let go a burst of laughter, shook her head and blurted. "I'll give it a week, I will." But she hated herself for not holding out. Yet she would have hated herself all the more if she had.

"THE LANGUAGE OF THE FLOWERS," he whispered after they walked into the now gleaming apartment. Startled, she uttered a small gasp. At the last minute, he had filled their lovely Waterford vases with yellow tulips from the local flower shop. As she gazed through the rooms, it was as if dozens of bursts of cadmium yellow united to form one all-encompassing blinding sun that set her ablaze with a warmth she'd all but forgotten was possible. Standing behind her, Noah continued to whisper. "I couldn't get the white roses tipped with red on such a short notice. But I remembered that when you gave yellow tulips at the turn-of-the-century it meant—" He paused and put his hands on her shoulders. "It meant that you were hopelessly in love." Then he slid his hands down over the silkiness of her dress to her already yielding breasts. "And— And that you were utterly consumed with passion."

ABSENCE MUST NOT only make the heart grow fonder but another major pump as well, Noah delighted after her shower when they were in bed and in the throes once more. Fonder and, as to the latter, harder thank god. He was bringing back the creamy rose blush to her milky flesh. He so adored that and so longed to do it all the while she was away. Things were going to be all right now. This was their new beginning and it would take care of the past.

Nora was amazed at the deftness and power of his lovemaking. And it continued on through the evening pitching her into one explosive orgasm after another just as it had when they were first together. At one point he asked if she wanted something to eat. "No. I just want this and you." And in-between the bouts, he held her tightly and she whispered how much she loved and missed him. After she fell asleep, Noah struggled to bask in his new sense of well-being. But slowly he felt it begin to slip away and he couldn't prevent an edginess from creeping in and taking control. Then it wasn't long before he felt the dire need to take something. "God I don't want to leave you, but I've got to take a leak," he whispered as he slipped his arms from around her. When she didn't react he knew she was still deeply asleep. So he darted out to the bookcase, reached under it for the vial and knowing the recent failure of just one nemmie extracted two. After he flushed them down with a glass of water, he snuck back to bed, slipped his arms back around her and she barely stirred. God how can I fight myself out of this, he agonized until he fell asleep.

"DAMN, THOSE BLOODY HORNS blaring away." He jumped up from reading the paper and paced back and forth by the windows. "They're enough to drive you bananas." It had been a few nights since Nora's return. After that first night, he'd forced himself to go cold turkey but it was unbalancing him.

"They'll settle down in another hour," Nora insisted as she left her easel and put some Vivaldi on the hi-fi to quiet his growing agitation which she only prayed wasn't a sign of drug withdrawal. "I'll make us a nice cup of tea."

By the time she returned with the tea tray, he had forced himself into a calmer temperament as he sat on the sofa looking out at twilight on the park. "I guess I should have told you before you left," he said as she sat beside him and handed him a cup.

"Told me what?"

"Doubleday dropped the book from their line," he sighed.

"Oh my god, why didn't you tell me? What happened?"

"It was all too grim at the time. Marie McCloud was fired and the new chief editor started pitching out a lot of her stuff including mine. It happens all the time they say. But anyway they started giving me a hell of a time wanting my advance back. Lawyers and all. So that was a double bitch. The book was a failure again and then they were going to steal my pride—well my ability to pay for the house anyway. That would have totally blown my mind. But at least the money part is a moot point now. Carole banded together her lawyer friends and they screwed Doubleday."

"Oh Noah." With that, she took the tea from him, put her arms around his shoulders and kissed him. "I hadn't a clue you were going through all this. I feel even more the *louser* now." And she went teary.

"Don't." And he hugged her tightly.

"I'm so worried about you. You're not still on those vile tablets are you?" she asked pulling back and looking him in the eyes.

"No. No," he answered feeling the presence of the bookcase looming behind them and his stomach churning.

"Noah would you not think of taking a leave of absence from Wilton a few months from now. I'll tell you why. And hear me out now. While I was in Dublin, I was able to ring Hughie at his neighbors' house across the way. He told me they had a grand bit of fine weather and that the house is all but complete now. I didn't have the heart to travel all the way to Donegal. Not without you. But if it's ready, why would we not take advantage of at least a short bit of time. Let's not think long term any more. That may have scared the daylights out of us to begin with. And that was my fault. Look I have my next showing coming up in early August. And I gather you'll have done two more issues of *Connoisseur* by then. It's still every two months isn't it?"

"For now anyway."

"Well by then we'd be organized. And you'd be truly set with the new magazine. So—we'd be able to borrow some time. And let me just be saying this. That book is going to sell. It came so close it just has to. And in the meantime we'll be over there. You could be working on your other book. Free from all your restraints here."

"Yeah. You make it sound truly easy."

"So would we not do this then?"

"Sure. Why not," he said hugging her and fending all thoughts of drawbacks.

19

BY NOW APRIL had slipped past and the park's English elms had long since burst forth with their greenery in unison with the current crops of azaleas, tulips and dogwood. Along with this, Noah had resumed his morning and evening bookends to try to cover what he now considered to be the disease of his anxiety. It was exhibiting itself through his racing pulse, trembling and vertigo. While these were confined mainly to late evening or early morning, he wondered how long it would be before they would become ever present. Although she said nothing, he knew Nora was most likely aware of his slide. Well she would have had to since his sexual desire had begun dwindling again.

In an attempt to prevent everything from splitting away, Noah began seeking advice. When he went to Carole's apartment for tea after John's funeral, he confessed to his pill popping aided by alcohol to ease his fears. Maybe she knew of a bright doctor who could give him some sort of a stabilizer. "Well I do," she said without hesitation. "I saw him for some time after Peter died. He was a great asset. Dr. Hartley. I would have suggested him sooner, but I had no idea you had problems that had progressed like this, until just recently when I began to wonder."

So off he went to see a rather elderly white-haired Dr. Hartley who he was shocked to learn was a psychiatrist. He reminded him of his stern philosophy professor from Ithaca. "You look like you were once a fine young man of action on all fronts but I guess you're just letting that disappear," he said with firm voice as he pulled on his horn rims and stared directly at him. Noah already felt himself weakening and unable to flash a concealing front as he squeezed his hands together.

"Well I don't know how to say—"

"I know you don't. But you don't have to. I can see it there in the background. And this is my own vision because Carole said nothing of your problem. The pills, the booze, the anxiety. I think you're doing a pretty good job of hiding it from your workplace. I've seen your new magazine, and it's a fine piece of work. But I must ask, have those who were close begun to abandon you?"

"Well no. No. Well—my wife did leave and go back home to Ireland for a short while. But she's back now. But things are so complicated here. Like the beginnings and the ends of days are getting so messed up. And the more I try to straighten them out—and I want to—the more snarled they get. Now I don't feel I can get—Oh bloody hell. What a tangled web." And he felt himself begin to sweat.

"Well now you're talking. Sir Walter serves you well, I fear."

"Oh I didn't mean—"

"Oh I think you did whether you know it or not. *Oh what a tangled web we weave.*"

And Noah jumped. "Well I'm not practicing to deceive anybody."

"No? Just everybody. And most of all yourself."

"Well can't you give me something? Some sort of a straightening agent that will bring back some sense of well-being."

"No. You've fenced yourself in and now you have to do the deconstructing."

"But how?"

"Well no drugs, no magic. But there are a number of good clinics out there. And there's AA. Oh I can guide you to the best. But you have to have the will-power to follow through. And let me just say this. If you don't follow through, I fear young Lochinvar you will be no more. And that would be a true tragedy."

And that was that. "It has to be a lie," Noah muttered too loudly to himself as others on board the descending elevator in Hartley's Park Avenue building turned and stared. He felt like sticking his tongue out at them. Oh what the hell and so he did, giving them all whiplash as they turned away registering shocking disdain. It was an elevator and a building he'd never be in again, he told himself as he fled into a taxi that foggy morning. And so he came full circle back to Pete's.

"I've got something here that's pretty terrific."

"What?" he asked as his scrambled brain latched onto the word *terrific*.

"Christmas trees."

"Christmas trees! Don't give me jokes at this point."

"No. They're for real. At least some call them that. Green you see. Oh big in England and they're getting hot here."

"Jesus." Noah shook his head. "I've taken everything else. I guess I can swallow a Christmas tree."

"It's dexamyl—a combination barbie and amphetamine. A dexie. Everything in one pill. It'll elevate your mood and counter the side effects of the upper at the same time. Could be perfect."

"Are you sure it will work?"

"Sure does for me." Yet he was still trembling as before. "But I'll give you some stronger nemies and bennies just in case."

Sure something should work, he told himself as he walked back to the office. But then Dr. Hartley's words began repeating on him and he started to quiver. God he hoped Murphs would be there. She'd be calming, he figured as the Wilton elevator rose to fifth floor editorial. But when the door opened and he stepped out, he found Murphs waiting to get on. And it was like two nightmares colliding.

"What's wrong?"

"I just found out Maine won. We've split. Jimmy's gone," she gulped then stopped the elevator door from closing. "But he's not gone alone," she blurted out the words.

"Apparently he's had some woman on the side for god knows how long—and she's gone off with him. Oh god, I can't talk now." She rushed on in tears. "I've got to get out of here." Before he could stop her, the elevator door closed.

DURING THE DAYS that followed, Murphs just didn't show up for work. Noah tried phoning her daily but with no reply. One afternoon, he stopped by her Thirty-eighth Street apartment. When she didn't answer her buzzer, he rang the super's. "I see her most times every day," the old man said when he came to the entrance door. "She's not as chirpy as she used to be, and I haven't seen her boyfriend Jimmy of late."

"Well tell her Noah stopped by to ask of her."

When she did return to Wilton, she was like another person. "I can't talk of it, Noah. And I don't want to talk at all."

"But I always talked to you."

"I have to have my time and space." That's all she would say, and then she went about her work in a slow piecemeal completely un-Murphs-like fashion.

20

SHE DIDN'T KNOW WHEN IT HAPPENED. Since her return from Ireland, Nora had stayed heart and soul with Noah always watching, caring, encouraging through all the growing resurgence of anxiety. But then she awakened early one morning in late May with the bright light leaking though the curtains and it was as if a bomb had gone off inside her. She looked over at Noah who was still in a deep sleep. Too deep not to be induced. Yet she felt absolutely nothing—no fear, no pity, not even the slightest bit of anger. She remained in this torpid state until Julian from Winsor de Caine reached her by phone that afternoon. "I came back from my trip to Florence this morning and found our Nora Cliffords practically gone."

"Well that sounds grand all the same," she offered, barely able to muster the words.

"Yes, but where does that leave us? I thought I'd be seeing at least a few new additions when I arrived after the thrill of selling the Met and the Whitney. And what about your summer show? August is not that far off. I want to take advantage of that time when not much else is happening at the other galleries. Make people who are here really stand up and take notice."

"Oh I won't let you down, don't you know. Sure I've some things for you now and I'm really struggling ahead on the show." Struggling was the right word, she thought later. These days she felt herself in fair form if she was able to lift the canvas to the easel.

DAYS PASSED all seemingly a blur. Her hand moved of its own accord across her sketch pad doodling charcoal faces of strangers she must have at one time recorded somewhere in her mind.

One day with all the energy she could muster she snatched up a group of the sketches, forced herself to the easel and working with oils began to develop a Dublin street scene. It was her own northside street. Once she had committed the basic outline, the buildings and the characters, she found herself working at an almost frantic pace creating an illusion of the dispirited. Soon with her palette knife she was jabbing on paint, thick dark quantities that enhanced the airlessness and forced a sense of entrapment. The darkness was now eradicating all the light. At one point she dropped the knife and ran from the apartment to escape seizure.

If she were to paint at all—and more to the point not lose, truly lose her sanity altogether, she would have to flee the familiar and do as she had done once before, go out into the city to the unfamiliar. Now it was the only way to jump-start and bring a much needed new direction to her work.

IT HAD BEEN A CLOUDLESS fresh early June morning, in complete contrast to the mood of the city. She had been to the UN to sketch distraught students flailing their peace banners as disillusionment eroded their rage. Then she had gone on to Tompkins Square Park where she'd drawn indigent hippie couples all seemingly resigned to quiet despair, some dissolute, some floundering without any provocation. And those with children had already infected them with the same contagious disease. How different these faces were to those she and Noah had seen at that Sheep Meadow Be-In several springs before when all was abundant with hope.

This she thought was a graphic example of the current national zeitgeist, a youthful country unraveling at war within and without. Then it came to her that this was but a mirroring of her own growing mood. In stark contrast, a band of shave-headed Hare Krishna in their saffron robes and with their musical clappers began snaking its way through the park. Their faces in unison had been enveloped by a wave of bliss that seemed idiotic. As they ranted on their primrose path they came to appear more and more the buffoons. Now she realized she was interweaving this dramatic clash in her sketching. Suddenly she felt alive again as if a new dimension appeared in her work though she told herself it could be but temporary.

"Well, I see you're still very much at it," a male voice called from behind her bench.

Nora turned around and instantly felt embarrassed. "Yes," she replied. Who was this person? There was something about him that made her feel she'd met him before but she didn't have a clue.

"You don't remember?" he pursued.

"Um. I—do. I just can't place—"

"Subconsciously you do. You're just madly scrambling to forget." He laughed and shook his head as he came around the bench, walking with the slight limp that reminded her. "The Mayflower Coffee Shop."

"Oh I don't believe it. You're Conrad. Conrad—"

"Conrad Landis. But call me Connie," he said shaking her hand, then sitting beside her and shrugging off his mail-pouch bag that held his cameras.

"That's right," she said as she closed her sketch pad and slipped it into her knitted tote along with the drawing pencils. "But you look so different." And indeed he did, she thought. He was the exact opposite of what he once was— a ghostly visage from one of German artist Otto Dix's works—one that had only terrified her. Now he looked and acted as if someone was actually living behind what now were incredibly green eyes.

"Human, you mean?" he asked as he laughed heartily and drew his hand through his now long curly black hair. It had previously been nearly skin-head short.

"Did you go to Ireland?"

"Sure did. And it was the right move too. I got myself together there. Well--" And he hesitated. "That is--somewhat together." Then he grinned a slightly condescending toothy grin. "I got a lot of great material too. My *Life* magazine feature's coming out next month."

"Oh I'd love to hear all about it," she replied almost without thought.

"Well if you'd grant me one more chance. I mean if you'd dare, we could go for another coffee. Or better still a late lunch."

"Ah I don't know. I think it's a bit too late, and god only knows I've loads to do."

"Oh come, we won't be long. Besides I'm a changed man, I'll tell you." And suddenly she realized his once unforgettably grating voice had gone to a much more appealing softer gravelly tone.

"Well okay, just a bite," she said. As they started walking, he talked of all the places he'd fallen in love with in Ireland, and she noticed how ruddy his skin had become compared to its previous ashen state. Although he was still very thin, he no longer looked seedy. To the contrary, he was quite the handsome lot in what appeared to be new jeans, hiking boots and a denim jacket that was winningly set off by a brilliant white T-shirt. The more they walked the less apparent his limp became. They ended over on the west side at Minetta's on MacDougal. "I come here when I want to splurge a little and get away from the grubby East Village. They have great cannelloni, and wait till you taste their zabaglione," he enthused with delight as he opened the door for her. Once inside the rustic old tavern with sawdust on the floors and walls laden with caricature drawings, he hesitated. "I hope you like it now. It is pretty rough-hewn. But I mean a lot of artists hang out here. Franz Kline, Mel Bernstein, Jake Spenser. Some of them did these drawings before they were famous."

"Ah this is grand," she said. "I love it." And he seemed very relieved.

After they were seated in a booth and had ordered, he continued to rhapsodize about Ireland, and she still couldn't believe this was the same man who had once nearly scared the wits from her. "I woke up each day there with a sense of peace and a feeling that there might be something of value."

"And you didn't have those feelings here?"

He shook his head. "Still don't. The war changed all that. Along with the aid of retroactive wicked headaches."

"Oh I'd forgotten you were there."

"Yeah, I was there alright. With everything that surrounded it. It took everything."

She noticed the fire in his eyes dim and remembered that look from before. Only this time instead of finding him off putting, she felt herself caught by his sadness. "It's like looking up one day and finding no one's there. And no one will be there. I can't put it in words. I don't know if I'll ever—"

"A wipeout?"

He scratched his head, looked at her for a moment, chuckled and nodded. "A wipeout. That's good. I wouldn't have thought an Irish person would come up with that word."

"Oh I've learned it well." Then she suddenly felt embarrassed and quickly went on to cover. "But how did you after come upon Ireland and as a subject to begin with?"

"Well I found out by accident that *Life* wanted a piece, and I knew they were interested in my work. My Vietnam stuff. I mean I'm no Larry Burrows, but it's pretty good. So they gave me a chance. Suppose it didn't hurt that I gave them my leprechaun imitation." With that he shrunk his torso, made a cocked hat of his napkin, let his bright eyes dart about and with a goofy grin began wiggling about in the booth. "This is supposed to be a jig. But I don't dare to stand up here and do it. Do I?"

"Don't you dare," she warned and then she burst into roaring laughter. "That without the least bit of doubt in my mind was the worst imitation I've ever seen."

As he pulled the napkin from his head and straightened his torso, his grin became a soft smile and his face glowed. "I liked that."

"What?" she asked.

"Your laughter."

"Go way out of that. You haven't heard anyone laugh before?"

He looked at her and then he looked away in thought as the lines of his angular face tensed. Then he looked back. "No," he replied in a dark somber tone. "Not in a very long time."

"Oh come now," she said shaking her head to break the mood.

"No," he said again holding himself there. "No. Not that I'm aware of. Not like that."

She shook her head again in disbelief. But it was really to mask her embarrassment for she couldn't deny or control her rush of caring. "Well anyway, tell us more about your trip."

At that point their lunch arrived and he went on about how Ireland had cleansed him of much of the war and why he wore the white Ts all the time. Then he walked her back to Third Avenue. "I'm sure I'll be seeing you around. I've got a lot of freelance jobs going here to keep the wolves away for a couple of months."

"Good luck."

"Oh and mind that laugh," he called after her as she started uptown. "Tell that husband of yours it should be a national treasure."

As she walked back to Gramercy Park, she thought him a bit cheeky for that last remark since she hadn't mentioned Noah once. Still it didn't erase the fact that he was attractively errant and genuine.

21

"OLIVER I'D LIKE TO SPEAK TO YOU before the *Connoisseur* meeting," Noah said as he dropped by his office early one morning. It was the first chance he'd had to snare him into a personal moment after several weeks of trying. And all this time he kept seeing Nora fade and felt himself slipping away.

"Well *ah* feel *ah* need to speak to you as well. Come in Noah and have a seat. *Ah* am thrilled with the work you and the others completed for the June *Connoisseur*. *The Houses of The Hamptons and The Players Inside Them* is truly fabulous. *Ah* don't think there's ever been such a complete roundup. But now *ah* must ask you for even more. Right off the mark, we have to start moving—"

"Wait. Oliver before we get into this I must tell you something," Noah insisted as he sped along on his two after-breakfast bennies. "As you said we have a great group working on this magazine. They really know what they're doing. So in light of this, shortly after our June issue goes to press I want to take a leave of absence."

"W-h-a-t?" Oliver nearly choked.

"Yes. Somewhere around six months."

"W-h-y, what forever for, forevermore?" Even though he was now gasping, he managed to add: "Do you have an illness to reveal, Noah? Oh heaven forbid."

"No," he laughed. "I don't have an illness. It's just that—"

"Not because of that book that hasn't sold yet? Or the new one that might be trying to steal you away?"

"No. No. No. And it's not trying to steal me away. It's just that my wife and I need some time away to be closer again. Could you not understand how important that is?"

Oliver sighed, and sat forward at his George IV desk. "*Ah* could. Not that it would work with my wife." Then he suddenly stopped, closed his eyes, tipped his fair-locked head back, shook it and drifted for a few burning seconds before snapping back. "But listen to me Noah. *Ah* have such plans for you, and there just isn't time right now for leaves of absence." And then without a pause, he went straight into it. "*Ah* think in the August issue of *Connoisseur*, we are going to bulldoze conventional high society. Shiver their timbers once again.

We'll do the whole thing, every page on the youth culture we've only been touching on in *FCD* for the last couple of years."

"But Oliver isn't that a bit remote. It is *Connoisseur.*"

"Oh *ah* would agree, some of the grunginess is pretty deplorable. But that's not the idea. The one thing these people have is the ability to change at a frenetic pace and that's not just their clothes it's everything about their life styles. Even with Viet Nam, the drugs, the protests and all that, so many of them still have verve and a freedom that's lifting up all these exciting ideas from the arts, the counterculture, the underground. They*ah* alive and what's the Establishment these days—all dreary and in near reposal. We'll pull out the most attractive of these young people from all over the country and our bureaus in Europe will follow up. We'll unfurl the banner of youth across all of *ahwa* pages. When we're finished, we'll have the stale doddery Establishment drooling over what they have. Of course they*ah* too far gone to ever be able to catch up with it all, but they'll try. *Ah* think we should call these young people *The Jeans Generation.* Oh the delicious envy they*ah* all going to feel for it. Don't you see the dam has burst and all these great ideas are gushing forth. Ideas that will affect everybody's lifestyles and even reach deeply into the world of the up and coming connoisseurs as well. Now Noah we'll have to get going on coordinating all these assignments."

"Yes we'll do that for the August issue," Noah said but shook his head. "Oliver won't you please stop and consider what I've asked for? I'd *need* a leave after that."

"Noah, *ah* can't even put to mind such a request. You know you *ah ahwa stah* of *stahs.* We need you involved here in everything including some of the traveling. Now—*ah* can see that you *aha* exasperated. But m-o-n-e-y! *Ah* would only hope that will calm you down. Three hundred a week more." And he watched Noah's face which did not change. "Five hundred then. No, make it a thousand. *Ah* know Stan Archer would fully concur. You *ah* worth that for the amount of advertising we're pulling in alone. And you*ah* getting better by the day. *Ah* never have to concern myself with the quality of your work. So does this make it for you?"

Noah first in shock, then experiencing involuntary shivers of delight nodded in the affirmative. God why did this appeal to him so much, he fretted. Why indeed couldn't he turn himself into one of those he'd be writing about? Why couldn't he do that for Nora?

22

NOW HE WANTED TO QUIT the pills more than ever. Just toss them all down the nearest toilet and let the money solve everything. This is what he told himself through all the working bustle of that day. But by its end, he knew he couldn't. The guilt prevailed. This time the money increase seemed to make it worse. Take more pills to cover up— everything. He thought of the dexies—those tree ones that worked both ways. He hadn't tried them before, even though Pete said they were the coolest things out there. But it was the idea that maybe they might make you feel as if you were going in opposing directions at the same time that riddled him with fears. Well he had to do something. So he dared one that night and prayed that Nora wouldn't notice.

NOW WHEN NORA WORKED outdoors, she always tried for the brightest days to do her sketching. It meant that she could struggle to elude the full-scale existential by cornering it with the brightness of the day. As she did she would immediately make note of the lightness of those colors for later translation to her oils.

Seated on a bench at the top of the Great Lawn on a sunny unusually hot day for the middle of June, she forced herself to sketch joy under the bright blue—joy of the passersby, the runners, the vendors. But when it became obvious it was an empty endeavor, her concentration shifted of its own free will to one of impending alienation and foreboding. It was the oblivion of one young couple as they shared a joint at a neighboring bench. She, braless in a tie-dyed tank top and demim cutoffs cradled her lover's head as he stretched shirtless with his tattered bell-bottomed legs across the remainder of the bench. The merciful western breeze carried the drift of their conversation. His raspy words that it could be their last hours together caused the girl to lean forward, kiss his unshaven face and stroke his long mane of hair. "I want to go with you." He took another drag, released the scented smoke. "How can you when I don't even know where I'm going? How crazy is this? I just get the gig at the Vanguard and a review in the *Voice* that says I'm the most intelligent, inventive player of the day and now I've got to fuckin' flee into hiding." "I gotta hang in there with you." "Where in Canada or Mexico as the babe of an anti-war dropout?" As he took the last suck on the joint, he sat up, pulled his clarinet from its case under the bench and began hitting some mournful notes while a crowd of hippies came up the lawn and gathered round them.

Nora lost in her sketching barely noticed a photographer some distance away rapidly snapping shots of the group. It was when he finished and started over to her that she realized. "I can't believe my luck," he called out beaming and came right up and sat beside her. Instantly she felt the waves of working exuberance still emanating from him. "It's like a fluke that I'm here." And she caught the thrill of his green eyes. "I got this rush assignment from *Newsweek* for an update piece they want on all of this," he went on motioning to the group. "But you know I almost didn't come this far." He said it with so much fervor that it was clear he would have considered it almost tragic if he'd missed her. She felt a sharp twinge of embarrassment. "Well you're looking great," he continued as he smiled broadly and glanced down at her sketchpad. "And working great," he enthused.

"Ah it's too initial to be sure. It would take a good lot more to put this right."

"No. You've captured what they're all about in a first sketch."

"Maybe so. But I'd say you've done far better," she insisted glancing at his Rollei as he stuffed it in his camera bag. "That raw image of the moment, only the camera can capture that today." They both looked over at the crowd, and Conrad shook his head. "I used to think they were so wrong. I used to think the war was such a noble cause."

"You really did?"

"Oh yeah, I was gung-ho all the way. Supercharged with valor. Really wanted to be the warrior at all costs. God I wanted it so badly, I could think of nothing but glory of the flag."

"Well I wouldn't say that was all wrong, if you believed in it."

"Huh. No one else felt that way. I was on the razor's edge from the get go."

Nora shook her head at the shame of it.

"Yeah. I was very close to my parents and my older brother. But they were pacifists and as such they were dead set against my going into the Army and off to the Nam. It was an unforgivable criminal act. An act against god. Well I was so possessed I went anyway, and I haven't seen any of them since. They won't even talk to me. And my friends, they were worse. They all thought it was a bad joke. When they realized I was serious, they wanted to shit can me. Excuse my language, but it's the only way to call it. They were all into U.N.

demonstrations and Pentagon protests and when they didn't work the next step was running away to Canada. All the while I was dropping out of NYU to do my John Wayne thing. I met one of them just before I left, and he said how does it feel to betray your friends? Then he spit in my face. So much for eight years of binding friendship."

"I guess abandonment comes easily for some." Staring across the Great Lawn at the maze of distant city buildings, she was completely caught in the emotion of what she was thinking and blinked tears. The words that followed, she didn't think she had spoken. "What you think is permanent, is solid, is real—it all unravels."

"I'm sorry, I didn't mean to—" he whispered and reached out to stroke her head. When she turned back to him he seemed shocked and disturbed. Then she realized she had spoken them.

"Oh no." She jumped and pulled away, stunned at what was happening. "Sorry I was just thinking. I mean how it could happen to all these people. Well I mean to you as well." She was rambling she knew, just trying to hide.

"It's alright. Don't be upset. It's just—well that I guess things happen to you too. And I'm hearing your losses."

Now she was letting herself be soothed by his words while she yielded all the more to his green.

"I want to hear them you know," he continued earnestly.

She had no idea how long she sat there before she felt her sketchpad and charcoal pencil slip to the ground. Suddenly she realized he had his arm around her and that his warm broad hand was stroking her shoulder.

Instantly she jumped up, collected her sketchpad and pencil from the ground, tossed them into her large knitted tote as in a complete state of fluster she gasped: "I don't know how I could be after gibbering on so. You must think me the fool."

"Oh no, I'd never think that. To the contrary, I—"

Avoiding his eyes, she checked her watch. "God, look at the time. I'm only dead late. I was to meet my husband ages ago," she said in a rush. It was a lie but she was trying to cover as many bases as she could. "I'll have to hurry so I will," she continued as she began her get away. Then looking back at him as he leaned against the bench, she caught in a flash the warmth of his being and the truth of his concern. It swept around her and she had to push out the words. "Well maybe I'll see you soon." Barely able to escape, she felt as if she were moving in slow motion with his soft gravelly words slowing her all the more. "I hope so. I sure hope so. I mean—I'd like that. I'll keep looking. I will."

His words: *I'll keep looking. I will*—followed her all through the park and all the way home.

23

SHE ACTUALLY BRIGHTENED when Noah told her the news, chancing the hope that in some way their presence might bring him round once again and somehow set him right. And indeed he did seem almost cheerful that Sunday afternoon as they set to preparing that evening's food. "I am happy they're coming for dinner. I know they mean so much to you."

"Well it will be good to see them again," he said and was delighted knowing how she once felt. As for himself, he thought they might spur a return of the youthful optimism that had once buoyed them, well at least Russell and Tim and maybe by now Janet as well. But maybe they wouldn't. After all, it had been a long time since he'd seriously talked with any of them."

He was relieved when she went off to tidy the living room. From the kitchen cabinet, he quickly snatched the bottle of Stoli they used when they were preparing Italian sauces and wolfed down a fruit juice tumbler full. God what was he doing this for, he'd been so good about the booze until now.

"WELL YOU PROBABLY HEARD my new production company is going great guns since we released *Thunderstruck* last year. Why it even out-grossed *Romeo and Juliet* and *The Odd Couple.* Now everybody's knocking at our door with great, great production ideas. Mike Nichols has one that I think could turn into a Golden Glober, maybe even Oscar. And there's so much more," Russell, dressed in California linen casuals, gushed forth over the Beefeater martinis Noah had made with aplomb.

"Hey don't get too cocky there, buddy," Tim chimed right in. "I've already made it award-wise. I've nailed three

Cleos for my agency. And Mary Wells of Wells Rich Greene, a pretty hot agency in its own right, would do anything, pay anything to get me to abandon ship and head over to them. That of course could capsize my place if I were to leave with a cargo of juicy clients. "

"Well I'm sure, and I'm not being cocky. I'm just so thrilled that we're all rolling right along. And I saw that great new magazine of yours Noah. What a production."

"Well it's not really mine it's Wilton's," Noah conceded as he polished off his martini feeling sharp pangs of envy over their achievements. "But--I do have some other news. Yes. Doubleday is publishing my novel. It'll be out this fall."

Nora instantly went into shock. Was it the drink that was allowing him to lie, had he taken some of those vile tablets? As yet, she couldn't tell, but she feared maybe he'd already gone over the top.

"Why I had no idea it was that far along, pal. Why didn't you tell us?"

"Well I was so busy I didn't get a chance to talk about it," he shrugged.

"Didn't get a chance to talk about it? How could you hold out?" Russell exclaimed.

"It's kind of boring to talk about work after all this time."

"But what else would we talk about?"

"You said it Russell," Janet snapped. "What else would we talk about?" And with that she polished off the last half of her martini in one go.

"Well what's that supposed to mean?" Russell huffed.

"That you don't talk about anything else but work. Ad nauseam. That's what I mean. Honestly I came here because I wanted to see and enjoy our friends. And all you've done is ramble on about your new production company and your dear properties that are—s-o-o akin to *Midnight Cowboy* and *Butch Cassidy* only I think they're much better by far," Janet ended perfectly imitating Russell's words and speech pattern.

"Well, you've certainly made your feelings utterly clear," Russell retorted in a more hushed tone. "But what you haven't made clear is just how much you enjoy spending the money."

"Yes, at least doing that makes me feel like the kids and I have *something* out there. But I just wish you'd shut up about work at least for tonight. And Noah, I wish you'd make me another delicious martini so I can enjoy myself."

"Of course I'd be only too delighted," Noah leapt at the chance. "Anyone else?" The rest declined as they continued to sip their first drinks. Noah went over to his marble table and with his back to them dumped a good portion of the Beefeaters into his glass and downed it. Then he set about making proper martinis for both himself and Janet. Meanwhile Tim, who now looked more like a well-groomed hippie dressed in a trendy new jeans outfit with his long golden red hair in loose curls, drifted over to Noah while Nora and the others talked away. "I think I will have another refill," he said. And then in a whisper: "I'm certainly glad to see the two of you together like this, pal. I was really worried when she wasn't with you at the Four Seasons on your night of nights. And then when you didn't call me—" "Oh no. It's rough with all this work. But we're okay," Noah shrugged as he finished mixing Tim's drink. "Sure? You wouldn't lie to me, pal?" "Sure." And he nodded and smiled. "Well don't you two enter the war torn zone yet," Tim warned as he took his fresh martini and looked over at Janet and Russell.

While this was taking place, Nora had tried to engage Russell and Janet in conversation about their twins and living in California. But this quickly shifted to a pleasant two-way chat as Russell turned back to Noah and Tim with yet more news of his production company. By dinner time, after a third round of martinis and Noah getting looser by the minute with his false words of Doubleday's promotional plans, Tim's current girlfriend Beth arrived full of apologies for her tardiness because her new quarterly magazine called *Free World* was about to go to press. Younger than Tim but stunningly attractive and dressed in a jeans outfit as well, she took the time to French kiss him before they seated themselves at the elaborately fitted dining table.

"Well Timothy," Russell smirked. "Do you and your new acquaintance here have some news for us?"

"Oh I always have some news, buddy."

"Oh he's just being shy," Beth chirped and boldly reached down and squeezed his thigh. With that, Tim leaned over and they kissed again.

"Hah, he hasn't a shy bone in his body," Noah blurted.

"Maybe you could lend them your bedroom for a while," Russell suggested noting the thigh action.

"You would suggest such a thing ," Janet snapped. "It would be right up your alley, wouldn't it?"

Nora utterly embarrassed began discussing the food she was passing as Noah poured the wine.

"Well maybe we are being a bit far out," Tim said as he laughed.

"We are not, Timmy," Beth insisted. "You see it's all part of a new or I should say *the* new philosophy. What we all want to be and should be are Consciousness Three People."

"What is it, a disease?" Russell jested.

"Well if it pertains to you, it is."

"Hon enough," Russell said glaring. But she merely began drinking her wine as soon as she finished the remains of her martini.

"No," Beth laughed. "It's a whole new wave of the future. A law professor from Yale hit onto it. This ad guy friend from Random House sent me the galleys of this new book they're about to do. It's going to be called *Greening of America* by Charles Reich. I nearly flipped out when I read it. What it does is define with certainty a great quiet revolution that's going to sweep this country. It's a new form of humanism that will overtake everything in its way and replace it with freedom. Even the Establishment will finally go. Of course the whole idea is to get out and be what we are. To reject the work ethic as we know it today."

"Well I'll concede that the old work ethic exhausted itself long ago," Russell obviously dying to interject agreed. "But I've already moved on to greater, far more sophisticated forms of achievement. That's what we're doing with my new production company. You know we've called it *Star Reach*. And we *have* reached them. Why we've got some of the biggest names out there coming to us."

At this point Janet burst into spontaneous hysterical laughter. "Hon!" Russell gasped in shock. But she paid him no mind and continued until she was quaking. "I'm sorry," she finally said. "But you don't know how farcical that is. Russell deluding himself about work ethics. Can you just believe it?" And she quickly polished of her glass of wine and nodded to Noah for more. "I'm sorry," she said to Nora who sat beside her. "But I get so exasperated."

"I know. I know," Nora commiserated and gave her a hug. It was then that she realized how Janet's once youthful face had aged with lines. Her big wondrous eyes had surrendered their sparkle. And her slender figure had lost far too much weight, a fact that her silky gray pants suit did little to conceal. But even more upsetting, her bright lively sense of humor had been all but buried in bitter cynicism. "I feel like that so often. Even when Noah's here he's working away. I get so little of him anymore, you know." And suddenly there was a prevailing silence where Janet grew sullen and began staring at her wine glass as she twisted its stem. "You know it's stolen my faith from me," Janet finally whispered. "I don't even go to Mass anymore. I never thought there'd come a time when money meant more to me. But it does."

"Oh Janet, why don't you just turn the whole evening into a wake?"

"W-e-l-l," Beth suddenly burst forth in a defusing exuberant tone. "We're going to start controlling our lives, aren't we Timmy." And she was back squeezing his thigh. "We're getting out of this city. We're heading west to the mountains."

"What?" exclaimed Russell. "You're not serious?"

"Oh yes we are. And that's not all. We're getting hitched." Beth confided suddenly bringing everyone to attention and Tim to a pallor that obviously none of them had ever seen. Then there was silence again. "Well say something Timmy"

"What? You've already said it all."

"But you seem so sad." And she squeezed his thigh again. This time he pulled away.

"I didn't think we were going to announce all this tonight."

By now everyone was turning to the wine and Noah was struggling to pull himself out of his slowly developing haze so he could go off to collect more bottles. On his way, he stopped by the bathroom medicine cabinet to collect a bennie from the bottom of the green Buffrin bottle, his renewed hiding place since the back of the bookcase became too risky. When he couldn't find one, he popped a dexie tree hoping the morning side would work a long while before the evening side took over.

Back at the table with open bottles in hand, he began quickly pouring to the anxious group as Beth still carried on. "All the rat race anachronisms are going to be passé. Freedom's the word."

"Well what are you going to do with all this freedom, Timothy?" Russell probed. "And out west yet? Open a stud farm?"

For the first time ever, Noah noticed Tim cringe.

"Oh we're looking at mountain properties," Beth pronounced. "We'll invest in all these small businesses. Well you have no idea—"

"We aren't ready to do anything quite yet Beth," Tim interjected sharply with an uncharacteristic flash of anger. "Especially with the market zigzagging about and my stocks right along with it."

"But you said yourself that we couldn't put it off much longer. We'd both be better off out there. Me as publisher of my new magazine and you doing the real writing you always wanted to do. You said your friends here are going to do that when their house in Ireland is ready. You can't fade from this brave decision, Tim"

Nora looked over at Noah whose spirit had suddenly kicked back in as he determinedly added: "No, you can't fade away from such a brave decision, buddy. You should follow our lead."

For a moment Nora's spirit leapt as well until it was brought to a full stop when she realized his was most likely drug induced from everything else he was saying.

"Well I suppose if you've all got the cash flow and that's what you *yearn* to do," Russell went on with as much condescension as he could muster.

"Cash smash," Janet snarled. "It's always all to do with money. Oh give me some more wine Noah so I can forget what we never had because of it."

"Janet you've had enough," Russell warned.

"Oh, we've all had enough. Enough of nothing," she replied.

"Yes, I think we've talked enough of all this for one night," Tim said, polishing off his wine and setting the glass aside,

"Well that's just it, we haven't," Beth, who approached being sloshed herself, insisted as she poured another full glass of wine. "I don't know why you're being so distant about all this Timmy. The last time we got into it, you were so excited you got a hard-on the size of the Empire State Building."

"Lucky you," Janet piped from her haze. "I wouldn't even know what one of those is anymore. Russell never shares them with me."

With that, Tim expressed complete shock. "I think it's time we all disappeared and left the Masons with some peace for the rest of the evening. At least they're on an even keel."

When they were on the steps outside saying their goodbyes, Noah slipped his arm around Nora in an effort to make it look as though Tim, being the only one in the crowd who had remained sober, had made a proper assessment. *Ave atque vale*, dear buddy, he called back.

"Well I wondered what happened to all the Latin," Noah replied.

"Oh I guess I lost some of It along the way," he replied as he looked at Noah and frowned.

"Ah you're just short of a few extra drinks."

"WELL I'D HAVE TO SAY you put on a pretty good show for them. Fair dues to you," Nora snipped as she and Noah began carting the dirty dishes down to the kitchen.

"How do you mean?" he asked as the dexie that had lifted him began its reversal far too soon.

"Oh Noah couldn't you have bloody well stopped yourself after they praised your work on *Connoisseur*? Did you have to go and lie?" she asked letting her anger build as they tossed the dishes into the sink.

"Well I guess I wanted them to feel I was as important as they are."

"That's what you call important? Why except for poor Janet, they've turned into a bunch of gasbags. And for you to turn into one as well. Why you're only just trashing yourself."

"That seems a bit unfair."

"It's not unfair. It's ugly. And god only knows how much your letting yourself erode again." And she looked him in the face as she waited for his reply.

"Really?!" he sternly replied returning her stare. "Well I thought I was doing pretty well of late."

"Look Noah, I know you're on the sneak again. When you're here you may as well not be. I've noticed that for sure since the night after we talked about your taking a leave."

"Oh you don't know what you're going on about." And he turned from her, went to the cabinet, took out the Stoli bottle and poured himself a drink. "Do you want one as well so you can calm down?"

"You must be joking. Feck the fizzin' dishes, I'm going to bed." With that, she stormed up the stairs.

Noah just stood there staring out at the street as he continued to drink. But it was really doing him in and as he turned to head for the stairs he could feel himself stagger. It was then that he couldn't believe his eyes. He was seeing a vision of Tim standing in the kitchen doorway. Noah blinked and blinked again, but he was still there. "You forgot to lock your door," he said.

"God you scared me," Noah mumbled as he wove about.

"You're scaring me," Tim replied as he continued staring at him.

"Wha—what's—wrong?"

"You for one, buddy. What happened? And so fast after we left?"

"You're here. Wh-a-t?"

"Beth forgot her handbag. She must have left it in the living room."

"O-h-h. I s-e-e. We will just have to go u-p-s-t-a-i-r-s and get it." And he nodded as he staggered for the stairs while Tim, first locking the door, followed suit. After he helped guide Noah up to the living room, he quickly snatched up Beth's bag.

"I'm a little w-o-o-z-y right now. Nora's gone to bed," he just managed as he squeezed Tim's arm.

As fast as he was dipping, Noah could see more shock register in Tim's face. "Well you'd better take a cold shower before you join her." Then as he left through the front door, he turned back. "And you better damn well call me before you let yourself get like this again, pal. I need to save you too, you know."

24

"HELLO NORA? I hope it's all right that I called you."

She instantly recognized the voice. It was late the next morning after Noah had leapt up as though nothing had happened, made toast and coffee and went off to work.

"I mean—" he continued a little nervously. "I found your number in the phone book and—Are you angry?"

"No," and she laughed a little. She certainly was surprised.

"Well something happened this morning, and I thought of you right away. I thought maybe you could advise me."

"What's that?" Already she felt a hesitance considering her last reaction to him in the park.

"This new gallery that opened on Fifty-seventh Street called the Witkin. It's all photography. Well they called and said they were interested in my work."

"Ah that's grand. But sure what can I advise?"

"Well I've got to get a collection together to show them, and I have so much. I don't want to overwhelm them and kill the whole thing."

THEY MET AGAIN at Minetta's for a late lunch, and as they ate Conrad talked on about how everything was changing for him. "I think it really is pretty incredible. Even after coming back from Ireland I was still zonked out. But in the last few weeks it's like I'm moving out from under some of this stuff and I'm beginning to see things again. Crazy huh?"

Magical, she almost said as the slight rasp of his whispery words seemed to be buzzing inside her. "No," she said finally. "Not crazy especially with news of the gallery."

"I guess that's encouraging it. That's why I need your help." And with that having finished their lunch, he came around to her side of the booth and prepared to show her his portfolio. Suddenly she was far more aware of the dazzling brightness of his white T-shirt tucked into his snug jeans and of the heat of his body that hit her with such intensity it was as if an oven door had opened. It swept over the silk of her muted peach peasant dress overwhelming her until all she was aware of was this extraordinary silkiness. His broad hands moved deftly, eagerly extracting photos and flashing them in front of her. After a moment she realized she was watching his hands instead of looking at his pictures.

"You're going too fast," she snapped. "I can't think about them."

"Oh sorry. I'm sorry. I really am. I'm forcing this stuff on you."

"It's not stuff. And you're not forcing it on me. It just takes time." She wanted to close down these feelings, to switch them off like a light. Finally in an effort to stifle his entrancing mobility, she took the pictures away from him and began to leaf through them herself. All the while she could feel his stare. At one point she glanced back at him and realized that there was more to the stare than just curiosity concerning what she thought of his work. It was distracting to be sure, but it wasn't at all upsetting to her. "Why don't you go to the men's room for a minute."

"You don't want to do this," he said as he shook his head then he smiled and laughed. "Let's—Let me—It was a bad idea." And he began to take his work from her.

"No." She stopped him. "It's not a bad idea. But I can't do it with you staring at me. Would you not go off for a bit and come back? "

"All right. Okay." And he put his hands up in front of her. Then as he rose, he asked with big eyes and all seriousness. "Just long enough to take a leak? Or should I go help them wash the dishes?"

She burst into laughter. "Get out of here."

"See I like that laugh. None other." He turned away then turned back. "But you know I think I like the way you feel when you laugh even more."

She watched him as he ambled off with that slight limp, and she realized she didn't want him to go.

HE WAS FAIR. He took his time in the men's room and after that, because most of the lunchtime patrons had left, he went about examining all the artist sketches that adorned the Minetta's walls.

"The character studies are by far the best," Nora said when she finally motioned him back to their booth. "You have a way of picking out things in people that I don't think most photographers would even notice," she said flipping through some of them again. "You just catch them at the strangest angles and at the perfect moment to tell a story in a different way. They get to you."

"Oh well—" he said tossing his head. "If you want to make a guy feel good." And he grinned.

"No, I don't want to make a guy feel good. I want to make a gallery feel good. And as such I have to tell you I'd lose a good deal of this landscape stuff. I mean it's all good. Excellent if you like. But there's only a few that are really unique. And you don't want anything that's not unique or dramatic. Which makes me wonder, what happened to your Viet Nam stuff?"

He jumped as if she had given him a fright. "Oh—"

"I mean it must represent a major segment of your life."

"Yeah—" he sighed. "I guess after I got back I thought once I got my foot in the door with a few of those things I could put them away and forever forget them."

"Well to be very frank with you Conrad, I don't see how you can. I mean I think those would be only spectacular."

"Oh they're spectacular all right." His face blanched and as he moved his now trembling hands to his lap. She realized she had tapped veins that had sent shock waves railing through him. "I'm sorry," she said.

"No. You don't have to be. I know."

"It's just that I'm sure the people at the gallery will want to see them." But even as she said this she could feel his hurt reverberating through her.

"It's just that it's hard to face." And he reached up with one of his hands and squeezed hers as it rested on the table. In that touch she could feel his need. But when she looked at him, his eyes hadn't gone dead as they once had. Instead they were still alive with the hope that she'd seen when he'd returned from Ireland.

In those few seconds his hand had ceased to tremble, and she slowly slipped hers from his grip. But she could still feel the heat of it coursing through her. "I'd say it might be best to leave it for now," she said. But he was still with those hopeful eyes. "Rather—Well until you're able—You just feel a little stronger about—"

"Would you do it with me?" he asked abruptly without releasing her vision.

"Oh-- Well-- It's so-- Personal. How could I?

"I can't do it without you. At least not now. I-- I guess I knew I couldn't leave it closed forever. But I didn't know it would be this soon."

"Well sometimes circumstances force you to do just that-- when-- when you think you're least prepared." Where did that come from, she thought. Right out of her wellspring, and it came for herself.

"Will you then?"

THE NEXT THING SHE KNEW, they were in a cab headed for his apartment. She was only aware of a constant shivery buzz caused by the look of his eyes and the sudden rush of his words. "I hope I'm not frightening you or that you think I'm taking advantage. God, if you do please tell me now."

"No," she said as her mind locked on *God if you do*. He was so good and so caring.

"I'm not in control. And I'm almost never like this. I thought I'd gotten beyond it all. Zapped it off I mean. Look I don't want to scare you—" He squeezed her hand again but let it go immediately.

"You're not. Stop saying that. You're only making it worse for yourself and making me feel useless."

"Oh never. Never ever." And there was that smile.

THE APARTMENT WAS ON Styvesant Street. It was one of those fine 19th century brick townhouses that instantly made her think of Noah and all the pain of that world. "How did you get this place?"

"Oh I just lucked out when I got back from the Nam. This young couple was transferred out of town for a year or so and they wanted to sublet. Don't get any crazy ideas," he said as he unlocked the door and they went inside. "It's pretty ratty and it's just a couple of rooms at the top." As they climbed up the four creaking flights of a worn carpet staircase, he continued in his rush of now raspy whispers: "I guess they must have been madly in love to be able to exist in such cramped quarters. But I guess I kind of like that idea. I mean what else do you need? It's really the way it should be if you're in love. Tight if it's right. The closer the better."

She had lost her breath and her head was reeling by the time they'd reached the top. The wooden door had been shamelessly painted orange as had the rest of the building's apartment doors. "They're horrible. Every time I look at them I think Agent Orange barrels." As he unlocked the door, he apologized: "Excuse the mess." He opened it and they were faced with his living room. A multi-paned window saved it from complete disaster. "Here, town dump really pertains," he said gesturing to the scruffy sofa bed, the worn overstuffed armchair, the rickety coffee table and the scattering of faded cushions on the dull bare wood floor. "The walls are aged New York white. Well aged," he continued as he switched on the hoodless bulb light that hung from the high ceiling to take away some of the dimness that even the window failed to resolve. "Hideous, isn't it? But this junk is all I could afford or wanted to afford when I got the place. The rest of my funds went into the photographic stuff and my dark room-kitchen combo. He pulled back the heavy drapes that closed off the tiny kitchen to reveal a fridge, a miniscule range, a sink and a dark room table, lights and supplies. "Toilet's back there somewhere if you can find it." As he scrambled around picking up dirty T-shirts, jeans and underwear to toss in the sagging, split-sided wicket basket, he gasped: "God, how the shit did I have the nerve to bring you here? Maybe we should just leave. Just pretend this never happened." And he began to spray the living room with air freshener.

"It's better if you open the window." She chuckled and shook her head.

"Oh yeah." And he did so. "It's hot in here, isn't it? There's no ac, but let me turn on the fan. With that, he switched on an enormous floor fan that was so powerful it sent sheets of newspapers, photographs, even laundry from the wicker basket cascading through the air. A T-shirt slapped across Nora's face as she was nearly blown out the door. "Oh shit, that damn fan. Let me save you." He grabbed her, pulled her away from its force and slammed the door. Then he quickly turned the fan down. "Are you all right?"

"Yes," she said as she pulled away the T-shirt that by now had landed on her shoulder. "But I have a feeling you might be entering into a cyclonic mode. I just hope you don't have any freshly brewed coffee around."

"Oh shit, you really do hate this."

"No I don't."

"Okay then." And he grinned. "Maybe a little lemonade though. I'm pretty great at that."

SHE WAS OVERCOME. She'd seen Vietnam pictures before. She'd seen all sorts of pictures of war. She'd studied them because she had an abiding interest in photography especially as a burgeoning art form. But these were something else. She had gone through one large cardboard box of blowups. And he had another whole box packed to the brim. All the while she looked, he stood staring out the window at the slow approach of a late afternoon summer storm. Lightening streaks and jags seared the room highlighting his grim face.

God in heaven, she thought, how could this man have gone through all this and still be alive. Physically and mentally. These were not just painful pictures. They were excruciating. To walk through hell, come out of it and be standing here now was all she could think. She ached to go over to him, to put her arms around him, to hold him. But she couldn't.

She went through much of the second box, put the pictures back and closed it. Then she leaned forward in the easy chair, looked down at the floor and began rubbing her forehead as if it would snatch away the unbearable horror. The only sound in the room was that of the thunder and the fall of cloudburst rain. Suddenly powerful gusts of wind began to sweep the rain through the open window soaking the floor and Conrad who seemed oblivious. With that Nora rose and watching the chain lightening streak across his face, she crossed the squeaky floor to him. Then she reached up with her right hand and stroked his forehead and his face. Very slowly he turned to her, and she could see the pain reflected there. With the rain pouring in on them, he lifted his arms and slide them around her and with a gasp clutched her to him, held her as if his life depended on it while his whole body shook.

She had no idea how long they stood there or how long the rain continued. She was aware only of the blinding lightening that seemed to fuse them. Then she was stroking his head hoping that she could extract some of the ache, draw it out as she would a poison.

When he was calm again she pulled back and looked at him. A couple of tears fell from his eyes, but he smiled at her, a soft tender smile. As he leaned forward and his full moist lips brushed hers as he closed his eyes. Again she had gone lightheaded as she had when she climbed his stairs. His lips were more insistent now, and she was yielding to them. When she realized what was happening, she gently pushed him back. "No," she whispered. "We can't."

"I know. I'm sorry."

"No. Don't be sorry. It's just that you need someone. Especially now. Someone to mind you and care for you. Don't you have a girl?"

"I did," he sighed and walked a bit away from her.

"What happened?"

"Oh, it's a story for another time," he replied shaking his head. Then he turned back to her. "Look, I can never thank you enough for helping me face this."

"Well all you have to do is dip into either box and take a handful of those pictures to the gallery people. You don't even have to look at them. You'll stun them with every one."

"Can I do something for you? Anything? Can I get you a drink?"

"No. God I've got to be on my way." The storm had passed and it was already dusk. "Oh look at my dress it's soaked and so are you. I don't know why we have this thing with liquids." She laughed and so did he.

After he hailed her a cab, he took hold of her upper arms and giving them a firm squeeze looked directly into her eyes and said: "I'd all but given up on people."

"You're using the past tense."

"Yeah, I am," he said amazing himself. "I really am. And I guess that's because of you."

"Well all the best," she said as she got into the cab and closed the door.

"Hey," he cried as the taxi moved away. "At least I owe you another lunch. Oh and I promise faithfully to be careful with the liquids."

WHEN SHE ARRIVED HOME, she found in their post box an envelope of pictures Hughie had taken of the Irish cottage as the workmen were finishing the roofing. It was lovely, she thought. A testament to some couple's dream. *Fine and proud and whitewashed be. And stand it will till judgement's due...love's covenant that...* She just stood there in her soggy wet dress staring at the pictures but not seeing them anymore. Finally she slipped them back in the envelope. And then Noah arrived home. "Oh you're all wet. You must have gotten caught in that god awful storm."

"I did," she said blithely.

"What's that?" he asked of the envelope in her hand.

She shrugged. "Oh just some pictures." And she handed them to him.

He took them from her, slipped them from the envelope. "Oh they're something else. I guess we really have to do something about them now."

"I guess," she said coldly as she went off to the bedroom to rid herself of the miserable feel of her wet clothing.

NOAH SAT IN A PUTRID uptown subway car anxiously awaiting his now two dexies to cut in before he met up with his photographer for his Jackie O *Connoisseur* interview at her 1040 Fifth Avenue apartment. Across the car and still with his early a.m. dimmed vision, he could make out a transit ad for American Airlines promoting sunny California.

--I'd get out of this place if I could." His mother icily muttered to his father on one of his wintry morning-afters.

--And go to California. Just as I so faithfully promised and never fulfilled."

--Anyplace out of here. It couldn't be worse."

--Why don't you just go then?"

--And leave Noah with you?"

"Sorry mama—*Sunlight on the garden hardens and grows cold.*"

"Hey, are you all right there?"

Noah jumped. It was a transit policeman. "Yeah, sure." When he looked around even the nut cases were staring at him.

He got out of the subway at Lex and 77th and wandered in the light misty rain still waiting for the dexies to cut him some verve. But as the mist turned to rain and MacNeice's poetry returned to submerge him, he darted into the Metropolitan for safe keeping. No glittering ball with Nora on his arm now. There he climbed the high banks of gray stone steps to the second floor where he drifted through the halls and rooms of European paintings until he finally sat on a bench in front of the Monet *Debacle*. For a long time he didn't look up. It was as if he knew. There were no bright signs of life in it now. Only the frost. Panic seized him and he rushed away before he lost the impetus to cross the street for the Jackie O interview.

25

NOAH HADN'T SEEN MURPHS for over a week. Rumors abounded and drifted from the fashion department that she had excused herself from covering the Italian openings that season in favor of Mae. Noah figured her loss of Jimmy had brought on a pretty ruinous effect. That was why it came as somewhat of a relief when he spied her drifting by the other side of the newsroom one afternoon and called out to her. As disenchanted as she looked, she smiled and almost in slow motion crossed past the dozen or so desks toward his. The closer she came, the more life's blood seemed to drain from her. The pallor of her face and the great loss of sheen from her once radiant red hair was only supplemented by the frightful darkening of her eyes.

"What's wrong? I've tried so often to get in touch. But with no reply," he said and she quietly suggested they go out to the stairwell to talk, something they never ever had done before.

"I'm finished here, Noah."

"They fired you?" he asked taking hold of her cold hand.

"No. I quit."

"But that's mad. Why?"

"Oh I don't know. Since Jimmy left me I've been pretty crazy. I haven't been doing my work properly. My heart just isn't in it. That's why I dropped out of the Italian openings this time."

"Well anyone can have a bad time. I'm going to go to Oliver and—"

"No. I've already been to him. As soon as he heard about the Italian thing, he called me to his office. I told him I was going through a rough patch and that I needed some time. He was really surprisingly supportive. He said that he didn't want to lose me, that he had been thrilled with my work and that I should take all the time I needed-- that the company would continue to pay me."

"That doesn't sound very Oliver-esque to me," Noah said as he took hold of one of her her arms and stroked the now dryness of her hair.

"Well not to me either. But I was so drained that I just sat there as he went on wanting to know why this was happening to me. Then in his waspish speech pattern he said: '*Ah* have to admit *ah've* been pretty obnoxiously rascally with the staff at times. Wrongly so, *ah* have to confess.' Pretty incredible from him, I guess. At least something good has happened."

"Oh Murphs this place will be bloody miserable without you," he agonized as he let go of her and looked directly into the emptiness of her eyes. His dexie high was slipping.

"No. Don't feel that way. This will give me the chance to do something I've always dreamed of and never dared to pursue. I want to design clothing. But with Jimmy, I never really had the chance. We were so close for so long."

"But will you be able to get over that?" he asked as they both forced back tears.

"Yes, I think so," she shrugged. "I have to. Anyway I'm going off to Bermuda for a few weeks to try to clear my head." Then she sighed and hugged him. "Oh Noah, I have to talk to you before I go. Come take a few minutes and we'll go for a drink." Then she pulled him down the stairs and out into the near blinding sun swept afternoon streets. "You're sort of scaring me. Are there worse things?"

"Let's wait till we get inside."

Inside was the rather stately interior of the Fifth Avenue and Twelfth Street Longchamps. Murphs quickly looked about and seemingly decided that the massive oak bar was not suitable. Instead she pointed to a secluded black leather banquet that had already been set for dinner. There they ordered bloody Marys from their steady bartender Victor.

"What is it?" Noah asked anxiously.

"I don't—" she started then paused as tears came to her eyes. "Noah—" she said gripping his wrists with her hands that had gone from cold to downright icy. "Noah, I love you. I-- I love you so much."

"Wh-- what?" he could scarcely get the word out as he began to draw away. Her tears were now flooding her eyes as she grabbed up the folded cloth dinner napkin to dry them.

Noah was so nonplussed he sat there in shock while Victor delivered their drinks. When she finally composed herself and saw his reaction, she gasped. "Oh I don't mean what you're thinking."

"I don't understand" was all he could manage.

"Well I've kept a secret from you from the first day we met at Wilton. Oh I wasn't certain at first. But it didn't take long to find out I was right."

"Certain of what?" he asked as he felt fear creeping in.

"God." She sighed and her strained face went even more ashen as she nervously stirred the celery stalk in her drink. "I feel such guilt now for waiting. But I couldn't before." Then she shook her long hair in an unsuccessful attempt to revive it. So she pulled it back over her shoulders as she took a couple of deep breaths. "Disney. I suppose that's the best place," she finally blurted.

"What in god's name?"

"Oh, it makes sense. Just bear me out."

Noah just sat there frozen in place with one hand gripping a napkin and the other clutching his drink but daring not to partake of it because there was so much undiagnosed fear.

"Easy," she said stroking the hand that gripped the napkin. "I once told you my mother put me up for adoption back during the Depression years and that the woman who got me was pretty horrible. Well—she never wanted me to know who my real mother was. I think that was part of the mean streak in her. But when I graduated from high school, I insisted. She acted like she was doing me some big burdensome favor. But she finally gave in and when I forced her she told me she thought my mother was living somewhere on the lower east side. So I found her in the phone book, called her and went to see her. That was fortunate because it was only a short time after that she had a stroke and died."

"At least you got to meet her."

"Well she was frail then, but managing and in her late sixties. Except for a few solid streaks of white, she had red hair just like mine. I remember she stroked it, put her arms around me, wept and said she was so thankful I had come to see her so she could know I had survived and was doing so well. Then she told me she had never wanted to give me up but that she was about to be evicted from our west Village apartment and we would have been living in the street. So that's when I asked her about my father. She told me he had been more of an *acquaintance* and that he had gone away without ever knowing he had made her pregnant. Well naturally I wanted to know more about him so I pursued it with her. And that's where Disney comes in."

"Disney?" Noah gulped. "That's really weird. You know my father worked—"

"For him, here in New York," Murphs finished.

"You know? Why I never told you that."

She looked at him for a moment, then took a deep breath. "Well she worked for Pat Powers. He was the head of *Cinephone Process*. That was a sort of bootleg sound recording company. You see *RCA* owned all the sound recording patents for the movies in those days. Disney and *RCA* had conflicting artistic ideas so Disney needed Pat Powers."

Noah could see she was stretching this story as she smoothed away at her napkin. Then she took another swallow of her drink. "What is all this?" Noah asked shaking his head. "Can't you just tell me?"

"All right I will." And she struggled for the determination but looked as if she might cave at any moment. A couple more tears came and as she wiped them away Noah surreptitiously slipped his hand into his pocket, extracted a dexie, slipped it into his mouth and then took a first and deep swallow of his drink.

"My mother met your father when he was working with Disney on the sound for his first talkie *Steamboat Willie*." And she forcefully exhaled.

"Oh my god--- Well how do you know that?"

"Paul Mason. You never told me his name."

Noah was so bewildered but for some reason he was trying to prove her wrong. "Well maybe I did. I could have at some point."

"Well you didn't. And I can tell you he lived in Yearnington in western New York."

"God that's right. Why that's why I was so surprised when you mentioned once that I was from western New York."

"Yes. That was a slip on my part. And you remember how important it was that I met your mother. I was so moved by that."

"Well--- What--- What does all this mean?" he asked stopping from thinking any further. "So your mother met my father—"

She stared at him while he stared back. Then as he leaned closer to her, her eyes dropped down and he felt something give in her. Suddenly the blood began to drain from his head and he was gasping. "Oh my god."

She looked back at him and nodded. "The *acquaintance* was your father."

He could scarcely breathe. His hands grasped the side of the table and Murphs reached up and stroked his hair. "How this ever came to be? That you came to work here? And I was so afraid to tell you because you're such a nice guy and I thought that somehow it might hurt you deeply. Maybe you wouldn't even want to know and you would hate me for telling you. Then even though she's gone, I thought I might be betraying my mother. All the while there was a war going on inside me with all this guilt stuff." Then she lifted his chin to face her and asked to his shocked eyes: "Has it hurt you?"

"I don't even know what to think."

After a period of silence with her still stroking his head, he finally spoke. "It all makes sense now. Why you were always so caring and worried and good to me." Then after another silence, his first emotion came with a touch of disappointment. "But you should have told me. You should have known I wouldn't hate you."

"I know."

"After all, we're kin. Oh god, and so much more." And he moved closer to her so he could hug her tightly. Once they'd calmed each other, she asked him: "What was he like?"

Noah nodded his head. "Good. Real good. Unhappy. Only of late I've begun to put all the pieces together." He stopped and wiped his own tears. Then he looked at her. "He would have loved you."

"Would he? Would he really?" she asked anxiously.

"Yes. Absolutely."

"That's so good to hear. I've wondered about that-- I guess all my life."

"I'm sure." And they hugged each other again.

Finally, Noah called out: "Victor would you please get some Beefeater martinis going over here and make it a whole pitcher. By the time it arrived, fortunately they had calmed themselves for the late afternoon Wilton ad men were arriving and taking their usual seats at the bar. They exchanged waves with Noah and Murphs who were now pretending to be very businesslike to dislodge any possible thoughts of gossip.

"It's something, isn't it?" Murphs went on. "You can't in any way know what those times did to people. That's what my real mother told me that day. In only a matter of months, even less, all the will, the determination, the hope—most of all the dreams—they were gone as if some god awful hand had reached down and pulled the plug. You could see it in their ghostly faces. They had stopped believing in themselves."

"Yes I guess I could see that. I guess I could see that all along in dad," he said realizing for the first time he was now speaking to his sister.

"I could imagine how it could happen," Murphs continued. "I could look into my mother's lonely eyes and it was there. I suppose like the rerunning of a gritty old film. Suddenly being without a job and no money. It was after she had been let go by Pat Powers that she saw this man that she thought looked a little like the dynamic guy who once worked for Disney and was so certain he was going to California to be with him. Except now he was a grim vestige of his former self. When he saw her, he looked mortified and hurried away. But she remembered his name and called out to him." Murphs suddenly stopped to take a few swallows of her drink as if she were remembering too much.

"It is too much isn't it?" he asked as he followed suit with the drinking.

"Well you need to know." And she continued. "My mother said she would never forget the loss in his eyes. The energetic young man with so much pride could no longer even get relief work as a picture projectionist. And he blamed himself for the whole mess he'd gotten into. To make matters worse, he said his wife was in the hospital."

"Well they never told me anything about that."

"It must have been pretty bad because my mother said he couldn't even bear to talk about it. I wondered about all that the day I met your mother."

"I wonder why your mother—" Noah started.

"How they became lovers?" Murphs finished. "I don't think they did. It would be better to call them lonely hearts who shared each other's pain. My mother had been going through the loss of the man who was her true lover. He had been a broker who had gone totally out of it after the Depression hit. His parents had long since committed him to some upstate looney bin because they were shamed by his mental state and that he'd lost his job and couldn't get another. So--- that afternoon your father and my mother went off to her dismal boarding room to share a bottle of illegal prohibition hooch. And that escape led to another. To put it pretty bluntly, I gather that the carnal moments that followed were a desperate evasion of all the torturous agony of the times."

"Did dad ever know the results of that?" Noah asked as a sharp pain seized him and he refilled his glass from the pitcher.

"No, she said she never told him. It was shortly after that afternoon that he met her in the street one day and he said that he'd scrounged enough money from janitor jobs at movie houses to pay for train tickets back home. And now that his wife was well enough to travel they were going back. She said it was the saddest thing to hear him blame himself for his failure.

Later when she realized she was pregnant he was long gone, so how could she crush him anymore by sending him that news. His dreams had done enough to him, dying as they did."

"Oh I wouldn't say that," Noah offered while the alcohol and the dexie tree started sweeping his brain. "I'm beginning to think dreams don't die, even though you may sometimes want them to." And these thoughts suddenly shot down the drugs, and all he could feel was the pain so he gulped more martini. "I don't know where this is coming from, but it's suddenly taken up residency in my head."

"Wanting to kill dreams?" she asked as she too summoned more aid from the martini.

"Shaping them. Putting the breaks on them. I don't know. But I don't think you can. I wonder if they don't run wild and follow you right through to the grave. The whole kit and caboodle."

"Well lately since Jimmy's disappearance along with all our multitude of shared dreams, I dared hope I could change them or kill them if I tried hard enough. Especially if I convinced myself it was a very wise thing to do. That's one of the reasons I left Wilton."

"Oh I don't know, Murphs," he said with a shiver. "I think dreams can overpower wisdom." And as soon as these words were out, he wished he hadn't spoken them. It was as if he'd swiped something from her, and she fell silent. "But it will all come around," he finally forced himself to say. "Hey, its already started." And he smiled at her.

"What? What are you smiling at?"

"Us. The more I think about it-- The more-- well jubilant I guess I feel."

"Do you? You're sure? Because I know I do, now that I know you're not disgusted with me."

"Oh Murphs, how could you ever think such a thing?"

"I don't know. But I did."

The Wilton ad men were still at the bar, but they were so pissed by now they could hardly see. So Noah leaned over and kissed Murphs. Then squeezing her hand he said: "We have to stay close now. No matter what."

"Yes we do. Even when you go to Ireland. We'll have to be sure you have a phone. You are still going at least for the leave aren't you?"

"Well we want to when I get all these things untied don't you know?"

"No I don't know, Noah. And I'm not sure you do. But you must untie them for yourself and Nora," she insisted.

"Of course. I just wish you'd meet somebody before we do."

"Huh." And then she chuckled. "I don't know how to *meet* anymore. I've been with him so long. Stayed by him and helped him all through law school. And then when he did the worst he could do to me-- I can't leave those feelings behind." Then she looked away and chuckled again. "Oh well, who knows. Maybe around the next corner-- and all that stuff."

So they wove out of Longchamps and into the still fairly blinding now westerly sun. He hailed a taxi for Murphs saying he was going to walk it off to Gramercy Park. But she seemed disappointed, as if she had wanted to talk more or tell him something else or maybe she only wanted to curb more impending loneliness. As her taxi pulled out, she turned to look back at him and flashed a bright smile as she had so often done in the past. But now he wondered how it could be at such an extreme to the gravity of her eyes.

26

JIMI HENDREX BLASTED from the turntable speakers. *Have you ever been to Electric Ladyland?* As couples gyrated suggestively, images flashed on towering juke box screens at dizzying speeds—whizzing hallucinatory posters, gaudy psychedelic art, old movies, old newsreels, couples making love. And all this was set off by streams of ever-changing colored lights. It was Bob Goldstein's Lightworks installed in his L'Oursin disco in Southampton. It was the hot young place to go where all the senses could be engaged at the same time and often aided by a fantastic array of drugs and hallucinogens. As part of its trendy youthful coverage for Wilton, Noah stood in the midst of it all. He was a little high on trees. His photographer had already dropped some acid. And everyone was moving to the loudness of the beat. To join in with the excited almost frenetic crowd, Noah decided on a double martini as his companion.

No sooner had he done so than he heard a burst of giggly voices cut through the throng. As he swung around he realized one of them belonged to the snake. When she noticed Noah, she quickly waved off the rest of her nest of vipers and slithered right over to him. "Well here you are again. Surely the loneliest man of the hour. Let me give you a kiss, you poor sad man." Noah pushed her off in mid-embrace. "Please do not. I don't want those fangs of yours coming anywhere near me."

"Oh come now Noah, how can you be so reclusive? Surely we can share a moment." Then she drew a finger down his pale blue linen shirt as he pulled away again.

"I'll tell you what I'll do Gloria, if you'll bow out. Since short creamy chiffon dresses are hot this summer, I'll get my photographer to snap you for *Connoisseur*." With that he called out to him. "Carlos could you do me a favor and *shoot* Gloria Hamilton Collins here."

"Drop the Collins and you're right, Noah."

"Oh you mean we missed something for our *FCD* column?"

"Not exactly. He wasn't worth missing." And with that she tossed back her blonde hair and started gyrating to the music for the pretty stoned Carlos who was getting more and more turned on as he shot her. It was Noah's chance to escape into the crowd of moneyed live-wire explosives the likes of which he had never seen in all his days at Wilton not even at Max's. Boy, were they high flying. What in god's name were they on, he thought as he popped an emergency bennie to keep up. Stopping by the bar to collect another martini was a mistake because that's where Gloria attempted her next assault. "I'm glad I didn't lose you."

"Well I'm not."

"Oh loosen up. Put some liquid in that liquid." Then she quickly whipped what looked to be an antique silver vile from her silver clutch bag, unscrewed the cap and before he could stop her dumped a few clear drops into his martini.

"What the hell?"

"Oh it's nothing, It just enlivens the drink a little."

Noah tried to get the barman's attention to change the drink but there were so many people it was impossible. "I wouldn't put it past you trying to poison me, Gloria."

"Oh no you're too beautiful," she said stroking his face. "Even though you have been so mean to me."

"Well I'm here on assignment. I have to circulate. Take care to get lost," he snapped and went off. He stopped by several clusters of gyrators where he recognized some of the faces but talk was impossible so he merely made love to his drink forgetting it could have been contaminated. After a time, he began to feel numb. It was most likely from the constant bombardment of noises, images and colors that were the light show, he told himself as he waved to a distant Andy Warhol. He waved back, but the wave was like something in slow motion. Then Noah wasn't even sure if it was Warhol or a vision he had conjured. He felt around in his pockets, but there were no more bennies to pull him through.

"Come Noah, it's past your bedtime," she shouted in his ear. "Your photographer has already taken off with Edie Sedgwick. Or so they say."

"Well that's the blind leading the blind. Did you poison him too?"

"Come I'll drive you."

"No you won't. I've my own car. I'm only going back to the Southampton Inn."

"You're already on a trip," she said as she followed him to the parking lot. "I'll drive you—for safety's sake."

"N-o-o-o. Why do I feel this is just the opposite from safe? I want to be away from you." But he was slurring his words.

She laughed as she pushed him into her Mercedes. Then she clicked the radio buttons until she came to *Light My Fire*. Noah hissed at her. "You did that to my drink. I was an asshole." Then he blinked and blinked to try to clear his vision to save himself. When it didn't work, he nodded off. Later he was vaguely aware of getting out of the car. "Where's the hotel?" And he blinked and blinked again. "This isn't my hotel." But he was seeing all those lightshow colors again, and he felt her pulling him up steps. So many steps. "Just take it easy and lie down here, Noah." He was vaguely aware of cool hands on his hot face and then on his bare chest.

Later he partially awakened out of a weird dream of distorted figures. Or was it still a dream? He was blinded by bright reds and ugly greens. But he could feel himself being aroused by Nora who was licking his penis. And this felt good because it was responding magnificently. He reached down to stroke her hair. Then she was crawling up his body and bringing her soaking vagina down onto his erection. She began moving, sliding up and down at a fantastic speed. Finally he was aware of a voice shouting out in the darkness as he exploded and collapsed back into the spooked out void where all the freaky figures remained.

AWAKE. SUNLIGHT ROARING in the window. Where was it all coming from? He began to jump up. Jesus. What time is it? Oh Southampton, thank god. As he let himself fall back into the bed, he vaguely realized the room wasn't right. He turned and to his horror saw Gloria sprawled on the bed beside him. "Oh my god. Holy hell." Gloria stirred and opened her eyes. "Jesus, we're both naked. What am I doing here," he gasped.

"Something wonderful," she purred. "You're a great lay."

"God, don't say that. I've got to get out of here," his voice rasped as he found his clothes and began pulling them on.

"Don't tell me you have to work this early," she said through a yawn.

"God, where are my shoes. Hell I wonder did anyone see us?"

"Stop fussing and come back to bed. I'm not through with you yet. Make me your assignment for the day."

"Where's my car? Did I drive here?"

"No. You left it at the club. See, now you can't go anywhere."

"Get up," he roared pulling her nude body out of the bed. "Drive me there immediately. Jesus, god almighty, you evil bitch."

"Oh god, you fool," she said with disgust shaking her head. "What a waste of talent."

"YEAH, I KNOW. There was something wrong with my room phone," he told Nora when he called here from the inn after he'd dumped Gloria and retrieved his rented car. "No, I'm fine. I just wish I could come home now. I've got the weekend though. So I'll see you Monday." Thank god she believed him about the phone or at least he thought she did. But as he hung up and with the horrible thought of facing the next two days out here, a sudden image of Hurd Hatfield as Dorian Gray flashed through his mind along with the words he spoke from the Omar Khayyam. *I sent my soul through the invisible, some letter of the after-life to spell. And by and by my soul returned to me and answered: I myself am heaven and hell.*

Noah collapsed on the bed. It's too late now, he thought. I can only turn my face from you in shame.

"WELL I SEE OUR GUY who's corresponding from the Hamptons has a lot to correspond," Jack Warren said with a smirk that Monday morning. Noah had driven in, returned the car and gone directly to the office.

"What are you talking about?" The smirk sent shivers through Noah. Jack hadn't treated him with anything but respect since Oliver elevated him to pedestal level.

"Oh, just this article in this morning's *Daily News.* And he plopped it on Noah's desk delighting in doing so. Noah saw the pictures first and felt his temperature drop below zero. One shot of Gloria clutching Noah next to her Mercedes outside L'Oursin with the caption *the heiress and the hot FCD society snoop at L'Our--Sin* butted up against a stunning one of Nora *the new wonder of the art world.* And the headline over both read: *The Perfect Triangle?*

"Rubbish, rubbish, rubbish," Noah said loudly enough so the rest of the nearby staff who pretended disinterest could hear. Then he pitched the paper into his basket. "I was only trying to help her get her car started."

"Well I suppose there are ways of helping. And then there are ways of helping," Jack quipped.

Then lowering his voice, Noah turned bitter. "I would watch it if I were you Jack. You haven't the power to support an attitude like that anymore."

"I CAN EXPLAIN all that truck in the *Daily News*," Noah trying to control his inner trembling told Oliver later that morning as he sat on his leather sofa. "She was soused and I was trying to get her home before she killed somebody. I was certain—"

"Stop, right where you *ah*. *Ah* don't want to hear any of this. Just let it play the way it plays."

"But Oliver you must be angry. It's obvious what everyone will be saying."

"Y-e-s," he delighted as he rubbed his hands together. "It's a whiff of scandal to catch everyone's attention. But don't be tense about it. We can easily turn this around and create even more mileage for *ah*selves. We'll take your side of what happened and rub the noses of those fools at the *Daily News* in it. We'll suggest how kindhearted you were to be helping one of the richest women in the country in her dipso condition and in doing so were saving lives. Why the photo they've used just backs it up."

"But what if it backfires? It could be bad for us all."

"It won't backfire. *Ah* won't let it. But *ah* do know what you're saying. Your real concern is your marriage. And of *cause* that's as it should be. It is of grave concern to me as well. And if the truth be told it has been so for some time. Way back to the time of the *Connoisseur* party when *youah* wife wasn't present and even before that, I began to realize that *youah* work here might be taking too much of *youah* private life. And this brings to mind that you have my full permission to back out of that western trip we had planned to cover the most beautiful of the young out there. *Ah* can easily appoint someone else for that assignment."

"Well that might not be necessary now. But my god, I never thought I'd hear words like that coming from you."

"And they most likely wouldn't have, if things hadn't begun happening to me privately."

Noah looked at him and wondered if the strain of his face was for real. "Oliver, I have to ask you if this is just another of your power-play games."

"In so many ways, *Ah* only wish it were."

WHEN HE WALKED INTO THE APARTMENT and saw her sitting in of all places his wingback chair his blood iced again. He knew she knew.

"I had to see your face," she offered immediately.

"Ah Nora," he sighed and began wringing his hands. Hands that she once thought were so unquestionably beautiful when he worked the keys of his typewriter. Now they were ugly in their messing. Messing had become the operative word in the way he handled everything between them now. She said nothing but after a moment rose stalwartly. "I'm doing what I should have done when I came back from Dublin." She began to walk to the door.

"Don't tell me you believe in that *News* gossip shit?" he asked as he followed. "Ah Nora, she was drunk, and I was doing the honorable trying to get her back to her home so she wouldn't kill anybody. She's a snake. Don't take those words as gospel."

"I didn't have to read anything, Noah. I believe in what I see before me." And he had never in their worst moments known her to be so cold. He sort of gasped as he turned away. She snatched up her over-the-shoulder, over stuffed knitted tote and continued out the door and started down the steps into the sweltering afternoon. Pausing halfway and only half looking back at him, she went on to profess without feeling: "I don't know how others see you lately. But you don't look young anymore. You've lost that. I don't know when, but it's gone. You're untidy now. Your hair is too long. Your skin has gone patchy. You used to glow. You have lost, Noah. And you'll continue to lose. I don't think you can stop now."

He was in white-faced shock, but when she was at the bottom of the steps he managed to call out: "You don't have to go, Nora. Because I'll be gone tomorrow afternoon. Oliver is sending me on an extended assignment. I'll be gone out west for several weeks, maybe a month."

As he managed to walk down a few more steps, she turned back and this time looked directly at him again. "Why did you do it, Noah? I think I could have taken almost anything." But she didn't wait for his reply.

27

SHE WAS SCARCELY AWARE of the elevator ride to

the tenth floor of the Gramercy Park. She entered the icy dim room which was a shock from the bright haze of the heat. Without thought she dropped onto the bed, alone except for the sounds—the hum of the air conditioner and the short quick intakes of her breath. She seemed unable to summon enough air. It was as if she were encased in a tank and at any moment the supply would run out. All the while her body exchanged the heat for the cold. And soon not just her outer layer of skin but her entire being was entering a state of deep freeze. Then there were no thoughts, just the sensation. At some point she pulled a thin pale flowered coverlet over herself. After that she must have dozed and in her light sleep came the awareness of change. She awakened with a start to the sound of a chipping against the windowpane. It was so loud that it eclipsed the sound of the a/c. Even though darkness had descended she could see from the reflection of the streetlights that a wind-driven rain had come with the nightfall. Strangely it was soothing, and flashes of lightening sped comfort through her. She was no longer cold. The rain and the lightening, she thought. The rain and the lightening. And—then she could make out the reflection of a man's face on the window.

NOAH'S GUILT THAT LATE AFTEROON soon drove him into a stage of such uncontrollable torment that he had no cognizance of what pills he was popping or what booze he was imbibing. In the middle of the night with rain lashing the front windows and thunder exploding over the city, he regained consciousness and barely managed to stumble to the toilet where between hiccupping and vomiting he spent the remaining hours till dawn on his knees accompanied by the words: *I myself am heaven and hell.*

AFTER SHOWERING in a daze, Nora didn't know how long she had wandered through the crispness of the next morning's cleansed air before she came to it. The heavy dark door entrance to the old Federal-style building. It was ajar, and she went on to push it open. Then without hesitation, without even thought, she climbed the creaky stairs and tapped on one of the garish orange panels. The door opened to the unfamiliar yet merciful soft coolness of a new a/c. "I'm sorry. I need to talk. I thought—" He put his fingers to her lips. "Sh-h-h. I know." His eyes clouded, and she knew he felt her sense of loss and had most likely felt it for a long time. He gently pulled her head against the blinding snowy white of his T-shirt and into the warmth of his being. As he stroked her hair, his other arm came around her for support. The peace of his warmth infused her and she felt a sudden release of spirit, a spiraling upwards of feelings long lost, a blessedness that she had so needed to retrieve. But once they were inside and he closed the door, her whole body seemed to seize up

"What?" he asked with even greater tenderness.

"I don't know," she replied almost as an apology. "It's something within me that's only holding me back."

"But you do know Nora that you could trust me on all counts." Then he gently kissed her as he moved them both over to the sofa. "I know," she whispered. "I'm so sorry for behaving like an eejiot."

"Well never. You're not that." And once again from his gentle kisses came the balm. Then she closed her eyes and let that and the soft whisper of his breathing be her only awareness. As time drifted into a lovely forever, he held her and his caress was so gentle that she couldn't be sure whether it was real or imagined. In that distant future she was vaguely aware of the heat of his face pressing against her and she reached up to hold it there. It was then that she realized he must have imperceptibly undone the front buttons of her dress and his lips were softly kissing her naked breasts. In her headiness she felt more of her rigidity fall away. In the midst of the peace flowing from his warmth, she felt him leaving her and she opened her eyes to see that he was grabbing a clean white sheet from the sofa's arm and unfolding it. Then he was lifting her up with one arm so he could spread it over the sofa's cushions beneath them. As he lowered her back, he slipped the rest of her dress away and for a moment she was stunned that in her mindless state that morning she hadn't worn as much as a shred of underwear. But he was softly smiling with such tenderness that she let herself fall back into the peace once more. When his face returned to her breasts again, his kisses were more passionate and this time he let his soft curly hair brush back and forth across them. Soon the sensation was so great that she found

192

herself stopping him. This time when she opened her eyes she could see he was naked except for his boxers.

"Oh Conrad I don't know," she whispered.

"Yes you do," he whispered through his soft breath. "Love is the only way out of these prisons I think we're in."

"Well I thought I was out on the right path."

"It takes two you know. And I'd say—neither can diverge."

"But I didn't go diverging."

"I know you didn't. But I can guess who did. And you know as well. I think you've known for a long time."

She sighed and nodded in agreement as she felt the flickers of rage once again.

"You need to let go. To stop this from marring you anymore. Just as I need to let go. The bad things of the past can corrupt the present you know. Once they take hold, it's pretty damn rough shedding them."

And the thought rushed her—god how could she ever— and how could he? But he was ahead of her and already stroking away the thought.

Then gently he began lifting her around on the sofa. In the dimness of the room he appeared much stronger than his thinness had revealed. His chest and the muscular stomach lent credence to this. But it was his long lithe legs that startled her, especially the right one with the jagged wide scare above the knee that moved at an almost perfect though more jagged right angle down along the knee cap. It seemed stronger than the left one most likely due to the overcompensation of the limp. Just looking at it caused her to feel a sudden ache. She wondered as before had it been a result of the war? She thought of the horror of those photographs and reached out and stroked his knee, then leaned over to pull him closer so she could kiss it. Once again he stroked her hair then turned her face up towards him and smiled softly through his own pain. When she lay back on the sofa, he pulled off his briefs and freed his strong erection Slowly he moved towards her, lay beside her, touching, kissing, stroking so gently that again it was as if imagined. Then he shifted, and she felt the strength of his entire body come over her bringing such security. Soon he was building the pressure as he entered her. Little by little he went all the way and for the longest time he held still in her as she felt his need for her build. Then moving slightly he groaned with the wonder. This touched her so deeply it sent ripples of pleasure sweeping over her that summoned the involuntary spasms of her first orgasm. Unable to be still any longer, he began moving. Moving, moving. And she was moving with him, going with him. The shine of his curly jet hair framed his face and the green eyes shone with love for her. "Oh god, I love you," he uttered as she cried out and kept coming from the intensity of his orgasm. He stayed inside her, holding her, his whispery breath skittering over her. As the morning grew longer, the white light creeping through the dark window blinds rose up to fill the room with its brightness. She let herself go to that light. As she did she felt a further mending of body and spirit. And their sharing of need produced a surge of euphoria. Once more he groaned in ecstasy. With the flush of their blood, his penis rose up inside her and this time he held back even longer so that she lost track of the number of orgasms and the white light became a red radiance.

28

NOAH AFTER ALTERNATING under hot and cold shower blasts proceeded to spruce as best he could then made his way still accompanied by nausea to the office via Pete's. "Oh you look so *c-r-a-p-u-l-e-n-t.* I've n ever seen you like this."

"God almighty Pete, could you not come up with something slightly more poetic than that?"

Pete smoothing his straggly beard pondered for a moment. "*The world which seems to lie before us like a land of dreams, so various, so beautiful, so new, hath neither joy, nor love, nor light--*"

"Bloody hell Pete, don't give me the Arnold yet. I need your help not your abandonment."

"Sorry Noah, I get it." And he went off to one of his dark dusty shelves and came back with a large container of orange pills. "Thorazine. Take a couple of these and they'll pull you together fast." He gave Noah some water to gulp them down and insisted he sit in a rickety old chair until they took effect. "What else do you need while you're waiting?"

"Plenty. I've got to go home at lunch time and pack for the west coast. I leave on an extended trip this afternoon."

So dutifully Pete went back to pack up a half dozen vials of barbies and uppies and mixtures of the two along with what Noah was by now considering the wondrous new orangies. "God I can't thank you enough," Noah said hugging him after he'd bagged the goods. "By the way, I'm dropping you down a pile of Lacoste alligator shirts on my way home. You'll look like a million dollars in them if you only get rid of the beard. Won't be able to keep the babes away from you."

"NOW NOAH, if *youah* really sure you want to go ahead with this, *ah* want you back in time to cover this thing whatever it is upstate in the middle of August. That festival," Oliver stressed in a definitely softer tone. "Youth is our mantra now and we're going to ride it high. Of course, as *ah* say we'll make it very clean cut. All those beautiful bodies with purified minds. If there are any up there"

"Yes, I gathered what you want by now, Oliver."

"But *ah* want you to have a good time out west now,' he added with an even more kindly note. "Oh and *ah* wanted to know how things went with you and your wife about that little matter that concerned you so yesterday?"

"They didn't," Noah replied sharply as he walked out of Oliver's office. "But don't worry Oliver, I'll look after our mantra."

"Noah," Oliver gasped and started after him. But he was gone down the stairwell.

AS ABHORENT A PROSPECT as it was, Nora did return to Gramercy Park just after dusk that evening when she felt with certainty Noah would be gone.

"I have to go home," she had told Conrad after they'd spent the whole afternoon together. Without acknowledging her words, he had pulled on a pair of boxers and gone about rummaging through the cupboards and fridge producing ingredients that when put together resembled pale imitations of sandwiches. They had been so hungry that they had wolfed them down with a shared quart container of milk. "It's not that I want to go, but what else can I do? I mean even though he'll be gone, I just can't *stay* here." It was when his eyes blinked with the hurt that she had realized the stress she had placed on the word *stay*.

"I mean I have to go somewhere else." But those words had only made it worse.

"No you don't. I don't ever want you to go anywhere else," he had gone on as he took her hand and looked at her with his bright consuming eyes.

"But I can't. I just can't. Not just like that."

"I understand and I'm with you on this. But—" Then he'd paused and gripped her hand. "You must come back."

"I will. I will." And she had tried to reassure herself as well.

"I mean after we've gone ahead and—I can't go back if—Well I wouldn't have started it if—But I did."

"I know. We both did."

"I'll hold you together Nora. I'll look after you through everything."

He had walked her part of the way back to Gramercy Park. "Now leave me," she'd told him when they were just a few blocks away. "Let me do this my way." And with a kiss he had.

SHE HAD ONLY ARRIVED in the apartment when the phone rang. It was Noah. "Thank god you came back. I've been after calling and calling. I'm at the airport and my flight is about to depart. I was so worried."

"I didn't come back," she snapped.

"Well at least you're in the apartment and you're safe."

"Yes, I think I'm safe now."

"I can't say how devastated I am about all this."

"Well don't, because I don't want to hear it."

"I'll keep calling you from the road."

"Don't be bothering yourself. At least not right away. I need time apart from all this."

"Okay. I guess it's right for you not to care."

"Oh I care. That's my trouble. But you wouldn't know that." Then she sighed. "Regardless, look after yourself."

"You mean that?"

"For whatever it means. Bye." And she rang off.

After that she went and collapsed on the sofa resting her head against its back. The apartment was darkening in the dusky light of early evening. She closed her eyes to let go of all thought. But the light of the hour stayed with her and soon she was remembering teatime in Dublin and how afterwards in such a light when the family had scattered away her ma would pull out her rosary beads and in the quietude whisper. And those words haunted her now: *Holy Mary, Mother of God, pray for us sinners, now and in the hour of our death.*

THAT NIGHT Nora brought out the rollaway bed. As long as she continued to live in this apartment, she told herself, she would sleep in the living room close by her work area. This way she would close out as many details as she could of her life with Noah.

And indeed in the days that followed a pattern enabling her to obscure the past began to develop. Mornings were devoted to her work and as such commanded complete attention. For some reason she knew not why nor dared question, she had never before been able to work with such speed and agility in converting more groups of her sketches to what she considered to be some of her best oil work. And to her surprise what only a matter of weeks before would have become some of her darkest endeavors were now contrasted by startling flashes of light. There was no directed effort about it. It just happened now as did the rest of her life.

Afternoons came and she left Gramercy Park for East Tenth Street and Conrad. He managed to plan his assignments so they were always left with a few hours. Together she loved the way he never stopped. The way she felt he adored her. His gentleness grew into a strength that roused her sense of passion and pure love for him. And just as it did, she could feel his love for her building in intensity along with the sense of spiritual awe revealed in his eyes at the culmination of their lovemaking. Afternoon is life, she came to believe during those days. And their bodies convulsed with the surging joys of it.

But at night, lying on the rollaway with true sleep as elusive as self-forgiveness, the voices would return. Sometimes, as at first, it was just her mother's. Later it was the long ago voices of church parishioners at confession. She the child waiting her turn in the queue as the near-deaf elder priest commanded penitential voices that pierced the confessional door. *Oh my god I am heartily sorry for having offended thee. I detest all my sins because I dread the loss of heaven. I have sinned against you whom I should love above all things.* Then as often as not her baptismal vows would return. *Do you reject Satan and all his works.* And panic from this would bring her back to full consciousness. To save herself from the crush of guilt she would listen to other words. *Nora, I'll look after you through everything.*

She played that familiar voice over and over in the pitch dark. It brought with it a light, the white light that she had known the first morning they were together in his flat. A saving light in the darkest of hours.

Noah had drifted away, she told herself to ease her conscious. Conrad had come, taken the dark and made it light. She had to hold to this now. But not just for herself. He needed it as much as she. And to run from that would be a sin. Could she commit a sin by not committing one? I could, she whispered to the night. By abandoning him I would be doing just that. But by continuing I would be sinning as well. How could I be in such a torturous trap, she kept asking until it became unbearable.

Then came the beginning of a weekend. Alone in the deep dark when persecution was relentless, the neighbors began pounding on the piano keys which brought the full focus on Noah. And the image that came to her was one of him when they had first met. Furiously she tried to battle it from her mind as if it were attacking her. He caused all this. He's no one to blame. But is it right for me to be blaming him for my sins? Oh god, where is he now? The poor feckless eejiot. Spirits and pills and anything could happen. He could be victimized. Slashed. Beaten to death. Yet he was victimizing himself. God if things could only be right for him, had been right, she muttered as she tossed about the skinny bed to the noise of the piano. If only—*Go way out of that,* her ma's voice called out to her. *I'd have thought more of you than this. To be going off abandoning your man like a common trollop. I'll deliver one pronouncement of it all and that would be the truth. You're after putting the Clifford name to shame with your sins against the lord and the holy Catholic Church. But I'll have no more of your disgracing us. Be gone with ya. You deserve no place in this family.*

Oh god, she gasped. I've truly pitched myself into hell. Then suddenly as the piano music reached a crescendo she sat up in total panic. "My god!" she roared. "When did I last have my period?"

AFTER THAT SHE WAS AWAKE the rest of the
night. Finally to calm herself, she struggled out of bed at dawn
and set to work at her easel. When she was about to take a tea
break, the door buzzer sounded. Startled she jumped up and
anxiously answered the intercom. "Who is it?"

"Conrad."

She was taken completely by surprise. She had never
expected him to come here. She opened the door preparing to
grouse about his boldness and then go on to blame him for the
wounds of her sin. But the instant she laid eyes on him all anger
fled.

"How soon can you be ready?" he asked, all eager and
intense. He was wearing hiking boots, snug Levis and a usual
bright white T-shirt.

"Ready for what?" She was in her dressing gown, and
with her hair all tousled she felt more than a bit embarrassed.
He had never seen her like this.

He laughed obviously sensing her embarrassment then
brushed her hair into place. "We're going to the country for the
weekend."

"Just like that?"

"Well that is if you will," he replied with an apologetic
tone. "I mean there's good reason. The Witkin's decided to do a
showing of my work."

"Ah god, that's great news." And in a rush she hugged
him. But before she could stop herself she was thinking of Noah

and that Saturday morning in Queens when he announced with great joy that *The New Yorker* had accepted his short story. Then she pushed back from him and wished he hadn't come here.

"Listen now," he went on. "Please get ready to go. It'll be perfect. There's this guy who works for *Esquire* who has this house in Connecticut that's way out in the woods away from everything and he's not using it this week. Come on, my trusty old Valiant stands ready to speed us there."

"But I can't. I haven't heard from him." And she began to back away.

"You know you might not even if you did stay here."

He's right, she thought. When she looked at him his eyes drew her in along with his smile and his love and suddenly she was reeling at the thought of being away with him. For the moment it banished all sin.

29

NOAH'S TRAVELS began in San Francisco's Ghirardelli Square with its promenade of shops and cafes. There he was met by one of Wilton's west coast photographers. A tall whiskery blonde guy named Adam who no matter what Noah said seemed to head for the scruffiest characters. The ones like the yoga guru who was spouting: "The leaves have all blown the branches now. Only the brittle sapless limbs remain. We're all experiencing the death of the trees." After that he began gravitating to the bearded guitarists chanting the likes of *Everybody's Talkin' At Me* and The Doors-- *We Want The World*. It was when he went over to *The War Isn't Over Yet*— poster carriers that Noah dismissed him and began using the Yashica 44 he had borrowed from the photo department before he left so he could take his own on-the-road pictures. Concentrating on those clean cut types in their late twenties who seemed never to have lost or had regained their sense of hope and promise, he made quick notes of their remarks and prayed the camera and its settings worked for him.

After a good few of such, as he headed off to the nearest café bar, he thought of Nora. Well truth was he never stopped thinking of her. But now regardless of what she had said, he was determined to call her. So after a tooie and a couple of bloody Marys he went to a phone booth but to no avail.

IT WAS EARLY SUNDAY July 20. He hadn't remembered much of the past few days other than what transpired during his working hours. He had stopped wanting to remember since only once had he been able to reach Nora and then she just clipped him off saying: "I'm far too deep into my work." It was after he'd had a few somethings so he guessed he completely blew his chance. Well even if he'd been in the best of form, she wouldn't have wanted to hear from him. And this really cut him so he let everything go to bits except his work. He did write copious, depictive notes with quotes to accompany his youth-driven photos that as they'd say at Wilton would *sing* for them. He'd have them processed in the Portland bureau praying they'd be first rate so he could send all this material off to Oliver posthaste. As for the bits, they included an underground bar in Sausalito where an Indian girl who came from the Chichi—something or other nomadic tribe from Mexico was doing weird things with peyote buttons and he was eating stuff she was feeding him, swallowing it with tequila to curb the nausea. Creepy-crawlies abounded. After that there were blissful reveries that soon faded from view as he finished this weird trip down to the docks. Then he was on a fiery dawn ferry but that began blurring from the loudness of tom-toms not real ones but bloody painful ones in his head. Later somewhere north of San Francisco, he drove into the mountains, miraculously without accident. Then more peyote with shadowy night people. This time vomited away. At dawn driving to an airport to catch a flight to Portland that heaved itself through a vicious thunderstorm. Saved only by some oranges. Not the fruit, but Pete's blessed Thorazines.

The Cascades, the rivers, the streams, all shimmering for him as he drove onward. But it became too much. It was blinding and the tom-toms were tuning up again, tightening the membrane. He fished for his sunglasses, fished for another orange. God once I would have thought this was so beautiful. I would have felt the thrill leaping in me. Then I would have suffered the hurt of Nora not being here to share it with me. Now I feel nothing. But what am I supposed to feel? Rhapsodic, after I shit all over her? Christ what's going to happen? Oh orange, work more. Please.

He switched on the radio hoping to soothe his head. *Is That All There Is.* Peggy Lee. "Terrific." He started to switch stations when an announcer cut in to say the station was going to Mission Control in Houston. *"It's great news. They're down! They're down! It's a beautiful landing."* Then came the jubilant relief from Houston. *"We copy you on the ground. You've got a bunch of guys about to turn blue. We're breathing again. Thanks a lot."*

"Well at least something's going right in the middle of this fucked up mess." He punched the dashboard hard enough to feel the pain rip through his hand and up his arm. "Nora, I gotta get it right for us," he roared.

"UP TELEMENTARY COMMAND reset to reacquire on high gain."

"Oh don't stop," Nora cried out of her orgasm. They were kneeling on the sofa in the small Connecticut cottage with the sunlight streaming in on them. Conrad had already brought her to several climaxes. Now with one hand brushing back and forth across her erect nipples and the other deftly stroking her clitoris, he was bringing them both to a powerful coming.

"Copy. Out."

"Oh god," she gasped, losing her breath and nearly her consciousness. And as she continued to come, she heard him cry out. Then they collapsed in exhaustion.

"We have unofficial time for the touchdown of 102 hours, 45 minutes, 42 seconds and we will update that."

Both burst into laughter as the words from the television registered.

"I think we've been to the moon ourselves," he said.

"Yes," she replied, but before she had a chance to hold to that feeling a wave of fear swept her as she remembered her missed period.

THERE WERE HITCHHIKERS ALONG THE HIGHWAY in Central Oregon. Young people, pleasant looking with the freshness of spirit on their faces. Spirit still unencumbered by the burden of dreams that time would clutter with addendums. Once he was like them, he suddenly realized. Then the sorrow of what he now considered to be his longings for more. And they had robbed him, consuming all he had.

At one point he stopped to pick up a couple. After all, they seemed the special types he should continue to interview. Maybe they can resuscitate me, he snipped to himself as they prepared to climb on board. Both sported deep mountain tans, shorts and T-shirts. The guy with long sandy hair and granny glasses had a broad toothy smile and the girl who was shorter and Twiggy thin had long brown hair loosely pulled back and tied with a wide blue ribbon that reminded him of the color of Nora's eyes. They were headed for the Ochoco National Forest. As they pitched their sleeping bags and knapsacks onto the back seat, the guy introduced himself and his girlfriend. Their handshakes were powerful and they enthusiastically expressed their thankfulness. "We're going out here for jobs. We used to head up a travel agency in Portland," he said using a bandana to wipe the mountain sweat from his brow. "But since coming back from the Nam that doesn't make it anymore." She got in the back seat, he in the front and they both cheered when they heard the radio. "Oh the men are on the moon." "That's great news."

After they listened for a while, the guy said to Noah: "The Sea of Tranquility. So that's where they are now. Look how far they had to go to find it."

"Yeah," Noah said. "Must be pretty great. A *Sea of Tranquility.*"

"Just think, after the revolutionary war days in this country how noble and honorable our thoughts and actions must have been before the greed and power mania took over."

"Yeah. How it just slipped over into that," Noah replied but it was more to himself than his fellow travelers.

"God, we need to go back to simpler ways. That's where our roots were. I think we need to begin all over again."

"Sure do."

30

"I CAN'T! I CAN'T! OH GOD, HELP!"

Nora jumped out of bed to the cries. Not knowing where she was she tripped and fell over a nightstand as the cries continued. "Help! Get us help!"

Awake and shuddering with fear, she realized it was Conrad and remembered where they were. Pushing herself up from the floor, she rushed around to his side of the bed and pulled him into her arms. "What's wrong? What is it?"

"Can't you see we need a medic!" he screamed out of his sleep as he grabbed her around the shoulders and began shaking her violently. "We need a goddam medic here now. Immediately! He's gotta stop the pain for this guy. He's gotta help."

"Hold on," Nora cried as she saw his face drained and contorted with pain. The sweat was streaming down his naked body. "It's all right. It's over. It's gone. Everything's all right now."

"Oh my god," he gasped almost breathless. Then he was panting for a time as he stared at her in horror. "Oh my god. Jesus. It's not real this time. I thought it was."

The faint light of early dawn barely registered through the meeting point of the blinds as he quieted himself. "I don't want to talk about this," he managed as his whole body shook and trembled.

"I can understand. Don't be worrying yourself."

He looked at her with such gratefulness. Then he hugged her tightly, and she could feel his tears graze her shoulder and back. But just as quickly he seemed to snap himself together. "Let's go out into the light. I don't like the dark. I'd like us to go out for a walk around the pond."

"Yes," she delighted as he got up and lifted her out of the bed. "It looks like it's going to be a beautiful day," he enthused pulling up the blinds. "Let's go out just like this. We're so far away from everything. Take advantage of the freedom." So they went out onto the porch and then down the knoll as they let the soft warm breeze envelop them and the early spears of dawn's first light darken their skin.

"Jesus, I don't give a hoot about anything but this," he said as he kicked at the cool misty water from the pond's edge.

"What?" she asked as he held her around the waist.

"Just this. Nothing else in the world," he went on as he squinted at the pond and then the distant Litchfield hills on the horizon. "I don't think I would have said this before. Well before the war that is." She could see him drifting for a few seconds and she shivered. But then he was back to the present again. "Well what I mean is before that I was so dead set. Gung ho to be this great photographer. There was nothing that could clip my sites. But because of that, I was this kind of guy who could have gone right on through the whole drift and missed all the really true stuff."

"But you wouldn't have—"

"Sure I would have. You see all those prizes that I thought were out there, that you had to bee-line for, they're here. They're not fortunes way off in the distance waiting for some bulls-eye hit. They're here now. They're this and they're us."

He watched her and she knew he could see the truth of his words come over her. Then his hands stroked the sides of her face and gently he kissed her. Wild geese cawed in the distance then streaked through the pale lemon billows of pond mist. In the rush of that moment he held her tightly and once again she felt surrounded by love and care and giving. Later they guided each other down to the silky long grass still sprinkled with dew and slowly began to make love as the lapping water and the remains of mist turned rouge from the sun's ascent.

But suddenly he stopped them. "God, I have to run up and get a condom."

"No," she insisted as the whole baby thing came hurtling back at here. "No, I'm just about to have my period," she lied pulling him back to her and then tried desperately to lose herself in their oneness.

Afterwards they stayed in the dewy grass holding one another and for a time he dosed in the peace of the rising sun that warmed them. But then a small cloud of mosquitoes began to approach and as Nora tried fanning them away, Conrad flinched, jumped and opened his eyes to the fullest.

"Oh it's just some mosquitoes. I'm sorry I woke you."

"No. It's not that," he said as he staggered to regain his footing. Then he squatted down beside her and shook his head. "It goes like this sometimes. Like in clusters. One bad one after another." And he pressed the left side of his head tightly against her shoulder. "I call them nightmare memory headaches."

"Why don't you talk to me about it then? Maybe it would help." And she began a deep massage of his head.

"I don't know if I can. I-- I thought if I pushed it away I'd be able to live with it." He shrugged his naked shoulders and looked out across the pond again. "Keeping it way in the distance. But—"

"I hope my presence isn't an omen."

"Oh how could you ever say that? I love you so much. No never. If anything, I think being with you is quite likely making me face more of it. As it should be." And he suddenly rose up, went for a dip in the pond, came back and sat shivering.

"Oh let's go inside, you're freezing now."

"No. It's not the air or the water. I guess I just need to feel like this to get it out." And he sat facing her as she began rubbing his shoulders in an attempt to warm him.

"You see the flashes of light. Gaudy awful flashes," he started. "So much there that was horrible happened at night. Not that it wasn't going on during the day even more so. But when you've got a camera in front of you and you're shooting you forget yourself and that you're a part of it. It somehow isolates you from all the horror. You don't feel anything. You just take pictures. But—at night we couldn't do too much picture taking." He shook his head and shivered some more. Then he braced himself and looked up at the sky for a time.

"And at night you really couldn't sense where the enemy was. Lots of times it wasn't even there it was just imagined. But when it was—that's when the light show came on. In an instant the darkness would explode into light. Grenade launchers, mortar rounds, flame throwers, cluster bombs. Could be any or all. The ground would be shaking like an earthquake. The sounds would vibrate through you until you were shaking too and the smell of burning flesh would just about consume you. I'll never forget that. And screams. Roars of pain. Yells. Always."

He continued looking at the sky and his tanned face had gone pale and blank. "Gaudy awful bursts of firelight," he finally continued. "Well I guessed it was like a Fourth of July in hell. And the horror. He blinked and closed his eyes then opened them and looked down at his leg. "The horror. That's how it happened. I panicked during one of those light shows. I jumped up from this ridge to run. Not just run. Truth is I was going to keep on running. Shit ass coward as I see it now. Well that's when I got it right through the leg. Probably deserved to. But that's what's so bad. There was this gung ho guy next to me. He was pretty green and still out for the glory of the flag. A kid, a real kid. He used to say to me—*think I'm a good soldier. Am I good enough?*" And then he was trembling again. When Nora reached out to touch him again, he stopped her, brushed her arm aside. "No!" And his face was no longer blank but full of rage. "Yes he was just a kid. No more. Well-- If I hadn't panicked-- If I hadn't stood up, caught enemy attention he'd still be alive. The bullet I took exited me and went right into his brain. Oh-- Jesus. You know how that goes down?"

For a long time they sat speechless. "Well at least you got past getting it out." She finally whispered.

"But I won't get past his face. Never. Because after he took it-- The whole shittin' sky lit up. That's how I could see the horror of what happened and I could see that he knew it. I could see that shock in his eyes that he was being taken out. He knew—and I knew. Just like that it was over. Just like that. The sounds of the shelling and the popping of the mortars faded into the night and the lights went out."

31

"OLD DREAMMAKER, YOU HEARTBREAKER."
He was sitting on a rock beside the Salmon. Alone in the red sunset swigging hundred proof vodka conserving Pete's rapidly vanishing saviors. The crappy booze was making him sing out Johnny Mercer lyrics to the river and the mountains. Then he tore a page from his notebook and began to write.

A breeze curls down the darkening canyon

The pines squeak their mighty life

The frosty milk water rushes west

The sky tones to sapphire for the heralding of the stars and the half moon

A place alone, except for giant birds scaling peaks, aiming for stars.

"Aiming for the stars. Would that I be aiming for the stars once more." And for a flash he was remembering that night seeing into eternity on Kilmurvey Strand with Nora. But it was fast fading most likely due to the vodka. Then he was laughing and tearing the sheet of paper into tiny bits and letting them scatter and rush away in the dimness of water. "What pollution!" And he laughed some more.

AS THE DAYS PASSED, Noah interviewed dozens more along the way. But he was having the bad knack of hitting on the disenchanted which didn't aid in suffusing the dynamism the Wilton material demanded. However he did notice that even some of these people held to the hope of effecting change. As such, they were going forward while all along he felt as if he were speeding in reverse. Yes through his job surprisingly he had earned the small fortune he had so longed to possess. But in the process he had dumped all over Nora and become a druggie. Perhaps as punishment, his real dream—his book still remained in limbo. So the sense of loss came to weigh heavily.

Taking pause from his interviews, he found himself detouring into the occasional ghost town. With the aid of one or two of his escapes, he could hear the voices of the dead murmuring their dreams. Over a century ago, they had come this far, to this majestic frontier. They must have stood in awe of all they were going to glean from this shimmering world of gold-laden streams that had awaited them. But then so often for so many something had gone terribly awry.

At one of these towns, he made his way into the patched-up remains of a church with a bell-less tower. There were a few slowly rotting benches along with a partial altar fronting a worn wooden cross barely held in place on a cracked wall beam. He chanced a bench and sat staring ahead as his heart sank. Not only could he not whisper words to God, to the Trinity, he couldn't even allow his mind to form them. In this place that still remained holy, he felt himself no longer deserving of that right.

INSTEAD WHEN HE WALKED OUT and without any prompting Dante Gabriel's words from college days greeted him head on: *What of the heart without her? A wayfarer by barren ways and chill. Double darkness up the labouring hill.*

"HEY NORA, I'M IN SALMON, IDAHO. It's beautiful in this country. I wish you could see it with me. Are you all right?" For the moment, he hoped he would get a favorable response, one that might faintly match Oliver's joyous reaction over the material he'd sent him.

"I guess so," she replied coldly. "How are you?" Well it was a bit much to expect.

"Okay, I guess. I—I miss you so much." But then there was silence. "Um-- I-- was wondering if we could talk some."

"I'm very much afraid we can't Noah. But look after yourself."

It was the end of the call.

DEADMAN'S BAR. How perfectly apropos. I should stay here forever. It was mid-afternoon in Jackson Hole, and his lodging was a distance down the road at the Jackson Lake. He'd cut back on the vodka because it burned and pained his guts. Now he was attempting to ride on some extra strength bennies that he could scarcely spare, and worse they weren't doing much good. To make it through, he lay on a sandbar bar at the Snake River basin. The pines were on either side of the river, and looking down at him from the rims of broken pure white clouds were the awesome jagged-tooth Tetons that rose thousands of feet above the timber line. He tried, just tried to remember what it was like to be calm and absorb such god given inspirational beauty. But he couldn't. Finally he got up and began to roam. As he did, music came drifting across his mind and then he was struggling to recall what it was. When he approached the sagebrush flats, it came to him. *The Call of the Far Away Hills.* The echoing voice followed: *Shane, come back.* Suddenly he had a vision of his father looking out of the booth window at the *Ritz* for every showing of the three-day run of that picture. Noah couldn't understand why it had appealed to him so much. But he could now. In a way his father was the same as Shane—that lonely figure who touched down in this part of the Wyoming frontier, a character drawn with torment and fatigue. He had missed or lost his chance somewhere along the way. "So had dad. So have I. The fizzin' Mason curse is real after all."

AFTER HE HAD a creamy Italian lunch for his stomach's sake, he returned to Deadman's Bar and fell asleep. Then he was back in Ithaca again. Young and sitting in his room writing through the brightness of the early day. Thrilled he was with the words. But as he read them back, the light faded and the room grew darker. They hadn't worked and he had grown into a withered drunk. When he cried out, a bright white light flooded him from above. He turned and looked up to see the arc light from one of his father's projection machines. And once his eyes adjusted, he could see his father's face in the booth window. His voice rumbled through the auditorium. "You're courting death, Noah."

It was almost dark when he struggled awake. "God, I've got to get to a phone and call her again." Before he drove away, he pitched nearly a full quart of vodka into the Snake.

32

IT WAS TEN O'CLOCK on that Sunday night when she and Conrad arrived back to Gramercy Park. For the second time they had taken advantage of the empty Connecticut retreat. Nora had been edgy the entire time because she was still without her period. And then she had her art reception coming up on the Tuesday. Although she had put forth the vague pretense that she wasn't troubled, she sensed that Conrad knew better especially when he insisted on coming home with her.

"God in heaven, what am I going to do?" she finally admitted when she came out of the bathroom.

"What?" he asked anxiously.

"My period. The damn thing won't start. I think I must be pregnant."

"Is that what's wrong?"

"Yes. I'm well over a month overdue."

"But how could that be? I've always used condoms until you said you were due. Oh god! That first morning when you came to the apartment. Shit! Why didn't I have the sense? I couldn't think of anything but us being together. But you should have told me you were scared and not kept it a secret," he insisted as he went to her and took her in his arms. "God I love you so much. It's been my dream for us to have kids someday. Don't you feel that way too?"

"Well yes. But—" she said as she pulled away and walked over to the window. "But we haven't even talked about anything. And now we might be having a baby."

"Yes we have," he said as he followed her, stroked her shoulders and then whispered. "We've said so much between us without even speaking."

"I know. But we aren't ready for this. And I wish we weren't talking about it here."

"I know. I feel the same way."

"I did start looking for an apartment of my own. But I've been so feckin' busy with all this work," she went on as she gestured to her easel. "And then the few times I did go ahead looking, I became so bloody sickened with the whole lot."

"But I didn't know that. Why couldn't you just stay with me as I've said before. I mean now that we're together."

"I can't you know. I still haven't made it right in myself."

"You still love him very much," he gently pursued.

"Yes," she said as she turned back from the window to face him. "In some ways. If worrying about someone means you love the person, well then there's no question."

"Does that mean--," he started and she could see he had gone rigid with fear.

"No. What it means is that I've got to use great care in sorting it out with him—and with myself. And even then I've still got to try to help him."

"Well of course. And I respect you for that."

"But it's going to make it all the more difficult if I am pregnant. Because it would be our baby. There'd be no doubt of it." She sighed as she went and sat on the sofa.

"I know. God I was an idiot," he said following her.

"Well there's nothing we can do about what's past. But what I've got to do is get out of here before he comes back in a couple of weeks."

"And there's something else too," Conrad sighed and then took a deep breath. "It only came up recently, and I was sort of waiting till I thought the time might me right. But I guess I can't wait too much longer. The Witkin is pushing me."

"What?" she asked already feeling fear. "Tell me."

"Well I've been thinking and hoping that when this is over and when you're certain you feel right about it that we could eventually move away together."

"Where?"

"I didn't know at first. But that's when the Witkin came into play. Seattle. They want me to consider moving there after my showing. They seem to have the hots for that area. They see it as a new frontier for me. That and Bainbridge and the other islands of Puget Sound."

"Well why when you've already begun to show so much promise here?"

"That's what I said. The material we're putting in the show they say they're thrilled with. But what comes next is their question. They feel I'm capable of all sorts of innovative stuff, and they raved about my talent. But the whole thing puts me on edge. I mean the situation has to work for the both of us, or it's not going to happen at all."

Nora sat there just nodding at him, trying to absorb the whole concept. It wasn't just the Seattle part that stunned her. It was the first time they'd even broached the subject of living together. And now all these thoughts were coalescing—the idea of telling Noah, of leaving him and moving away, of having a baby. And now Seattle. Suddenly she was completely overwhelmed.

"I think what they really want is for me to be traveling about opening my mind to all sorts of new dimensions," Conrad went on spilling out all the details. "They said they'd sponsor me, put me under contract if I'd give them exclusive gallery rights because they were certain my work would escalate in value."

"Well that's great all the same," she finally managed out of her numbness. "But—how do you know what it's like out there?"

"Oh I've been there before when I was a high school kid. My family had relatives in the area. And it is beautiful that whole part of the country. And the islands, the mountains, the forests. I suppose it's still the same."

She wanted to say—well Noah's out there now, you could call and ask him. It was the first streak of anger she felt toward Conrad. How could she be in the position of having to confront all this, she wondered and he just standing there breezily going on with more details. Then she looked across the way at her easel which reminded her that her showing was only two days away.

"They're paying my expenses to go out there in a few weeks to have a look around and see if it seems exciting and would work out."

"God, it's all too much," she finally gasped aloud as she sat forward.

"What?" he asked in shock as he went over to hold her.

"Oh I don't know how I can cope with all of these things. And I'm still married."

"I'm sorry. I went on too much," he said and then went on to kiss her across the cheek and neck and then to hold her tight. "You have to know I'll be with you through everything always no matter what." And she wondered if she hadn't heard similar promised words before back down the years. Could she ever believe again?

"Nora, you have to believe there's no one but you. And there never will be. Not now."

That brought her out of the one set of thoughts and jarred her into another. There was something in his words that had jarred her. She pulled away from him and went back to the window again. Lights flickered through waving branches of trees from apartment lights across the park as night descended. *Not now*, he had said and the distance between them grew.

"Not now," she repeated his words coldly. "But maybe later."

"How could you say that?" he went to the window and gently pulled her to him. "Please look at me," he said as he turned her face. "Oh I see. I shouldn't have said it that way. Please come back and sit down. You have to hear me out." And so she followed and sat beside him.

"Yes, there was someone. Yes. And I was in love. It was during the war. And like everything else I thought I'd put it away. But you can't," he sighed. When he spoke again his voice had become skewered with pain and then he went distant. "She was Vietnamese. A schoolteacher in this tiny village in the lowlands. It was peaceful and so lush green. A little like Ireland. They sent me there after I'd been chopped. I guess I was pretty crazy. Mad and sad—and miserable with the guilt. But I think they thought they could revive the gung-ho photographer in me. So they gave me a kind of half R&R. And god did I need it. So I was doing a little work from this quiet compound. That's when I met her." With that he got up and crossed to the windows. By now the street lights cast enough tone on them to catch the reflection of his eyes seeing visions of the past. "She was really beautiful. Her husband had been killed in the war. So out of all this death and desperation, we became lovers. We used to talk for days about how one day when the war was over we'd get married and live in America. One day----" As he paused and wandered about a bit, Nora felt an upsurge of regret having provoked him into this dredging. She also had to acknowledge that along with it she couldn't ignore the certain little waves of jealousy. Then suddenly she was wondering where this woman was now. And she held her breath.

"Her family," he finally went on as he stopped by the bookcase behind her. "They liked me. They did farming and fishing. And they even called me son. The last two weeks I was there I stayed in their home more than the compound. Then one morning after we'd been together and when it was still dark outside she went off to school." Slowly he wandered back to the windows and faced out again. "There was a VC ambush on the compound. Gooks killed a lot of our guys. I'd probably have gotten it too if I'd stayed at the compound that night. Anyway the school was between the VC and the compound. I could hear the shelling as I limped there. A lot of kids got it right off cause they didn't know how to get out of the way. Blood was everywhere. Some of them cried as they went, whimpering for their parents. Others froze in the horror of dying. Children. Little children. And the damn gooks couldn't have cared less." He stopped again, took a deep breath and pushed his hands against the framework of one of the windows. "She got it trying to save the kids. I got to her just before she died. And she whispered—America, we still go there."

He turned back to Nora, his eyes filled with tears. "So you see what *not now* means."

His head bent as he wiped his eyes. She went to him and without words held him tightly. And once again they were reunited through grief and pain. "But see," he finally whispered. "There's one thing I know for fact. I've been given a second chance. There isn't one person in this world who I could love more than you. No one."

"I know."

After a moment he broke away. "I better be going. It isn't the right place for this. I just wish you'd come home with me tonight."

She saw the hurt lingering in his eyes. "No. Whether it's foolish or not, I don't want to do that in case he calls. But wait." And she went to the closet and pulled out the rollaway and some fresh sheets. Then closing the bedroom door she closed all the images of the apartment behind her as well. All images in fact, all but one—this loving, caring and deeply wounded man before her. "We'll both have to sleep on this." He appeared so relieved that a gentle smile crossed his face and she knew he wanted to close out the world with her. He began undressing her as she made the bed, holding her around the stomach, spreading kisses down the heat of her sun-reddened back, rolling the tips of her nipples, touching the wetness of her vagina, massaging it. By the time she had finished with the bed she was in orgasm.

33

IT WAS 9:30 when Noah arrived back at the Jackson Lake Lodge to phone Nora.

11:30 IN GRAMERCY PARK. Nora and Conrad had long since collapsed into each other's arms and into deep sleep. Even the off-tune drumming of the piano in the upstairs apartment hadn't awakened them. Then came the ringing. Loud and persistent. Nora stirred and Conrad began to awaken. The proximity of the phone to the bed was similar to that in Conrad's apartment. Still full of sleep, irritated by the ringing and the now booming piano, not cognizant of where he was, he groped for the phone and answered. "Hello." He was yawning.

Suddenly Nora snapped out of her sleep and sat bolt upright. "My god, it's probably Noah," she whispered.

"No," said Conrad, now realizing what he had done. "This is OR 50209. You've got the wrong exchange. That's okay." Then he hung up.

"I'm sorry. I'm sorry," he said, slapping his palms to his temples. Then he pulled his arms around her shaking body. "I don't think he suspects."

"Probably not. But even so."

"Don't worry."

"He'll call back now." No sooner had she said the word than the phone rang. "God I'm frightened."

"Don't be. Be natural." And he held her more tightly.

"Hello. Hello Noah. Is anything wrong?"

"I just wanted to tell you that I miss you. I've been horrible to you. I know that. I love you. And I want to be with you so much."

God does he have to be saying this with Conrad's arms around me yet. She started shaking again. "Sure you'll be home in a week or so won't you?"

"It's just that I'm depressed as hell because I've been so wrong."

"You'll hold on," she said as the piano above boomed out another crescendo.

"Probably better here than there. They really seem to be going at it tonight. I can't take that, you know."

"Noah---"

"I love you." And he hung up.

"He knows," she gasped.

"I GOTTA TALK TO SOMEBODY," he told himself over and over again trying to shut out everything but that thought. If he were to talk and keep on talking, he might prevent his mind from absorbing all that was transpiring. Panic was already seeping in as he fumbled through his case for his address and phone book. "Murphs, I'll call her," and he quickly dialed as he sat on the edge of the bed. "She'll calm me. We'll calm each other through all that's gone wrong." The phone rang and rang. "Where is she? Damn." He finally hung up. "Tim. Maybe Tim." He dialed him. "Shit, no answer." He hung up and dialed Murphs again. Then Tim. "Shit the whole city's out on a toot." He slammed the receiver down and with his head in his hands he replied to his last remark. "Everyone except Nora—and her newly acquired. Or maybe not so new." Automatically he went to his bag and began fishing for some remaining tooies, found them, ran into the bathroom and gulped them with some water. "God I'm far too sober. Vodka! Oh shit." He'd pitched it into the river. There was the Stockade Bar here. He'd buy a bottle. Quick before closing time. He almost gasped relief when he found it open. He had three martinis there because he was afraid to be alone until the booze kicked in. Then back in his room he got into bed and proceeded to drink the better part of the fifth he'd purchased. "Oh god, I need your help. How dare I even have the nerve to ask?" he whispered as he crossed himself. "I'm in such trouble. Everything's going."

THE PHONE BLASTED HIM AWAKE the next morning. "Seven-thirty. God," he croaked. It was one of Oliver Wilton's secretaries. "I hope I'm not waking you. I know how early it is out there. But I wanted to give you time. You see Oliver would like to have you back in the office tomorrow morning."

"Tomorrow morning!" He leapt in the air and then crashed to the bed again, momentarily, but only momentarily, leaving the throbs of his head above him.

"Yes, tomorrow morning. The Seventh. He knows it's a bit of an inconvenience but he really wants you back to discuss plans for covering the Woodstock rock festival next weekend. He thinks it might be a much bigger event than anyone anticipated. So do you feel there's a problem."

"No. No problem." May as well add this to the mix as well.

He made it to the toilet and heaved up a pint including blood and bile. He knew he was almost out of oranges. But if he ever needed them it was now. Of all his barbs, he was finding that Thorazine was the only one that worked on his stomach while it calmed his brain.

It took over an hour to organize a flight to Denver where he would connect to New York. But he had to drive seemingly halfway across the state to get it. There really must be a guiding force somewhere in the universe, he thought when he cleared Avis at Casper Airport, because he had no idea how he got there. He didn't even remember the drive. Would that the same could be said for the trip from Casper to Denver. It made his previous journey from San Francisco to Portland seem smooth. This flight went through so many endless drops that passengers reacted with continual roller-coaster screams. Thankfully, no one sat in his vicinity to view his use of the barf bag that put the oranges out of commission.

Due to overbooking and flight delays, he would have to wait till 12:40 a.m. for a flight to New York. "T-e-r-r-i-f-i-c." He just sat there in the airport dazed, going down and down as foot traffic built around him. He finally moved to as distant a corner as possible. Still he could hear the clatter and the wailing of babies which made him think of Nora and how she longed to have them and how he wanted to postpone. Now quite likely they never would. God was it all over for them, he panicked. Finally he closed his eyes against the pain, the crowds, the noise and his mind began sorting through *R* words that one way or another pertained to him. *Revenge/Retaliation* because he could still hear the bastard's voice. Then a vision came to him of the two of them doing it. "God, I can't take that," he muttered opening his eyes to close it out. "But haven't I caused it," he startled himself with the words and closed his eyes again. Then came *revolting/reprehensible* for his long time behavior followed by *remorse*. He had arrived at this point because of *riches* or the persistent desire for such thereof. And now there was the *retribution* which could *raze* their relationship. Oh god no. There was after all—*retrieve/retract/reprieve/redeem.* "But it's too late, isn't it?" Shit what a fool. There is no *rebounding* from this, is there? No going back to my *raison d'être?* "Help!" It was then that he opened his eyes and realized a number of people were staring at him. I've got to get out of here, he thought as he jumped up, grabbed his bag and headed for a stall in the men's room. There he found a good handful of trees he didn't know he still had. He must have tucked them into a hidden pocket of his bag on some previous long forgotten trip to nowhere. He hadn't taken any trees in a good while. He hoped they'd work again, be his saving grace. He hadn't better think that too loudly he told himself. One thing god would not want to be lending him at the moment was grace. As he took them, the green portions reminded him of Ireland, of Donegal, of the house. He quickly popped two at the sink, cupped water in his hands and downed them.

Out in the hall the announcement came that his flight would be boarding in a half-hour. With that he quickly chased after a couple of bar-side martinis or was it three. Then he was on the plane where strapped in his seat he quickly passed out.

7:40 A.M. KENNEDY. Are all airport mirrors vicious? Noah didn't recognize the face he was shaving. He had lost that much during his journey. The cheeks had disappeared into hollows of gauntness. The eyes were now blotchy red yet tinged with yellow. And worse they stayed lifeless no matter how forcefully he tried to instill some brightness. His idea had been to shave here and go directly to Wilton because he wasn't ready for Gramercy Park. But I can't go into the office like this, he thought. So he stepped into a stall and changed out of his requisite jeans gear assignment clothes. By now they'd gone rotten or *manky* as Nora would say. He changed into a shirt and tie and a pair of cavalry twills. They were the trousers he had worn belt-less out to the coast all those days ago. Now they would no longer stay up without the aid of his jeans belt. After he pulled it on, he rubbed and pressed on his stomach, hoping in vain to relieve the now ever-present nagging pain. Then he went back to the mirror. God even his hair had grown far too long and unkempt. He had never ever looked this shabby. "Jesus, that can't be a mirror."

10:15 A.M. THE WILTON BUILDING. Noah decided to bite the bullet and went directly to Oliver's office. Oliver was outside with his secretaries and immediately shook Noah's hand and patted him on the shoulder. "*Ah* see how exhausted you look," he said with unusual concern. "No wonder with all that great material you've been sending us."

"Well also when you consider I've been traveling for over twenty-four hours."

"*Ah* know. My apologies for that. But there was no other way but to get you here quickly. Come into *mah* office, Noah." Noah followed and went to sit on the sofa before he collapsed.

"Oh we would need the door closed," Oliver insisted as he reversed himself to do so. "*Ah* need to speak to you in private." The word private loomed along with the sound of the door, but Noah was almost too tired to care as Oliver went and sat behind his desk. "*Ah* didn't call you back here for Woodstock. *Ah'm* afraid it's going to be grungy and not what we would consider worthy of our next month's *Connoisseur* theme *The Re-Makers*. And with your new western material added the issue looks fantastic as is. But we *ah* sending a few novices up there just in case of any *glamour*."

"Well then why did you call me back in such a rush, Oliver?"

"There's something much more important *ah* have to tell you and *ah* wanted you here in person."

"What? Am I being fired?"

"Oh don't be ridiculous Noah. *Ahm* absolutely certain you must be responsible for at least fifty percent of our advertising revenue on *Connoisseur* and it's escalating by the day. This next issue is going to hit two-hundred-and-fifty pages and heaven only knows what you've meant to *FCD* with your column.

"Well what is it then?" Noah asked with exasperation as total fatigue began setting in. "Are you leaving? Is Champ Com. dropping us?"

"No. No. No! *Ah* almost wish it were something about the business."

"Oliver, I'm a big guy now. Tell me."

"*Ah* just wonder how you'll take this."

"My god, it's not something about Nora," he panicked.

"No. Although *ah* have to say *ah am* concerned there."

"Oliver, are you going to wait till I have a stroke?"

He sighed and sat forward leaning with his arms on his desk. "*Ah* know how close you and Murphs were."

Noah shook his head in bewilderment. "Well, we still are."

"You have to take the present away Noah." And with that he closed his eyes.

"What!?" Noah gasped.

Opening his eyes that were now brimming, he struggled to continue. "Noah, *aham* so sorry. Four days ago, Murphs committed suicide."

Noah's mouth fell open and he sat there stunned, staring past Oliver at the blank wall. Finally he let go with a low visceral wail. "N-o-o-o."

"She walked up onto the 59th Street Bridge and jumped off."

Noah bent forward holding his head in his hands. When he looked up again, the room had gone into a blur. "How come you waited all that time to call me out there?"

"Why *ah* didn't know," he replied as he patted his eyes with his handkerchief. It was a whole day and a half before the Medical Examiners Office called me. There was no identification on the body. All they had from one of her pockets was a blurred Bloomingdale's charge slip. Her name, address and the account number were obscured. *Ah* guess investigators spent the best part of a day at the store pawing through records." Oliver shook his head and took a deep breath. "*Ah* had to go down and identify the broken body. How ghastly was that?"

"God—God! I can't hear this. I just can't." And he sat silently with tears falling all over him from he knew not where. "What are the funeral arrangements?" he finally somehow asked out of a mindless state.

"We haven't made them yet. I have Campbell's standing by. But we have to wait until they've completed an investigation and the *awetopsy*."

"Oh my god. Has this been in the papers?"

"Just reports of a suicide but they didn't know who it was. Now that they do, they'll all be certain to go with it in tomorrow's editions. *Ah* tried to keep it quiet as long as *ah* could for your sake. No one here knew. Now *ah've* called a full staff meeting for eleven this morning. They'll have to work on the extended obit for *FCD*." Then he sighed and once again fell silent for a moment before he got up and went to sit beside Noah. In a much slower, darker voice he spoke. "*Ah* can't understand it Noah. She was so vivacious. *Ah* offered her almost anything to stay. We were paying her full salary on an open-ended leave. She could have come back at a moment's notice. You knew her so well Noah. Why?"

Noah thought for a long time before he spoke. "Maybe—maybe she found the things she'd chased couldn't match the things she'd lost-----or never had."

IT WAS WHEN Noah stood to leave that he felt as if he had been walloped by a sledgehammer. He staggered a little while Oliver came over to steady him. "Noah, *ah* want you to go home to get some sleep. We'll be able to keep you up to date on the funeral arrangements. *Ah* just have such ill feelings not doing more for her long ago."

"Well they can't be as many as mine. I can assure you of that."

"And that's another matter. *Mah* other concerns right now are really you and Nora."

"Oh," said Noah snapping from his wooziness. "Those feelings of yours keep amazing me. What *has* changed you so?"

"*Ah'll* tell you. While it's strictly definitely *entrée nous,* my wife has left me. She's begun divorce proceedings. *Ah* don't want to see the same happen to you. *Ah* know Wilton is *mah* life. Through it *ah* thought *ah* could rule everyone's roost with my power. Now it seems that *ah* am the one to suffer the harrow."

10:45 CROSSLAND. "My god Noah, you look like a walking nightmare. What the fuck is wrong?"

"One of my closest buddies is dead."

"Oh I'm sorry."

"Someone I could have saved. Only I didn't. I was too caught up in my own shit." And for the first time since the news he let go with sobs for a release he could never deserve.

"Look, take it easy." He came over and gave him a hug.

"Yeah," he said and blew his nose. "I guess *easy*'s a word I don't know."

"Jesus, what can I get for you?"

"Oh--- anything," he shrugged. But make it strong. I've got this pain in my gut on top of everything else now."

"Well you know it isn't right if you've got a condition like that. You should be seeing a doctor."

"Oh it's just that I haven't been eating much since I've been out west. Just p-l-e-a-s-e give me some stuff for now. I've got to have something."

Pete sighed. "Well I guess some stronger Thorazine. Or some Percodan to ease you through the pain. But do not take them with alcohol."

"Of course not," Noah assured as he took the large vial and began to leave.

"Don't take more than one perc every three or four hours. Hold out as long as you can. You don't want to end up dead like your friend. And see a doctor. But don't tell him anything about this," he called after Noah as he began to rush away.

"Of course not. I told you I never reveal my sources."

Hold out? Was he kidding? The instant he was out the door he garnered enough saliva to swallow two. Thoughts were fleeting now. Maybe I do want to end up dead. *We're Depression babies,* she'd said. *We survive.*

11:30 A.M. AND THERE WERE NO BARS OPEN YET. The White Rose, that dump across from Luchows. That would be open for sure. So suitcase in hand, he joined the rest of the demented. But after a quick look in the bar mirror he couldn't escape the fact that he looked just like them. "I'll have a double Stoli on the rocks," he told the baldy bartender thinking the quality of the Russian would be kinder to him. Baldy raised his eyebrows and snapped: "We don't get much call for the fancy Jamey stuff over here buddy." And good morning to you too pal, Noah thought and was about to leave. But then he thought better of it. "I'll take whatever you've got."

Now his mind filled with images of Murphs, of her walking up onto the bridge. What would she have been thinking, what would have ever possessed her? And now he was remembering the gravity that shown in her eyes as her taxi sped off that day near Longchamps. She had revealed so much more than their brother-sister relationship. She was really telling him how lost she was, especially without Jimmy and after the shock of his betrayal. But more than that she was most likely saying she had been lost her entire life. And wasn't she holding out hope that after her revelation they would bond as faithful brother and sister and see each other through everything. Now all he could wonder was why he had been so *effen* slow on the uptake. "Asshole! Self-centered fool!" He'd betrayed her too. With that he pounded the counter bringing him back to the horrible awareness of this day.

Mercifully through the grunge of the window, he noticed that Luchows was opening. So quickly he headed over there, got his Stoli, a double on the rocks. After which he proceeded to call Tim from the restroom phone.

"God, I need to talk with you."

"That would be good right now. I just split with Beth."

"Great! It looks like we're two of a kind."

"You're not serious," Tim exclaimed.

"Try me."

"Shit you are serious."

"Look could we have lunch?"

"Hell, you picked the worst day of the year pal. I'm having lunch with the big chiefs at Bristol Myers. And we're doing a major presentation right afterwards. It could mean millions for us. And that would certainly be great right now, especially in this downward market when we're losing clients. If only I'd known sooner. But it's too late now."

"I guess that's just my luck."

"God, you do sound bad."

"Pretty much so. How about later? How about dinner?"

"Well aren't you forgetting? There's the reception for Nora's big showing tonight. Won't I see you there? Things haven't gone that far out of whack have they, pal?"

"Oh yes it has. But I'll be there. I forgot it was tonight."

1:15 AND HE COULD HEAR THE PHONE ringing away as he fumbled with the keys to the apartment. By the time he reached the receiver, the caller had disengaged. It meant that Nora wasn't there and that was just as well, he told himself. That would give him a chance to look around for clues of passionate reveling in his absence. As he did, his stomach began pitching again along with his slow burn of hatred for this creep. When he found nothing, those symptoms eased somewhat. Maybe the whole thing had been his imagination. Maybe there was no lover. Quickly he went over to her calendar that rested next to her easel. Yes the showing was tonight, six o'clock onward. I'll go there, he told himself. Go there and she'll see me, and she won't be angry in front of all those people. She'll talk to me.

It was at this point that the phone rang again. It was one of Oliver's secretaries with more details on Murphs. The body had been released and Oliver had arranged for a service at Campbell's the next day. In the meantime, the police had been able to contact Murph's stepmother who said she couldn't afford a burial. When Oliver offered her *a very generous sum* of money, she insisted that the remains be flown to some of her own relatives in a suburb of Cleveland where she would be closer to the kinds of people who loved her. "Hah!" roared Noah. "She didn't even know them." "Well Oliver thought that was pretty weird too," the secretary said. "The stepmother probably thought it would be cheaper to send her off to Cleveland so she could keep some of Oliver's money for herself," Noah snapped. "Well I think you're right. But what was he going to do have a fight over the corpse? So he drafted this weird woman a check." God, thought Noah as he hung up, how incredibly ludicrous for Murphs to spend eternity in some plot in a non-descript cemetery outside of Cleveland, so far from the lights, so far from her cherished Bloomingdale's. How had it all come to this?

Were there any signs of hope in this nightmare day? God, get yourself cleaned up, sobered up, he told himself. So there followed a long steaming shower in which he pressed his head against the tiles trying to stop thinking of Murphs, trying desperately to think only of Nora. What did they used to say in Yearnington when someone died...she or he would have wanted it that way. How easily people cover the truth when they don't want to face it. After a while the hot water began to draw all the blood to his stomach, leaving him lightheaded and bringing back all the pain to his guts.

He struggled out of the tub and without even toweling staggered to the bed where he fell onto it and let his head drop toward the floor until the blood returned. Then he managed to pull himself onto the floor where he crawled to his jacket and pulled out some of the new percs—or were they perkies? Oh what the hell, I'm worried about drug semantics in my condition. So he popped two swallowed without water, then struggled back to the bed and into sleep without even a sheet covering him.

4:30 AND THE PHONE JANGLED HIM AWAKE. Not bothering to answer it, he headed for the kitchen to treat his somewhat less painful guts with some food. He boiled some old but hopefully safe eggs and prepared an egg salad sandwich loaded with the standby mayo. It seemed to take away most of the pain. With that, he went upstairs, shaved again, cleaned his teeth and gargled vigorously with Lavoris then dressed himself in his most dapper sportswear, a deep blue cotton broadcloth shirt from Brooks, rep-striped tie from Turnbell & Asser, a Dunhill blazer and pale brown summer weight slacks from Ted Lapidus. At least these would take away from the dimness of his face. A smile would help as well. So he was ready to go and face her. But not so fast. His eyes caught sight of something strange in the storage closet. The made-up roll-away protruded slightly from its fold-out doors That was unusual for Nora, but more than that between the sheets was something of a coarser fabric. When he pulled on it, it became a bright white men's T-shirt with a Wallachs label and a hint of Old Spice about it. It certainly wasn't his. "Shit! Fuck!" he bellowed and pitched it into the air. Weirdly it caught and remained on the chandelier, dangling there as a brutal reminder. "I'll kill him! I will!" he continued to roar as he stormed about the living room purposely knocking over Nora's easel with its current canvas. "I'll go to that showing, and he'll most likely be there with her and I'll wipe him out!"

5:45 AND *EVERYBODY'S TALKIN' AT ME* drifted from the juke through Molly Malone's. Noah drank safer BMs because he needed to calm himself and not be too explosive too fast. No, he wanted to make them suffer before he surreptitiously exsanguinated the guy with one neck slash of the carving knife he would stop to buy up the street at Warshaw Hardware. It would be sharper than anything he had here.

6:15 AND HE WAS JUST ABOUT RIGHT. The short, curly blondie barmaid from Cork seemed very caring and pretty eerily psychic said he should have another drink. "You never know what you might be finding out there," she warned in singsong. "So you'd be better off by far staying on your mark right here where you'd only be safe and snug." *Snug*, Noah thought. Oh to be snug once more. What an important undervalued word that was. But he couldn't have another drink. He knew if he did it would weaken his resolve to polish off this bloody codger once and for all. The barmaid smiled but her worry showed through as he started to leave and that made him really want to stay, really want to talk.

Warshaw, should he stop in for the knife considering the psychic message he wondered as he stepped from the pub into big sprinkles of rain and looked across Third Avenue. The rain came stronger, but that didn't stop him. He walked down to the familiar store and went to where the knives were. Without any hesitation, he purchased a five-inch German-made utility knife. It would fit into the pocket of his blazer. In the taxi, he removed it from its packaging, drew his thumb carefully along the blade and realized it was far sharper than he had imagined. So sharp that it instantly nicked him making his body shiver at the thought of what it could do. Only now did he realize how far his mind had descended into the realm of madness.

7:10 AND WITH A HEAVY RAIN RIGHT ON CUE, he arrived at the Winsor de Caine on Fifty-seventh Street. There were a few limos doubled parked there meaning some BPs had already arrived. He jumped out instantly lashed by the rain and rushed to the building to find a doorman blocking his entrance. Had he learned of his plot? "Oh no, they moved four doors down the street a good three or four months ago." In the down pour, Noah burst forth again. Now he would arrive with killer intentions as a drowned rat. Even so he was immediately welcomed by a guard who had remembered him from past times. Inside he looked down an entry deck to the gallery floor below. Instantly he picked out Nora from the gathering crowd. She was dressed in an emerald green silky dress adorned with milky strands of pearls he had given her on one of her birthdays. Her face had regained much of the glow it had lost in recent times. How truly beautiful she was, what radiant grace. He couldn't bear to look away.

It was after she'd finished chatting with a small gathering that he noticed her glance across the gallery at this tall wiry guy with curly black hair. It was quite obvious that he stood out from the rest. Because it was a summer event, the emphasis was on casual dress. The men varied, some dressed like Noah while others wore cool color poplin or linen slacks and under light sport coats were the Lacoste polos or striped oxford cloth button-downs from Brooks and Paul Stuart and most had donned Gucci loafers. But this guy wore pale jeans with white sneakers, a jeans jacket and the giveaway to Noah a bright white V-neck T-shirt just like the one in their Gramercy Park closet. As he approached Nora, she looked intensely worried, no doubt because amongst the crowd were Mae Dupree and two *FCD* photographers. Noah had a perfect vantage point as he watched—and listened. "You shouldn't be here," she told the guy forcing a smile. "I know. I just couldn't resist seeing all this beautiful work you've done. But mostly I couldn't resist seeing you." "I know. But I think you should go, especially with the press here. Besides I'll see you later." "You're right of course."

At this Noah's stomach began churning again and his rage rose. Stealthily he moved down the steps with his hand in his blazer pocket gripping the knife. Just then the guy turned toward the stairs. Perfect--except Noah caught the full-front glimpse of his face. It stopped him cold. It shown with pure love for Nora. Jesus, he hadn't figured on this. He squeezed the knife tighter but he couldn't bring himself to pull it out. What was he going to do, slash this guy's throat for loving and caring for the woman he'd so much as ditched. In an instant it caught him. All he had destroyed for the want of wealth, for the uncontrollable need for success. And now he had reached the verge of committing murder over it.

Mercifully by now the guy was gone. Knowing he was going to cry, Noah turned to leave as well. But Nora saw him. "Noah," she called out and started for the stairs. Noah ran from the building into the drenching rain. Ran and ran and ran. Crying as he went. But he could hear footsteps pounding the pavement puddles behind him. "Noah wait!" It was Tim. He tried to run faster to elude him, but Tim finally caught him. He struggled to get away. As he did he vaguely remembered a time in the rain in Ithaca when it was Tim who was in tears and wanting to run away. "Look pal, let's go somewhere and talk."

"I don't want to talk anymore," he roared.

"Okay. But I'll go with you, and we'll just drink if that's what you want."

"No! That's not what I want!" And with that he pushed Tim with all the force he had mustered to deliver to Nora's lover. Tim skidded backwards, lost his balance and fell into a puddle. Noah ran and jumped into a taxi.

"You know something pal, you're an asshole," Tim roared as he struggled to his feet,

"Damn right!" Noah yelled back, and the taxi sped away.

7:45 AND THE TAXI PULLED UP in front of Max's Kansas City on Union Square. For a reason he couldn't discern, it was the first place to come to mind, the place where he and

Tim used to drink in the old days before Nora. Now as he went inside and plowed through the mélange of hippies, artists, writers, musicians and some high powered execs, he was recognized and waved to by many. God this is the wrong place to be if all these people know who I am, he thought with a rush of anxiety. So he dropped his head as he pushed his way through a crowd and ended in a seemingly safe bar space where he ordered a very dry triple Stoli as Lennon-McCartney's *Yesterday* boomed from the jukebox.

"You new here?" a young woman's voice asked. He looked up from his slump at the bar to first come across a tie-dyed T-shirt well filled out with oversized bazooms. By the time he got to her face, she was smiling suggestively. Her eyes were a washed out blue that made him instantly long for the intensity of Nora's. Her long black hair was braided in a ridiculous looking ponytail that cast her as all but ugly.

"Not really," Noah finally answered as he looked away.

"Oh been away?" she pushed to continue a conversation.

"I guess you could say that."

"Good time?"

"Some of it good. Some the best. Some the worst." He was vaguely aware that he was rambling to himself rather than answering her. So he shifted to watching her puffy pocked face sipping away at a Coke drink with a twist of lime that he imagined to be a rum and Coke. As his martini went down even the classy Russian stuff tore at his guts. That made him wonder if he wouldn't be better off with a fizzy cola drink.

"Poor baby," she whispered as she shifted her stool closer and rubbed a bare leg against his making him pull away from the familiarity. "You're kind of cute when you brood. But you're pretty far down there, aren't you?"

"'bout as far as I can get." Then he chuckled not knowing why. "*Look in my face,*" he said staring at her. "*My name is Might-have-been. I am also called No more, Too-late, Farewell.*"

"Is that you? Did someone tell you that?"

"Yah, an old friend haunting my mind. Dante Gabriel to be exact. Keeps bumming me up. Over and over again."

"Poor baby," she repeated, stroking his withdrawing hand which he used to pick up his drink again. "I'd guess it's a woman dumped you. I guess that's what it is."

"I guess you got the brass ring. Or at least part of one."

"She must be crazy. I know about those things. I'm an artist you know and I kind of like you."

Noah wondered the connection of these thoughts and decided it would be better if she used the word *artiste*. Then he was staring into his drink and back thinking of the real artist he loved so much, still loved.

"Hey!" She snapped her fingers, bringing him out of his thoughts. "You there?"

"Yeap. I'm afraid so. I am *Might-have-been,* you know.""

"Stop saying that," she snapped. "You want to go on a trip?"

"Where?"

"To p-a-r-a-d-i-s-e. Where else?" Then she suddenly stopped herself, drew back and looked at him. "Hey, you're not fuzz or anything?"

"No I'm not fuzz. *O-r-r anything.*" And Rossetti was starting up in his mind again.

"You really are in a bad way." And she leaned over, brushing her obviously excited breasts against his arm. "Want to do it then?"

"I don't know. They're freaky."

"Oh baby, that's what's wrong with you." And with that she produced a tiny corked vile, uncorked it and carefully sprinkled a drop of it into the remainder of Noah's drink before he could stop her. Then she did the same with her own.

"What is it?" Noah asked as a sudden vision of Gloria popped into his head.

"Acid, of course."

"Oh, I don't think I want this," he said putting the drink down. "I got in big trouble with something like this first time around."

"Yours was probably bad stuff. This is really the best, believe me."

Noah looked askance. Should he? Things couldn't be much worse. Maybe it would even trip him out of the reoccurring sharp pains in his gut and the sharper ones in his mind.

"Go ahead. I guarantee you'll see *Lucy In The Sky* with those diamonds, if you get my drift."

"I guess you may be right," he said as he conjured a vision of Nora's deeply caring lover. Then hoping to dissolve it, he went ahead and finished the martini. But as he sat the glass down, another vision rushed him. This one was of Murphs as she walked to the center of the 59th Street Bridge. With that he hastened the bartender for another triple and a rum and Coke for his next door neighbor who turned out to be Joelle from Sioux City. "How come you're not Sue then?" he giggled. "And how come you don't sound like you're from there?"

"The thing you do when you move to New York is work very hard on not sounding like you're from Sioux City."

Noah laughed but not about Sioux City. It was a nervous laugh that came out of his growing panic. Between gulps of his martini, he said: "I don't feel anything. Why don't I feel something? Maybe you should give me some more drops."

"Oh it takes a while. If we overdo it, your mind will totally explode."

"G-o-d, it would be totally worth it."

"No. Because then we won't have this terrific fuck trip later. And I know after dropping I could have a really fantastic scene with you," she said as she wiggled up her mini to reveal a peak of rose panties. Then she shifted her knee over once more, this time to nudge him in the crotch. But sex was the furthest from his mind. Escape was. So he ordered another drink and polished it off.

"I don't know if you should drink so much with LSD."

"Oh I don't think that stuff was for real."

"It was. You'll see."

It did take a long time. He couldn't be sure just how long. All he knew was that he went through another drink and nothing was phasing him. The shock of the day had been that great, he told himself. But then at one point, he looked down the crowded bar and saw another mini-skirted girl squatting on the floor performing fellatio on a beardy artist-looking type. No one else seemed to notice caught as they were in their own separate scenes. "Is that happening down there or am I finally hallucinating?"

"Oh it's happening alright. But that's nothing here these days. If you really want to see something, catch a glimpse of the action in the phone booths—or even better the rest rooms."

"Oh I seem to remember."

"I'll just bet you do." And she nudged his crotch again.

"Oh, oh. Something's happening," he said as he looked at the once familiar red laser beam that someone from the Minimalist school of art had designed to shoot across Max's bar. Now the light was exploding through clouds of cannabis smoke into dazzling fans of multi-colors. What Nora would make of them, he thought. So near blinding were they that Noah stepped down from his stool to gain support. When he did, the floor went all mushy, and his feet felt to be sinking into it as if it were composed of quicksand.

Startled, he turned away to see if that would change his impression. But at that point he looked directly at his father, hunched with steel hair and looking severe. When he started to speak, the sonorous words came dragging out like a record playing at the wrong speed. "You had everything I wanted. And you dumped it." He continued to drone, but the words turned into blobs of psychedelic colors growing bigger and bigger until his father's face disappeared.

Then an arm was helping him back onto his stool. He turned as colors shot around him to see Joelle. She was licking her lips with a tongue that finally extended all the way into his mouth. Then she retracted it and said: "Oh I feel so fabulous. It's like I'm in this pink orgasmic cloud a dozen miles away looking down on all of this. Everything's so pretty, and you're so sexy. And oh I want to fuck you in this technicolor, baby." And she seemed both close and far away at the same time. The jukebox boomed now and with every word came an explosion of color. But ugly color.

"Oh that music is going to make me come," Joelle gasped. "It's Sly and the Family Stone. I just love them. They're making me so feverish. So high. O-h-h-h."

"Yeah, they are pretty great," Noah forced himself to say just so his voice would let him know there was still some reality to his being. But the voice wasn't his, and there was no reality. A blob of color had stolen him, taking his pain and making him feverish and turned-on as well. Joelle slipped from her stool and pulled him down with her. The floor had stabilized, so he began to gyrate against her to the music of *I Want To Take You Higher*. It was a long set that kept building and building in an upward spiral. The higher the set, the higher Noah felt. Once again colors were exploding around them like fireworks. As they did, he had an erection that kept growing and growing. Then pressed in by the crowd, Joelle gripped his penis, unzipped his pants and pulled it out. To his horror, it looked to be the distorted proboscis of a small elephant. Joelle reached under her skirt, did an exaggerated wiggle that sent her rose panties that had now gone flaming red down around her ankles. With a broad kick, she sent them flying under the barstool. Then she rose up onto the stool, pulled her skirt out over his bobbing trunk with one hand while she pushed it into her with the other. As they squirmed, Noah caught a vision of a greased pig with a snorting human face as its mug. When Joelle squealed in unison with the pig, flames rose up and engulfed it. Then he and Joelle became as slimy as the pigman and entered into some sort of epileptic attack. This was followed by so many prismatic blasts of dazzling colors that suddenly they were separated. Still the music built. As he spun around the floor, other couples began to gyrate into explosions of color. The music boomed so loudly now that it seemed to be coming from his heart, and he felt any second he would go up in a blaze of color. Then as she stumbled and reeled around again, he came face to face with a beautiful vision. The only vision of worth in his life. A vision of Nora on the cliffs of Aran where the colors from the booming seascape highlighted her radiant face. But so soon she was gone and all her colors gone and everything went chartreuse ugly. His blood turned to ice at the same time he felt sweat pouring from his face. He reached into his blazer pocket for tissues and his hand came to grips with something sharp and hurtful. He pulled his hand out and dropped the object. He looked at his hand and it was pouring blood. His senses were there and then gone in an instant. He heard "Help!" coming from the distance through all the noise, yet this time he knew it was his own voice. Then he saw this man with long greasy black strands of hair, anxious eyes and beggar's clothes hurrying towards him. He remembered him as flaky Mickey Ruskin, the owner of Max's. But now he became a gigantic vertical lizard. As Noah spun around, he saw the upper bodies of the entire crowd turning into enormous menacing vipers when they saw his face. Fangs leapt out at him. He backed, turned and began to run when he spied the red laser shaft shooting in from the enormous front window. Suddenly ugly prismatic colors were back exploding, pulsating with his heartbeat. And Sly and the Family Stone's music was with him once more, pitching to its crescendo...*I Want To Take You Higher*. He felt the darkness from behind, its dankness catching him by the neck, and he flew forward, piloted by what he felt to be some saving inner force so strong that he knew he was headed for the sun. Through the fireworks he went into a shattering crescendo of his own.

FOUR

BLACKNESS AND VERTIGO. Then the sheer plunge that doesn't end. But screams won't come. And all goes so bitter, while that that was once so sweet is draining in the fall. The weakness comes too, taking everything even the sense of terror. Then abruptly it's the bottom, there without the crash or even a thump. The crazed sense of motion stops but not the ever-fading weakness. And now the cold. Cold like winter stone thunders from above piercing all awareness. It is impossible to move a hairbreadth under the weight of such cold or to find vision in what little remains. Just the fading. Fading into an ever dimness of farewell.

LATE THAT NIGHT after she'd received the phone call the nightmare at St. Vincent's began. In the midst of the flurry and frenzy, her mind failed to keep pace. But she did manage to grasp words that loomed. *Brain trauma. Hemorrhage. Perforated peptic ulcer. Critical. A battle on two fronts--head and guts.* "Plus," one of the doctors in scrubs added into the horror: "There's all the external lacerations. He's lost a lot of blood."

She did manage a one-word question. "How?"

"The paramedics told us there were some witnesses who

said he crashed through a plate glass window at Max's."

"Let me see him. I want to see him," she said as she began shaking.

"You won't be able to. He's already in the OR. But you'll need to sign these forms." Then through the blur she obeyed without even the cognizance of what they were or meant. After that a nurse was suggesting a waiting room, but she didn't go there. Instead she began wandering the gray green, ugly green corridors not knowing where they led but just wandering the late night's forsaken hours of hell. And she was cold, colder than she could ever imagine she had been. She pressed herself against the wall to control her trembling. Someone came by and asked if she needed help. She wondered vaguely if there was a chapel. Then somehow she was in a chapel on her knees at the altar sobbing profusely. "*Miserere nobis.*"

OPEN YOUR EARS, now open your eyes. The cold along with some of the dimness has begun to lift but not the weakness as he's hearing these voices piercing what seems now to be this sinister dark wood that slowly surrounds him. Even though he can't see them, there's enough of the real in their distorted tones to reveal. It's the old philosophy professor from Ithaca who always spoke with this strange but notable otherworldly accent. And Tim is there speaking in an overly resonant voice. In unison they go.

Follow us. The road to the city of desolation. Lost creation. Eternal pain and sorrows.

But these are Dante's thoughts that are vaguely scattered through my memory. I don't draw them forth. So why would you want me to go, he thinks but knows he doesn't speak because there's no strength left for that. Yet they can hear him.

Because you're ready, the voices signal, because you brought yourself here, fine fellow that you once were. So lay down all hope. Oh but you've already done that haven't you, you've abandoned all. And god has gone from you. Left you where you wanted. So you're ready to go in.

No! And where?

You know where. Waste no more of the little strength you've left to ask such drivel, the old man speaks alone now as he points to the words on the lintel of the gateway.

Yeah pal, you can no longer fool. We used to read from this stuff back in his class. Remember how we tried it in the original Tuscan? Smart ass true believers back then. Nothing was impossible.

But I'm gone right here. There is no further I can go. And even though he's still thinking, they're still hearing.

Oh yes there is, they speak in unison again. We'll be pallbearers of your now derelict soul and the rest of you will drag along. So in they go into the vertiginous spirals of velocity and all the while he is sensing the clamor of perpetual night.

Listen to those voices that you now hear. The words of them you know well from my class. The terza rima incatenata. I had you all take turns reading them aloud. They live here now.

Yes they do, once dear friend. You knew them when and they never left you. Open your ears to their roar.

Howling and crying and fulminating, he is aware. Tongues jumbled. Hideous vilifications in babbles he doesn't know but does. Piercing wails, discordant cries, murderous screams. And endless frantic handclapping without cessation. Even through this madding roar, the far greater horror waits ahead, he knows. So he lets go into another consuming dark vortex that's away.

WHEN ENDLESS HOURS HAD PASSED, a surgeon appeared looking so menacing Nora was certain it was all over.

"It's not good," he shook his head. The surgery could have been a success, but he was bad to begin with."

"What does that mean?"

"His vital signs aren't good. He hasn't regained consciousness. And there's evidence of brain edema."

"So it couldn't be much worse?"

"Oh yes it could. But this is bad enough. We've got to bring the edema down and under control. That's not always easy. We're going to have to keep him in an unconscious state with phenobarb until that eases. Then there's the fact that he's lost a lot of blood. A good thirty percent or more. Once that's straightened out, and it's coming along now, there could be an improvement. If he wants it, that is."

"What would you mean, if he wants it?"

"The condition he was in when he came in here with all the drugs that showed up in his system." He shook his head. "It doesn't really fit the picture of a man who's anxious to fight for his life. And that's what it's going to take."

"Can I see him?"

"Sure. For what good it will do. Maybe you can help him. Who knows. But we're doing the best we can do."

A nurse led Nora to Noah's stall in intensive care. It could have been anyone connected to the ventilator she thought when she saw him. His face, arms and legs were swathed in gauze bandages. Tubes were running out of him everywhere.

"Even though he's unconscious," the nurse said. "If you'd like to say a few words to him. You never know. Sometimes it gets through."

"Yes, I would." Then she reached down and touched his arm. Over the death-like gasp-sigh of the oxygen tank, she whispered: "Noah, it's me. I love you. Please believe me. You have to want to live. It'll all come right. You'll see. It will. Please believe me. You will get through this."

Then another nurse came over and said: "Pray all you can for him. You'd be amazed how that can help. People in here who don't have anyone to pray for them, they don't do so well. And I've been here long enough to state that as fact."

So Nora sat in the bedside chair-- watching, praying.

AWARENESS COMES AGAIN. And this time with a start. He can now see clearly the horror that's ahead. He is on a riverbank where only a few feet away in the dim greenish light is a boat filled with terrified passengers moaning with the torment. He tries to look away but is at a dead standstill, even his eyes won't shut. A nearly naked monster rises from the opposite side of the boat ugly with the dark glow and fetor of evil. The sinister flame-ringed eyeballs cause all the passengers to shriek as the demon violently hoists a giant oar.

Tim, are you still here through all this, he asks in thought.

Here in the background with the professor still. He asked that he bring my spirit along to watch your agonies.

Why? Why should you witness such?

Why shouldn't I since you turned me into a stranger, pal. That cuts.

And the professor forcefully admonishes You shed your fine honed youthful brilliance, cast it to the winds, all that you were given. And not only did that scar those so open to you but you destroyed god's will as you went. Avarice and prodigality, greed for success and all the vain pride that goes with it. Not forgetting in the least all those moments of stoned oblivion you eagerly courted. Evil took you right by the hand and you so readily followed, even to the point of adultery and the threshold of murder. So now you watch.

Wielding the oar the monster proceeds, just as in the Dante, to drive a crowd of screaming doomed souls onto the boat. And now of course the words and visions come together to form the picture. What he had read and thought he had dismissed those youthful years before are still there. The lowest depths of flaming hell.

EXCEPT FOR little more than an hour when she raced home to shower and change, she stayed at the hospital all through the next day. *Condition unchanged.* These words kept playing through her mind. Blame loomed as it had in the past. Only now it was far worse. *I never start anything I don't finish.* Long ago he had said this to her on the Aran Islands. For some reason these words were serving to soothe her now. They offered a logic of sorts. Noah was obsessed with everything he did, everything he wanted. There was no solution but to succeed. And no solace strong enough to contain him when he didn't. This would have happened with or without me, she told herself. No one could change what he was. Just maybe I did act as a buffer for a time.

But those thoughts quickly ended and the full jolt of guilt struck again along with the growing certainty that she must be pregnant. When a nurse's aide showed up that night in the ICU to announce that Conrad Landis was waiting out in the hall, her stomach turned. "I was so worried," he said as he hugged her. She automatically glanced around thinking someone might be watching. "I would have had no idea of what happened to you if I hadn't just seen the cover of the *Daily News.*"

"It's there?" she said as she pulled away from him.

"Oh yes. It's pretty horrible—the story. Is he going to make it?"

"I have no idea. Not a clue." And she burst into tears. He put his arm around her waist, and they walked down the corridor to a darkened secluded area. "I can't even bring myself to talk about it. I think he lies there dying. I don't know what to do."

"You really look terrible. How long have you been here?"

"All last night and all day today."

"Have you eaten?"

"Nothing."

"You'll have to come out. At least for a while. To get some food."

"I suppose. Even if just for the air. It seems so incredible." Once again, she was remembering the night they sat on the strand at Aran, and he talked of the stars.

"Come on. Don't think about it now."

"Where will we go?" she sighed, unable to shake her sense of impending doom.

"To my place?"

"Okay," she said with great hesitation as guilt continued to rush her. But where else would they go, she thought. "That way I'll be able to give them a number where I can be reached."

CONRAD'S APARTMENT MIGHT as well have been an extension of the hospital. It was like a waiting room with a phone that she expected would ring at any moment. He made hamburgers. "Something quick after so long." Nora was choking on each swallow.

"Would you stay the night?"

"I don't know if I could." And the words like the food stuck in her throat.

"I'd only hold you."

She looked at him and realized how sincere he was. But she didn't want to notice that. She had no right to it. "I just know I couldn't stay away," she finally replied. Then she sat in silence at the table, not eating anymore and soon not even remembering where she was. In the daze, a vision of Mrs. Mason came to her as it had numerous times during this ordeal and each time she thought of her belly swelling larger and larger with Conrad's baby. She felt regardless she must reach for the phone, but the thought paralyzed her. After this with her arms resting on the table, she nodded off and Conrad lifted her and carried her over to his sagging sofa. Then he took it upon himself to phone the ICU and got the same-- *Condition unchanged.* He sat and held her for the next two hours when suddenly she jumped awake in a panic. "Nothing's happened," he assured. "I called the ICU."

While she sighed in relief, the little rest had sharpened her senses. She looked at him at his gentle eyes. Despite all the concern, the undeniable love that came through, she felt distanced. "Do you ever go to church?" she asked.

"I used to go a lot before the war," he replied obviously shocked by the cold tone of her sudden inquiry. "We were devout Presbyterians you know. But then they became ashamed of my stand on the war and asked me not to go with them. I still prayed a lot while I was over there. That kept up no matter how bad things got. Now that I'm back I find myself getting onto some Episcopal churches when things start swerving off course."

"But if you do that, you must believe in god's laws."

"I suppose."

"What about remorse then?"

"I once believed in the cause as I've told you."

"No. Remorse over us. You and I."

"God Nora, don't let yourself be tortured by that. I know it's worse now, but you've enough to be troubled about at this time."

"Yes but didn't I start the trouble?"

"If you think about it in one way, we were loving innocents. We didn't mean wrong. Only goodness. And that's what should come of it."

"Goodness? Well I wouldn't be thinking we could breeze through something like this that easily. And if I'm pregnant yet. God I think I must be."

"Nora, you can't chalk up what's happened to us to wrong doing. We are in love, and we can only thank god for that. And even more so if we've been blessed with a child."

She was ready to continue her argument born of remorse and now anger. How could he say *blessed?* But when she looked into his eyes again they were so clouded with love for her that the distance she had put between them suddenly narrowed.

EVEN DEATH, if death it is, will allow him out of this. He feels in possession of his whole being now. But he wishes not. For there are scores of demented creatures flocking round him. And they are all naked and goaded by swarms of hornets and wasps stinging their hideous bodies. Then despicable worms come forth to suck their blood and tears. Already he knows the next as he becomes one with the rest and the insects begin their attack.

Now you see what it's all about, the professor calls.

Sorry pal, the stings are your call.

He hears his screams sounding just like the others and then the worms crawl forth.

AFTER SHE CHECKED with the hospital and still *condition unchanged*, she left Conrad and took a taxi to Gramercy Park. On the way, her mind began to flood again. In the rainy morning gloom, she was suddenly back with the nuns in her Gardiner Street classroom where the words of Jesus reproving the scribes and the Pharisees were expounded until they were emblazoned in memory. And those that now pertained to her leapt forth to castigate. - -*from within, out of the heart of men, proceed evil thoughts, adulteries, fornications, covetousness, wickedness, deceit, lasciviousness: all these evil things come from within.*

She barely made it from the taxi to the bathroom where she spent a good fifteen minutes dry heaving and wondering if it was the guilt or morning sickness or both. This along with the panic made worse by the loss of sleep left her with a torturous headache. The shower did little to alleviate and it took all of her remaining energy to focus solely on Noah's condition.

Before she went back to the hospital and still trembling, she began dialing Noah's mother. Halfway through she rang off. She realized she couldn't even begin to tell her. And surely what good would it do. If he were conscious, that would be one thing. But this would only frighten the wits from the poor woman. And then she would come down here and see him like this. That would surely kill her. No, she couldn't ring.

The throbbing pain is unbearable. Torch-like stabs of fire from the swarming wasps as they launch their attack on his entire bare body. His eyes are swollen shut from their savage stings. And once again his strength is all but gone. Go into the dark with your much-deserved wounds and let them engulf you in agony, cries the professor. The worms will not stay here

270

because they give you more consolation than you deserve. Oh and hark back to the reminder as you go—covetousness has made you its masterpiece.

"HEY BUDDY, COME OUT OF THAT. I know you're faking it," Tim said when he squeezed Noah's hand at St. Vincent's. "There's no bad vibes between us. Just open those eyes and we'll take it from there." But he may as well have been talking to a corpse. Shaking his head in disbelief, he walked out into the hall with Nora. "He's worse today," she said. "We thought for a time he was making some improvement, but--"

"I thought he was really putting the moves on his writing, going so far ahead with his column and that *New Yorker* short story and then launching that fantastic *Connoisseur* magazine. And now above all his novel coming up for publication."

"Well there have been some strange things that have been all but possessing him right enough. And for a good while now," she ended not wanting to carry it any further.

"Oh I thought something strange was going on with him that night in your apartment and that he was trying to cover it with the drinks. You know I tried to call him after that, but he never got back to me. If I'd have known he was this bad, I'd have called you. I can't believe he's my best friend and there's so much of late I didn't know. It just shows you what living in New York is like. Or maybe what I'm like."

"Oh don't blame yourself. He tried to keep a lot of things to himself. And that could be my fault. Strange the way things just happen. Things you can't control."

"Well there's something else that's pretty strange as well. That is if you don't already know."

"What?" she panicked.

"His closest friend at work. Well you knew her--Kathy Murphy."

"Murphs. Yes, she has crossed my mind. I wondered if she'd heard, because she hasn't been here."

"That's because she's dead!"

"W-h-a-t?"

"Yes. She committed suicide a few days back. Off the Fifty-ninth Street Bridge."

"Oh god preserve us, w-h-y?" For the moment she felt she couldn't breathe from the shock. Just as Tim shrugged his shoulders, a nurse approached them telling Nora there was a call for her at the nurses' station. "Do you know who it is?" she asked as the shock of Murph's death melded with the sudden fear that word of Noah might somehow have reached Mrs. Mason in upstate Yearnington. "No," replied the nurse.

Tim hugged Nora goodbye when they reached the station and made her promise to phone him with any news. "I'll be back every day. Of course if you need anything--" Then he paused. "Nora you *do* know, if one thing can save him it's you. You're the only stable thing in his life."

By the time she picked up the receiver, she was reeling

from his remark as if she had been struck by lightning.

"Nora, this is Carole Dawson. I can't believe what I'm hearing. How is he?"

"Oh Carole," she sighed both in relief and despair. "I'm afraid his condition is still unchanged. It's still critical."

"Well I'm out here in the Hamptons and I only just found out. Dear god, how are you doing?"

"Oh I'm okay. I just want him to come through this then I'll be fine don't you know."

"Does he have good doctors? What are they saying?"

"Some of them tell me there's hope. Others I'd say won't even go that far. So to be truthful I've no idea what to think."

"Are you satisfied they're doing everything they possibly can?"

"As far as I'd dare chance to ascertain it looks like the care is excellent. Whether they could be doing more, I don't know."

"Okay. Above all don't you despair. I'm certainly going to drive in right away, and if we think he needs anything-- better care or whatever, we can manage that. But you think about it and know that my prayers are with you and that I'll see you very soon, Nora."

When he is aware again and his eyes crack open, he is lying in black mud that oozes away some of the pain from his wounds. He has no idea how he arrived here, but knows from the

gurgling sounds that others have plunged deep into the broth of
putrid vile as well.

Soon morning gave way to afternoon with the same
pattern--some doctors saying it doesn't look good and others
advising not to give up hope because absolutely nothing had
changed. At one stage a clutch of writers from Wilton arrived
in the waiting room. Nora greeted them but was scarcely aware
of the conversation except it all seemed so inane. Even more so
when one of Noah's most hated Mae Dupree rushed in and
began to weep profusely over his condition, while the others
hastily tried to play catch up in grief demonstrations.
Mercifully, since the doctors refused to allow visitors other than
family into the intensive care area, the group soon prepared to
depart. But as they did they were suddenly stopped in their
tracks by a television set in an adjoining alcove. An announcer
on the six o'clock news interrupted a feature with a bulletin
confirming that philanthropist socialite Carole Dawson had
been killed in a horrific multi-vehicle car crash on the Long
Island Expressway that afternoon.

My god, Nora kept gasping as her whole body shook on
the way back to the ICU. She was on her way here because of
this. She'd still be alive otherwise. She cared that much for the
both of us. Instead of the ICU, she found herself back in the
chapel. God be with her, she whispered to the flickering candles.
And god be with Murphs. Two who were so close to him now

gone. Two who might have helped him so much. Oh god be with Noah and don't let him suffer the same fate.

Heavenly god I am choking to death on this horrid bile, he rages in mind for he knows he still can't speak. He is submerged with the liquid rot that's rancid to his inwards, while the wasp stings feel as if they're turning to giant boils on what once was skin. Help, help, his mind explodes the words. And through the slop that penetrates his ears comes the cruel wash of the professor's voice. But this is what you were doing before. Courting the poisons you are now crying out about.

Right. But I was trying in the end to run away from them. I was.

Run to where? Not back to before. Not back to the plenty. No you ran ahead to even more substances of loathsome drugged waste. But don't worry. You won't die here. Because here is forever.

Tim if you're there please for god's sake pal help.

Oh I'm here, buddy. But I'm heading off, because what good am I to you? When I think about it, you are now only a once buddy, because that's what you came to think of me.

No I didn't. I was wrong.

Regardless, it's too late. Brew away, pissaroo.

AS THE DAYS dragged to nearly two weeks, hope came and went like frequent shifts of the wind. The edema decreased, the edema increased. Every moment Nora faced the agonizing possibility that he might just let go without ever regaining consciousness. As she did she wondered if he hadn't plummeted to this state believing there was nothing left of worth. God, the idealism, the spirit he once had, she ruminated. And this came close to breaking her heart.

Even though she felt compelled to go to Mass every day, she was coming to the desperate conclusion that god had little time for her anymore. Often she wondered if he hadn't constructed a vise that was tightening with each passing day. Her mind constantly flitted from Noah's condition to her guilt, to Conrad and her pregnancy, to Mrs. Mason, to what would happen if and if not. Where would it end? Could there be at least some positive note? Through it all Tim never failed in his daily visits and his cheering words to comatose Noah. "We'll get you back," he would insist and that would help. But what became annoying were the frequent calls from Russell who kept telling her he'd come to New York as soon as he met his shooting schedule and then went on to detail it. Calls from Janet were far more plausible in that she expressed deep concern and said that she would be there as soon as their twins' bronchial problems were resolved enough for her to leave them with her nursemaid. Since these were always individual calls and since neither spoke of the other, Nora wondered if she and Russell hadn't already separated. This of course brought her back to the agony of her own breakup. Then that would lead to Conrad. For the past week, except for a daily phone call, she had kept him in limbo. He was never demanding, but the tone of his voice made her ache with pain. She knew that not only was he being battered by their situation but the whole Vietnam trauma as well.

"I do need to see you," he finally told her one late night when she arrived home from St. Vincent's "It's so damn lonely I've been calling all evening just to hear your voice."

"I know. We'd have to be getting together to talk."

"I just wish you'd come over here to stay at night."

"Well I can't, not with this going on. I feel such guilt."

"Will you at least come over for dinner tomorrow. I'll order some stuff from the local deli."

She agreed and after the call was over she felt a warm rush that overrode the guilt. That night she went to bed putting all but that feeling from her mind. It was the first night she was able to sleep since this nightmare began. In her dreams she was in a cathedral where magnificent stained glass windows of cobalt, royal blue, vermilion and indigo were ablaze with light from the sun. She did not want to awaken from this sanctuary, to let go the spell of its solace. But when she did she felt as if some of the burden had been lifted. It took a while for her to realize that the bed was wet. She quickly reached down to touch herself and brought her hand back to see the color red. Oh my god, dear god, thank you god, she gasped over and over.

AMONG THE WEEPING and the woeful in the darkness and stewed rotgut, he has no way of knowing the length of this spell. Will this go on and on with not even as much as some repose, he wonders. Repose, the professor laughs pitching an aphorism that gleans the Dante: For all the gold that is beneath the moon, or ever was, could not buy you as much as repose after your folly.

THE MINUTE she came in his door a much paler Conrad held her tightly without saying a word. Once he released his strength she found herself clinging to him for more. When their eyes finally met, he whispered: "God I want you so much." Then the passion of their kiss was all but overruling. Now she had to summon the strength. "We can't," she insisted as she pulled away and walked toward the window. "You know I tried to call you twice today, but I guessed you were out on a shoot. I wanted to tell you--"

"What?" he interrupted then held his breath in obvious fear.

"Well it's some good news. I got my period during the night."

"Oh," he said dimly.

"Well aren't you relieved?" she asked turning back to him. But the regret was undeniably there.

"Yes, I suppose it eases the situation somewhat."

"But you are disappointed," she said.

"I guess—Well—the baby would have been part of us, part of our love. I guess I see it as a loss."

"I know. I know how all of this must hurt you and all the more while you're trying to cope with the memories of that bloody war. I worry about that too, don't you know. How are you managing with it now?"

"Alright I guess, as long as I don't go to sleep." Then he laughed before turning grim. "I thought it would be easier by now. Some distance and all. But nothing seems to fade. Instead it keeps getting more vivid and starts looming right up front again. And worse what I go through at night, I can't always shake during the day. Even these friggin' sudden headaches. I know some guys who get like this, they do weed and drugs. But I can't do that. There's nothing now for me but you."

"Ah Conrad," she sighed and went to put her arms around him. "It will take time. But we'll have to get through this together. I wonder if it might help if you took a trip to Seattle. It could take away some of the torture you're putting yourself through and maybe much of this gloom. And well you should give it a try after all."

"And leave you even for a few days with all this worry?"

"Well I'm going back to my work," she said purposely brightening. "The doctors have told me I have to spend some time away from there, if I'm not going to lose my mind."

"Oh they're right. Because you're torturing yourself.

And likewise you may be right about me. I guess I will go out there for a look at the place. I only hope it's right for us. Of course I won't really be there. All my thoughts will be right here with you." Then he held her and kissed her and whispered: "But no matter what happens while I'm away, what would hurt me the most is if you didn't do what you felt was right on all counts."

ARE THERE NO SECOND CHANCES, he asks the professor. Oh yes, there would be second chances. But third, fourth, fifth—You seem to have forgotten much since you've been here. No I think when all is considered that the powers have decided that you should remain. But I think for your sake they would like to give you a little preview of the forever. And once again into a plunging vortex he is hurled. This time he arrives at a river of blood where hideous creatures boil for their sins. It's possible that you could join them, the professor suggests. But look ahead first. As he does his vision sharpens and he sees clusters of trees whose trunks ooze blood and beyond are nests of vivid green nine-headed hydras and swarms of asps and adders squirm round punishing other tortured souls. But look ahead again and see what the depraved can administer to one another, the professor insists. And there naked, pale, possessed they bite and savage their lot like gouging wild boars. I've seen and lived enough horror, he bellows to the professor. Would you not consider yourself a sinner for pitching these demonic tableaus and dragging me through the wastelands of hell? You proceed as if you were a saint. But are you not as much a transgressor? To this the professor roars back in fury: You're the one on trial here. And since is such, I'll have you look ahead once again. And there he sees in his clearest vision yet a seemingly endless desert of lost souls shrieking and howling their anguish under an on-going rain of fire. Now my student, the professor declares as he pushes him forward, let you have another sampling to your own being of what lies in wait. And screaming he stumbles and staggers onto the searing red-hot sands of the desert as flakes of fire scorch his skin. These I must warn will soon seem like mere flurries when they turn to flames. But they will not kill, just go on forever in the agonizing torture of hell.

WHEN NORA ARRIVED back at the ICU that night her heart stopped. Clusters of doctors and nurses were scurrying around Noah's bed and she thought this was the end. His condition had worsened while she was away. Suddenly he had started thrashing about and the brain edema was rapidly increasing. They were already upping the amount of the phenobarb drip to calm him, but from all accounts his condition was dire, really dire now. This was all they could do to reduce the swelling. So once again she stayed through the night making several visits to the chapel as the nurse assigned to Noah's case did frequent checks and kept constant vigil. As always she pleaded for god's help, but afterwards on this night she fell silent in thought and began to draw consolation from loneliness. It was becoming her silent companion in her ever-growing fear that she truly had lost god. This time she thought better of telling anyone the latest news, not even Conrad. The same held true the next afternoon when a surgeon arrived at the ICU and spoke of further complications including circulatory shock that had caused a serious reduction in blood flow to some of Noah's organs. As he spoke of ischemia and more transfusions and the possibility of operations, she felt herself sliding further into an aura of what she considered deserved reclusion. It will only grow with the hopelessness of the situation, she thought. And if Noah goes, it won't leave her.

I have dreamt only the most dreadful of dreams here and now know such horrors will never end because of my grave misgivings. But professor I find that through all the torturous fires of this hell I still hold to one hope that dreams they be. As such if I this lost wanderer would come forth to god with heart and soul and in faithful promise to expiate and follow in rightful justice all the days that might be given me, would I be given the chance to awaken and prove?

Heart, soul, god. You already buried those, dear student. Dreams? You still think all that has come to you here are but dreams? Awaken? You are at your darkest hour now. Earthly death hovers smothering your pitiable chance. Only one word of yours stops me though. The word—hope. There's a flicker of god's dazzling light in that word. And there now in your eyes. I know that well, because I was once here exactly like you. Oh yes, I had gone to the depths. But the mercy of god had granted me a return—under certain conditions that is. So I became a professor expounding the likes of the saints, the scholars, the philosophers. But often the young don't retain the wisdom of their redeeming values and go off on wild escapades of waste forcing me as part of my own continued expiation to attempt a savior role. This time it was through a reinvention of Virgil and Dante. But dear student if that dazzling light lifts you up as in Dante's world to once again see the brilliance of the stars you must remember there will always be a price to pay. I fear O Noah that price for your failings may forever bear the weight of sadness on your soul no matter how much atonement your conscience will insist you endure.

NO MATTER HOW PRESSING the staff became Nora insisted on staying nights at the hospital once again. She would sleep in the chair beside Noah's bed and in the early mornings the nurses would take such pity that they would allow her to shower in their quarters. Sometimes they would even sneak her coffee and a bagel from the food carts. More often than not she would wait until eleven when Sutter's the nearby French bakery and café would open then dash over for a brief respite with brioche and strong coffee. And that would be her daily diet. A few neighborhood boutiques saved her from going home for change of clothes and the hospital shop carried the essential needs, tooth brush, paste etc.

During this time almost on a daily basis, she received calls from one or more of Oliver Wilton's secretaries expressing Oliver's deep concern. Probably over guilt or the loss of a workhorse, she thought as anger flashed through her. So not wanting any contact with the outside world but especially the Wilton staff, she had the hospital issue a no-visitors order at the front desk. Fortunately Tim was away on a business trip, so she saw no one. Except for a few brief words from Conrad in Seattle, she took no phone calls. She even stopped going to the chapel. And nothing interested her except the doctors' reports. After five days and nights of this, she looked worse than the patients and the world was dissolving around her. But she could care less. Death hovered in the air over the ICU. You could feel its presence creep round and although it remained invisible you knew it was there like some poisonous vapor waiting to descend. There were those who escaped but more often than not a loved one's devastating wail like that of a banshee would pierce the unit signifying another passing.

On the sixth day Nora was in such a haze that she wasn't certain if the group of doctors standing in Noah's cubicle was real or part of another shadowy dream. "We do think we have a bit of a miracle on our hands," one of them reported.

"What's that," she said jumping to her feet.

"Well we don't want to be overly hopeful," the one

continued. "But for some reason almost beyond comprehension, the swelling is decreasing. So much so that we're cutting back on the phenobarb level. And if this keeps up we'll take him off it altogether. That means he could soon regain consciousness."

"Oh thanks be to god," she gasped.

"Yes, well that's the good news. And we think we may have avoided those operations due to the ischemia." "B-u-t," another said rather cryptically curbing her joy. "If this man recovers, you'll be taking his place if you don't get the hell out of here, get some food into you and have a few good night sleeps."

After they were gone, she whispered prayers of thanks for the return of hope while she held Noah's hand. Then she went on in a far stronger voice: "Noah if you can hear me please continue the struggle I know you must be going through. Know how much I care and how much I love you. Please dear god, help him through the rest."

But later after she'd struggled into a taxi, she was suddenly thunderstruck that if as she prayed Noah recovered, the power would be in her hands to sever a life or two. Maybe both. Oh god no matter what I do now---

So I wonder were you given this chance you so plea to possess would it bear the ever-lasting fruit of wisdom or simply lure you once again into that Lucullian world squandering all and send you plummeting back into this fiery terrain. Then I wonder too who you would dismay and crush as you went down the next time.

I can only say this to you faithful professor, and you are truly faithful, for accompanying me through all this horror, I can only say that having fallen on my sword for the crimes of my past I would spend each of my days proving that no matter how severe the going I would be loyal to god and his will. And I would care for the good of others who've touched upon my soul with loving abundance while I in return offered such pitiful misery. Other than that I can say no more.

Other than that you need not. For I can now see far greater evidence of the truth in your eyes than in your words. So dear student you have once again taken on the power and the strength of the stature given at your birth. Sometimes it takes hell for such a reconciliation. You have learned that well I am convinced. And you've learned the weight you must bear. It has robbed you and will continue to do so. Ah but Noah, as in the Dante, you will look once more upon the stars.

2

FIRST THERE WAS THE WHITE then there was the bright. Too bright to know what it was or where it came from. Only that it was far from the darkness. But then his eyes strained and the lids grew heavy, too heavy to keep from closing. Everything dimmed again and he fell back knowing he was sliding into sleep. Yet even with the great fatigue something far greater told him he dare not fall through to the deepest phase of sleep for fear it would carry him back to the gruesome world he had finally escaped.

He hadn't a clue how long he had struggled with this before he was able to push open his eyelids again. Now the white and the light came together. But it was far too dazzling to keep from hurting his eyes. As he forced himself into a blinking pattern, a voice came to him. "Are you with us again?" A male voice but such a blessed relief this time it wasn't the professor's. "Can you hear me?" And then he felt hands shaking him. It was another struggle to say "yes" but he must have and was hazily amazed at the sound of his own voice again hoarse as it was. "Do you have any idea where you are?" the voice went on. "Alive?" Noah managed. "Yes. And you're in a hospital. St. Vincent's. The intensive care unit. And I'm one of your doctors. You've been here over three weeks now." He tried to move his head to look around but he was too weak. "I thought I was dead." "So did we my friend." The word *friend* sent him right back to thoughts of the professor and the underworld and death which made him wonder if this was reality or another phase of perdition. If she were here he'd know. So he called out: "Nora! Nora!"

"Nurse, do you know where Mrs. Mason is?"

"I believe she's in the chapel. I'll send someone to fetch her." Noah gasped his relief as he struggled not to drift away again.

Then she was there in the distant blur of the room. His eyes widened as she came into clear view. "Nora," he whispered as she watched the inky veil of death fade a few degrees from his face. Then she came over and sat at the edge of his bed and smiling began to stroke his face. While she spoke something of god and the grace of his mercy, the words were lost to him as he felt the onrush of such soothing peace in the blue of her eyes. "I'm coming out of this. I am Nora. But I just have to sleep some more," he whispered with an even hoarser voice as his eyes blinked closed on the blue. "Sleep Noah," she whispered back. "I'll be right here when you wake up again."

She held his hand and watched him as he slept. He had gone so frighteningly thin, as thin as the bed rails she thought. One of the doctors had said that even with the drip he had lost about thirty pounds. His poor battered body and his mind. Would he realize now, she wondered. And even if he did, would he have the strength to overcome all this?

"THANK GOD of that," Conrad said when she rang him in Seattle. "It was unbearable seeing you suffer like that. I never stopped praying you know."

"Well I think it helped. I can't tell you how grateful I am for that."

His voice was so soothing that it touched her the way it had when she was falling in love with him. She had all but forgotten that in the midst of the recent madness. "Well how is it out there?"

"I hadn't told you before because I didn't think it was right. But this place is more beautiful than I remembered. The city and those coastal islands. I mean the quality of life is fantastic. And the other great thing is that there's lots of work, beside the stuff I'd be doing for the gallery. Good stuff too. Regional and travel magazines. And ad agencies springing up and looking for good photographers. The pay's is great too." But then he let his voice trail off. "Yeah I guess it's pretty great."

"Why do you sound hesitant then?"

"Well I had been thinking if we had a chance at all, maybe I could get the Witkin to give me a few months to get out here."

"To be sure I hadn't thought it out. But time has to figure into it."

"Yes of course. And I wouldn't have it any other way. But they want me in four, five weeks at the most. I mean the extra freelance work's here now. But there are other photographers in the world who could grab it away."

"Well then you'd have to be moving on it."

"But why do I freeze at the thought? I don't want to be anywhere you're not."

"I know but we can't do anything to take away from the gratefulness we feel for god giving us back this much."

"You're right. But anyway I'll be back in another week to take the edge off some of this loneliness."

The call ended but yet his voice and words stayed with her and continued to render the rush. She had said she loved him and now she knew it was still true.

DURING THE NEXT DAYS Noah improved rapidly and was moved from the ICU to a semi-private room in another wing. As weak as he was he began eating, thus dispensing with the drip, and was up and walking the corridors with the aid of either Nora or a nurse. Most of the remaining bandages had been removed, and even though there were some nasty body scars, the marks from his facial lacerations began to fade.

A number of doctors, including a psychiatrist, made periodic calls. They strongly suggested he stay another couple of weeks to recuperate from his injuries, gain weight and detox while they carried out a battery of tests to be certain there was no damage from the ischemic period before the transfusions.

Actually he was relieved that they wanted him to stay. He wasn't ready to leave yet. He needed time. Time to work out a strategy for living and working in the city free of drugs and alcohol. A strategy that eventually would allow him the freedom to move to Ireland for a few months to do his writing. Yes, he had to write. Come what may. He knew that now. But he feared that it might be a greater task than he could imagine, even just getting a job again. Yet no sooner had the concern begun to press him than as if by magic a personal note arrived in the mail from Oliver saying that he'd be in to see him as soon as he figured he was well enough. Meanwhile he was not to worry,

Wilton would support him through everything and his job would always be there. What a relief that was. It made him realize just how much he owed.

But even now he didn't know all that had happened to him—all that he had made happen to him. Nora would tell him when as the doctors said he was strong enough to ask. He had returned from his hall walk one day when he did.

"You crashed through the window at Max's Kansas City."

"My god."

"Fluthered and drugged out of it. You lost a lot of blood externally and internally."

"What do you mean?"

"Some of those scars aren't just from glass cuts. You had to have an operation for a perforated ulcer. You nearly hemorrhaged to death."

"God I'm sorry for your sake, Nora. All this."

"And there's something else you should know. A couple of days after this happened, Carole Dawson heard and was driving back from the Hamptons to come here. She was killed in a head-on collision."

"Oh my god." And it took a long time for his mind to grasp this. "If it hadn't been for me-- Jesus, she's dead? Are you sure?"

"Yes, she was killed instantly. Her funeral was some weeks ago."

Noah sighed and shook his head. "She thought of me as a

blessing. A replacement of sorts for her son who was killed. And now I've in a sense killed her. And she isn't the only one." Then he went on to tell her about Murphs and how she had told him that he was her step-brother."

"My god Noah, it sounds pretty incredible. Do you believe that?"

"Well yes. Why would she have made up such a story? But the worse thing is that I let her go off without trying my damnedest to help her. That's because I was half smashed."

"Well Noah, you can't do this to yourself. There's nothing you can do about these things except bring on more harm. Accept what's happened and look ahead. You have to change things. And the only way is to get past all this and go forward."

"I know. Forward. And as much for you as for me." He wiped his eyes and closed them as she nodded in agreement. Exhausted, as he slowly faded off to sleep holding her hand, a whisper of his words came forth—"but no penance can ever--"

AS THE DAYS PASSED, his spirits did lift. He was finding the return of strength. He was able to tackle a call to his mother convincing her that everything was perfectly fine. Then he convinced himself that he liked living again. But this was because of Nora. She came every day, and he grew anxious for her visits. He woke each morning thinking of her, and she never strayed from his thoughts. It reminded him of when they first met on Aran. Only now there was someone else.

While he hadn't talked about it, Noah knew she was

going to leave. It had to be that way. It wasn't in what she said but in what she didn't say. The lack of any plans for them. *I fear oh Noah that the price of your failings--* Why shouldn't she leave after what I've done to her? If there was any hesitation on her part it would be because of pity, and he would have to undo that. The past was past and right was right. No matter how much the regret.

So he charted his course. First assessing what had happened—and why. These feelings he put to paper because it made more sense than verbally dwelling on his abusive addictive actions with the psychiatric department here. *Covetousness had by degrees all but consumed my soul. It certainly had delivered me to the dark side while it wrought its chaos on my marriage. How had I continued so unawares for so long? How had I let this destruction carry us right to the brink when such wondrous love had been at our birthplace? Maybe it was true as in the Omar Khayyam. Maybe all along I was carrying the seeds of heaven and hell. And just perhaps those seeds spawned a pendulum that sent me swinging from the light to the dark. But if so, I do believe that it has booted me back to the brightness of the Dantean stars once more. No matter if it does seem way overly positive, I do believe the pendulum then crashed back to be consumed along with the dark side in the fires below.*

"HELP," HE CRIED OUT as spears of jagged glass gouged him and blood gushed forth.

"It's all right," a voice called as hands shook him.

"Wake up." Noah jumped and opened his eyes to see a nurse. "You were having a bad dream. Are you in pain?"

"A little," he answered dazed and groggy. "I don't know if it's the dream or some of the stuff from the operation still."

"I can give you a morphine injection if it you think it would help. It's on your chart."

He blinked his eyes, looked at her and felt the temptation rise. "No! I don't want any morphine."

"HEY PAL, what a way to lose weight and get attention," Tim called into Noah as he looked out the window of his room. Then he came in, gave him a powerful bear hug. "God I didn't think you were going to come back. Every day I came in here you looked worse."

"You came in that often? I sure didn't deserve it. Not after the way I seem to remember treating you that last fateful night. God I'm sorry for that."

"Ah you messed up my suit a little, crumbled my feelings. And *worst* made me late for a date with a pretty foxy one who didn't bother to wait. Now I'll never know." And he shook his head and laughed.

Noah laughed too, for the first time since all this happened. It seemed so long ago. Even Tim had changed again. He had cut away his long curly hair in favor of a far more spiffy business styling and was back in a blazer, gray flannels and a rep tie. Probably as a result of his latest split, he had left the jeans generation behind.

"But why didn't you talk to me, you pisser? Why wouldn't you let me help?"

"I don't think you could have then. I don't think anyone could have."

"But what about now? Are you going to be all right? Seriously?"

"Oh yes, I'm determined for sure. But I have to do it on my own."

"Jesus buddy, what do you mean? You've got me and you've got Nora. If you'd only stop closing us out."

"Well you're wrong. Partly wrong anyway. I haven't got Nora. Or at least I won't have her much longer. I screwed everything to hell. She tried and tried to help me. To help us. When I kept shitting all over it she fell in love with someone else."

"Whoa! God pal, are you sure? You said something during that phone call just before all this, but I thought you'd just gone a bit top heavy. Maybe on the booze. Like that night when our crowd was all together."

"No. It was far more gone than that."

"You wouldn't make another pitch. I mean now that you've been through all this. If you're that determined--"

"No I can't. I've tortured the woman enough. I went to hell for my mistakes, and now I have to pay for them if I'm to survive."

"A little bit strong isn't it."

"Oh no. It comes back to me in flashes now—what

happened while I was unconscious. You were there with me along with that strange but great professor of ours from Ithaca. Both of you were guiding me through making me see the horrors of my undoing."

"Well it must have been one hell of a nightmare."

"More than that I'll tell you. It was real."

"Whatever it was, I don't think it deserves splitting up. To me you two were the golden couple. I was so envious of you. I mean Nora's alive. She's still here." Then he blinked as if tears were in his eyes and turned away.

"Tim, you never really leveled with me either. Don't you think it's about time you did?" And Noah sat in the chair by the window.

"Oh, it's worse than you could imagine, pal." Tim sighed as he dropped down on the edge of the bed. "I don't know if it's the right time for you to hear this."

"Well it is the time, buddy. I can handle it now if I ever could." And he was demanding.

"Okay," he said with resignation. "You remember my old man who thought he could buy and sell the world. He bellowed around that palace of his in Marblehead bleating that he'd disown me if I disgraced him by not going to Harvard. But Diane— God do you realize it's the first time I've said her name in all these years? I never even told you. Anyway Diane encouraged me to go it on my own. We really were so much in love from first sight. Being with her—loving her was what life's all about." And Noah figured his grimness acted as a powerful dam to hold back any more tears. "Anyway we were going to be married and go through Ithaca together. Like Russell and Janet." Then he stopped and took a deep breath. "We were both working that summer at an inn in Rockport. She had the afternoon off and she just disappeared. They found her four days later in some rundown hotel in Boston. Dead from an OD of sleeping pills."

"God why?"

"My mother found out from one of the servants. She must have gone to see my old man to try to patch things up between us. She was like that. Always trying to make things right. So that bastard took her into his study and raped her. And that's just what her step father had done to her years before." He sighed and his face tightened with the bitterness. "The maid heard the screams, but she couldn't open the door. He'd locked it she said. She told my mom all this just before she quit. It was a week after they found Diane. Then my mom was killed---make that killed herself. She drove over an embankment into the sea. I know for certain because she left me a note."

"Oh Tim, Jesus--" Noah said as he came and sat beside him on the bed then put his arm around him. Tim had gone so unlikely spiritless and looked to be numb from the telling.

"I always felt troubled for you, you know that. But I never knew how much more I should have felt until now."

"Yeah," Tim sighed. "Keeping things hidden does that. A psychiatrist once told me that we do it under the pretense that it never happened and that one day we'll walk away from it and it will be so. But there's no such thing as going back to a blank sheet. The colors no matter how ugly are fixed."

"No but you could do what I have to do. Look ahead."

"Sure but somehow I keep getting caught up with the easy seductions. Money. Women who are always wrong. I even let myself get blinded to what might be good. Long ago I think Merrick gave up on that play he so encouraged me to revise. That's because the fuse finally blew in me. That's because I probably wanted it to. Maybe because I came to realize I couldn't bear to have a life after what happened." There was silence for a moment while Noah felt true regret. The same as he felt for Murphs and of course Nora.

"Shit!" Tim suddenly snapped out of it. "What the fuck am I doing. This is all you need after what you've been through."

"No. This is what should have happened long ago. The same with Janet and Russell. The four from Ithaca letting go and accepting help from one another."

"Oh god, now that you mention that I assume you haven't heard."

"What?"

"They've split. They're getting a divorce."

"You're kidding."

"No, I called to keep in touch with them about you, and Russ told me. Not too long after they were in New York that time, she went into one of those rest places for a short time."

"An asylum?"

"Well more up market. But still, she must have been pretty bad. Anyway while she was there, she met this doctor and now they're seeing each other. Russ is already moving out. But from what I read into it, he's pretty broken up. He wants the kids but she's going to fight him on that. Meanwhile he's just burying himself in his work. So what's new? That's what caused all this to begin with. Along with a sudden cascade of starlet flirtations. But who am I to talk."

"I can't believe it. You know Janet called me here yesterday and never let on that anything was wrong. All she and Russell were concerned about was me."

"Well they were right to be. You need to take care of yourself. Put some weight back on that frame of yours. And stop worrying. Nora finally leveled with me about that last rejection of your book. But she also told me a number of top editors thought it was brilliant."

"Well brilliance doesn't always work in that crazy publishing world."

"Look when this is over and you're out of here. I want you to meet this agent I've become friends with. We were doing some promotional stuff for Knopf and I met him at a party we threw at *21*. He's young. He's on his own. And his business is still small enough that he'll have time for you. But more important he's good. He's already discovered a number of really fine writers. I think it could be a good new beginning."

"Good. I sure need it."

"But pal I also think I'd try my damnedest to get back with Nora."

"I have to be honorable Tim. I know honor is a double-edged sword. And for too long I've been on the wrong side. Now that I'm on the right one I have to take on all the responsibility that goes with it."

"I KNOW NOW THAT YOU'RE AN EXCEPTION. And a rare one," Noah told Nora as they talked later that day.

"What's that about?"

"Your art. I couldn't see it before. Or I wouldn't let myself. For most of us, when we really want to do something—something big, something that's out of the ordinary, we have to go through rough times. I think they're tests, and we have to endure them or we don't stay on the path. But it sure takes mettle. My god. Then I messed it all up with my ever growing greed. That's when I started running. And that's when I really started losing it and finally came to the end of the line."

"Well what can I say? I can only thank god that you can see this and more important that you believe it. But Noah, I think of my art as something of the moment. When I think about it, it's just a few steps from whimsy. It's different with you. You were born with the drive. The complexity of your work and the enormous task of weaving it all together far overpowers anything I could ever put on canvas. But never mind me, do you think you can live with this knowledge now? Because you mustn't stop writing."

"I think I can. I *know* I can. But I don't in any way agree that your beautiful work is whimsy."

"Well whatever it is, it doesn't contain the weight of yours. But—I can't tell you how fantastic it is to see you like this. It truly is an answered prayer." Tears rushed forth and Noah put his arms around her as they sat on the edge of his bed.

"Don't cry Nora, you've been through so much."

"Oh these are happy tears," she said wiping them away. Then she kissed him on the cheek.

"Well I want you to be happy. To me that's the most important thing now. I know it's hard to talk about it, but I know you'll be leaving me soon."

"Oh there's nothing certain."

"Nora, I know you. I saw you with him at your opening the night of my crash. I know you've fallen in love with him and I'd guess from appearances that he's very much in love with you."

"Oh Noah," she sighed not wanting to hurt him.

"You do know. Don't deny yourself that. What matters here is— is he a good man to and for you."

"Well yes, there's no doubt about that. A fine man who's been through a hell of his own. He was in Viet Nam you know, and it was pretty grim. But he survived. And yes I do love him. I have to tell you that. But--"

"But what?"

"Well you--and all the complications."

"Well I'm not one of them. So you can rule that out.

But by saying so I don't want you to think that I don't love you. Nora, I'll never love another woman as much as I love you, and I know that. I don't want to give you up. But it's the only way after what's happened. So what are the other complications?"

"Well there's family."

"But you were always sort of at odds with them. I mean they would adjust."

"And then there's your mother. The hurt there."

"Yes, but she's been hurt before. I think she knew way back that things were going very much awry with us."

"And then the church. I really am a true Irish Catholic at heart. I'm only plagued by that. How could I be doing all this?"

"Because I pushed you into it, the same as if I pushed you off a cliff. I'm a Catholic too. But I see the remorse as all mine. Please leave it with me, because I'm handling it. And nothing's going to stop me, I'm going to continue to."

"Oh Noah, if only it were so simple. A part of me still loves you, and that will always be with me."

"Yes but time--"

"No. Not for either of us." And she shook her head at the truth.

"The important thing as I see it is that we are for each other. We are going to work our way through this with dignity and without losing our love."

DESPITE THE DETERMINATION there were the

continued drawbacks which Noah kept secret. Almost always they came in sleep. When they didn't evolve from the horrors of the crackup, they usually spiraled from vain attempts to pick up on his job again to other writing failures with little or no hope in sight.

"Noah, *ah* hope *ah'm* not disturbing you, but the nurse insisted *ah* just come on in."

"O-l-i-v-e-r," Noah struggled as he awakened not knowing what time of day it was but certain this was not a part of a taunting dream.

"Oh don't try to get up. Just rest there."

Quickly Noah looked down and was relieved to note he was fully dressed in leisure wear atop the bed.

"*Ah* would have come sooner, but *ah* relied on my secretaries to let me know when you were recovered enough to receive afternoon guests."

"Well I seem to be coming along fine now. But I'm certainly embarrassed."

"Embarrassed! But why? Noah, *ah* should be the one to be embarrassed. *Ah* feel in the end that *ah* put you here." Then as he pulled a chair over to his bed, Noah noticed for the first time how his fair hair was turning white and his once baby face was rapidly sprouting lines and frown marks. After he sat back down, he continued: "When *ah* think back *ah* remember how not too long ago you asked me for a leave of absence. *Ah* can't tell you how it grieves me that *ah* paid you no mind."

"Well it might have changed things had you acceded to

my request. But I have to wonder if by then compulsion's roots hadn't grown too deep for me to regain what I was losing."

"Compulsion is an ugly word. *Ah* should know. *Mah* ancestors fostered it and fed me on its bitter fruit. You know all the way back the men were Yale grads and each and every one was a Bonesman. Omnipotence swelled their hearts and souls. And because of that they were leaders in their fields. *Ah* used to call my father a warlock. Back then *ah* couldn't believe the dark conjuring games he used to play. All for procurement of greater enterprises of course. But then that advanced to the social stratum where he made devious moves on all those he knew— even me. He was game to outsmart everyone. Well everyone except his old boys network And all the time *ah* watched the greater the infection. And then *ah* became one of them."

"Well Oliver, I think I already knew some of this. But did your divorce proceedings really trigger all this change in you."

"Oh many things did," he chuckled and shook his head in disgust. "But that certainly turned on the light throwing the spotlight on those horrible memories. And *ah* began to see the losses. Then there was you—and Murphs. Something happened to me that day in the morgue when I saw her once vivacious body—broken and lifeless. *Ah* thought a cruel god was shouting down his rage at me." And he stopped for a moment as if to gather all that his mind had finally let formulate. Finally he sighed: "Now *ah* think in more simplistic terms, *ah* must been given a pretty poisonous dose of my own medicine." Then suddenly he snapped back in shock. "But *ah* can't trouble you with all this."

"What? And leave one of your star reporters forever wondering?"

"No not one of—*ahwa* only *stah*."

"Well thank you, but do go ahead then. There must be more."

"You know that secrets among Bonesmen *ah* supposed to remain secrets almost under the punishment of death. But *ah* suppose if one of them betrays another, a comeuppance of sorts is deserved regardless. A Bonesman from *mah* class did a number on me. Remember all that business *ah* had you go through over Bill Paley?"

"As if I could ever forget it."

"Well it was that Bonesman who told me he had certain knowledge that Paley had his eye on *mah* wife?"

"And?"

"Well he may have had his eyes on her, but as far as *ah* know that was all. It was my Bonesman who exploded it into the overblown lie it became."

"I didn't think Bonesmen ever lied to one another. Other than secrecy, I thought trust and honor formed their mantra."

"So did *ah* until *ah* learned that passion, even though premeditated, can trump all values—and worse thieve them. It was he who was playing the games and chasing after *mah* wife Martha. Just for the hubris, the self-glorification."

"Has she gone off with him?"

"Oh no. She was using him as a pawn because *ah* was so consumed with the Wilton empire. *Ah* really can't blame her for making such a strong statement after all these years. But she did wait until *mah* son was grown before she embarked on the divorce. That of *cause* brought on the next blow. My son has railed against me and will have nothing to do with me or Yale. So, he's gone off to Princeton. Perhaps wisely so. *Mah* games, *mah* Bonesmen and all the cruelties have left me with nothing."

"That's pretty rough, isn't it?"

"Yes it is. Though *ah* rarely saw them, *ah* never knew how much *ah* needed them. But more than that, *ah* realize now how much *ah* love them." Then he shook his head and pondered a moment. "Huh. *Ah* didn't even know *ah* had a heart until now."

"Recompense?"

"*Ah* was never taught that word. But maybe--," he added with great doubt.

"Could try."

"Well anyway *ah've* troubled you enough. Stan Archer and *ah* want you to take all the time you need to repair yourself. We'll stand by you through everything. That of *cause* includes your full salary and any medical costs that aren't already being covered. As much as we desperately need you back at Wilton, don't even think about it. We'll be ready for you when *you'ah* ready. But what worries me is what happens when you come out of here. *Ah* know *ah* made light of you and Nora and that situation that concerned you so a ways back. *Ah* was so wrong."

"Oh Oliver, as they say the past is past. We're managing to work it on out just fine."

"Well *ah* would so hope. It would be one blessing out of all this."

And indeed it was a blessing of sorts, Noah thought after Oliver had gone. Such a shift in insight, one that in virtuousness crossed with his own.

3

"GOD I MISSED YOU," Conrad anxiously whispered as he crushed Nora in his arms on the night he returned from Seattle. Since the accident, she would struggle inwardly to suppress these moments. But this time in his apartment she felt an enormous release as she welcomed the passion of their kiss. Conrad was so consumed that he could just barely separate them. "Look, we don't have to. I'll understand," he gasped breathlessly. "I don't want to hurt--" She stopped him there and pulled him back into the kiss. Then without breaking apart, they slowly undressed and fell back naked onto the sofa. "It'll never be over between us," he whispered. "I know," she answered. And slowly he began to edge into her. But then he stopped. "God I've got to get a condom. Let's not go through that again." "No. I just finished my period. Don't leave me." Smiling softly with relief, he pressed on until he was fully inside her. Then he stopped again and gently kissed her face and her neck and looked into her eyes as if he were overcome with worship for her. Suddenly with no build up a powerful wave of love rocked her body sending her reeling as she grasped his arms and he glided his way to joining her in the convulsive orgasm.

"WELL YOU CAN'T JUST LEAVE HIM," Conrad said when they went out to the Second Avenue Deli that night. "Even though he is coming along so well, he's going to have to face the world again, and he's going to need help for a while."

"What do you mean?"

"I know what you're going through," he said reaching across the booth and stroking her face. "I know the pain you're feeling."

"Well Conrad I probably will always have that."

"I know. Remember I've had it too. But what I want to say is this. I have no one now. No family, no friends, no loves. Just those nightmares. And still the headaches. So I look around my world and I don't want anyone-- except you. You're the only one that can make this mucked up planet come alive and be beautiful for me. Otherwise there's nothing."

"Well I feel that way too. And I've fallen in love with you, and that's what makes us inseparable. But I can never forget that I did love Noah and in some ways still do."

"That's what I'm saying. It's going to be harder on you than it is on me. But we have to do right by him. There are times when I think I'm tearing his life apart too. I couldn't possibly see us just flying off in a few weeks."

"But what do we do?"

"I suppose the wisest thing would be for me to finish off any bits of work I have left here and then go out there soon and start working. At the same time, I'd be looking for a place for us. Then as soon as you thought he was strong enough you'd come out."

"Go back to Gramercy Park with him?"

"Well we could keep my place. But that doesn't make a lot of sense. I mean he will have to be watched for a while won't he? So he doesn't slip. And then he'll have to be starting back to work if they'll give him his job back."

"Oh they will. They're even paying him through all of this. And he's sworn to me that if he feels himself slipping he'll be off to AA in the blink of an eye. Of course that remains to be seen, but I've never felt such determination coming from him."

"Well the other thing that I'd be worried about is that he still loves you and as he gathers his strength he might be tempted to put the moves on. Sure I mean who could blame the guy."

"Well he won't. He's already talked to me about our relationship and he's insistent that we go ahead with it. He's had some sort of major transformation through that whole trauma, and he's determined to set things right for all of us. He's even said that we'd have to be thinking of divorce and annulment. He is a good man. But rightly so it will be rough leaving. The way I'll do that is to keep you and our love front and center. So let's go back to your place and do it again."

"Yeah. All night long. I want to get blissfully wrecked by you woman."

IT WAS ONLY A FEW DAYS later when things began to change. She had stayed longer at the hospital than usual because Noah had been so enthusiastic about several short stories he was writing. The youthful bloom had returned to his pale cheeks and his eyes had gone back to that palest of browns which were so prominent before all the anxiety, panic and drugs took root.

Because it was so late, she took a taxi to Conrad's apartment. Her need for him was greater now than it had ever been. Suddenly it struck her. God it couldn't happen this soon. That morning before she had left for the hospital and while she was in a phone discussion with an agent about doing some commissioned oil portraits, Conrad had phoned her. "I felt lonesome," he said. "I just wanted to hear your voice." Then he finished the call abruptly saying he had to rush off on an assignment. Now when she thought about it there had been a note of sadness in his voice. Oh god, she panicked as she ran up the creaky stairs to his orange door. When there was no reply she anxiously fished through her bag for the key he had once given her.

The note was on the table. She already knew the words. She didn't have to look at it. As she approached it passing his empty closet, she began to freeze. He was gone. He had already taken a flight to Seattle. As she wiped her eyes she read some. *You need more time. Not time on our part, because I'm convinced your love is as deep as mine. But time for Noah. Time without my being there in the city. I think that would only complicate things for all of us. Nora I know how painful this is for us. But as I told you, you are my life. I will call you every day until you know its right to come to me. Conrad*

Fear overwhelmed her as she curled up on his dilapidated sofa and for consolation tried to imagine that he was there making love to her once again. But instead thoughts of Noah and Gramercy Park kept interrupting. How in god's name am I ever going to get through this without Conrad here?

CONRAD DID CALL later that day, and they grieved over there separation. He had booked a room in a small bed-and-breakfast place and would start looking for their apartment the very next day. The following week he would begin working he figured on a free-lance basis because that would bring the most money and give him a wider scope of possibilities.

Two days later the doctors discharged Noah. Nora forced herself to exude a cheerful air, but she was frightened for both their sakes. As he had requested, she had ridded the apartment of all alcohol and stray pills.

"I'm going to try it without therapy. It's too expensive, and I've had enough mumbo jumbo. I'm not even going the AA route. Not for now anyway. I'm going to do it on my own. I am, you know."

"Well it would in the least be very hard."

"Sure it would be hard for anyone growing up at my age." And he laughed at himself.

They were finishing dinner at their apartment from groceries they had picked up along the way at Walter the butcher, Sutters, Balducci's—places that had been so familiar to them. Noah wondered how long it would be before he would be doing this on his own. He knew Nora was thinking much the same.

"You know Conrad has already gone."

"Is that his name?"

Nora nodded yes. "You never mentioned it before. But gone where?"

"To Seattle."

"What does this mean?"

"That's where we're going to live. He's a photographer, and there's a lot of work out there." God she thought I hope I'll not be after doing Noah in telling him this so soon. But he has to know.

"Wow, Seattle. But what are you doing here then?"

"He wanted to go out early to establish himself with work and an apartment," she said hoping to avoid the rest of the reason. When he paused shaking his head, she asked: "Why? You don't want me to be here?"

"Yes." He replied too eagerly. "I-I- do—want you--" And before he could stop himself his heart leapt. Oh god, how can I live without her? But then he was remembering what the professor had told him in his unconscious state about the price for his mistakes and the weight of sadness on his soul.

"Well I will be going. But you could use some help for a while and I'd need to be getting my stuff together. Sure there's no rush."

"No. No rush. You could stay--" And he was thinking of what Tim said about making the pitch. "for—forever." Oh shit I didn't say that did I? I so didn't want to.

"You know I can't, Noah." God he really did look so young and appealing once again.

"No of course not. And you shouldn't. We've settled that already. I've spoiled enough. All those times. They were a lot."

"Not *all* those times Noah. There were so many good ones. So many happy times."

"Yeah. There were. Beautiful really. But I have to pay. And even if I didn't, I couldn't bear seeing you hurt again. Oh I talk about how I'm going to manage now, and I am determined to. But I'm shaking inside."

"Well don't go torturing yourself over me. That won't help your cause."

"But I do. I probably always will.--Because I love you."

THE NIGHTS THAT FOLLOWED were strange. After they'd spent a lovely evening together, they slept apart as it had been when he had trashed their relationship. This time he insisted on the rollaway letting her have their bed. How could it be any other way. But a couple of hours later, even after battling through nightmare Dante flashes, he would begin drifting into dreams of Nora and awaken with a raging hard-on that quite passionately shifted his attitude. God how could he hold to all his repentant promises in this state?

But regardless he did, and within a week he had returned to *FCD* and *Connoisseur* and yet another test. The luncheons, the little evenings, the giddy galas, the booze flowing, the people whispering about him once again—all could have resulted in his succumbing to temptation. Now there was no Murphs, no Carole Dawson to lend guidance. So he had to depend on himself and amazingly one other person. Oliver Wilton had obviously threatened the bon ton with his *you-better-watch-out* attitude, most likely promising a good few with verbal decapitation if they so much as attempted to wound or make folly of his prized columnist/vice-president/publisher. For that Noah knew he must prove himself still worthy of such attention even though it meant a good bit of fakery on his part. He had come to discover that all the glitz and glamour of the world of the lavish had disintegrated. He had lost that voracious need on his torturous journey. Now his job meant survival. And he would survive.

AND SO HE DID. Nothing would deter him. No matter how crazy things got at the office, no matter the piano-booming neighbors, even the pain of Nora eventually leaving or the occasional urge for some kind of sedation, he would keep his pact. For above it all there was god. Since before he was married, he had never gone to Mass as much as he did now— every day if it were possible. It was his linchpin.

Each morning he'd awaken with such strong feelings of determination. He felt years younger. He was up early. Five-thirty, six oclock. Hours he never knew existed. Exercising. Following the beginning of the city's running craze, he did dozens of laps around Gramercy Park. Oh how good it felt to be running when he wasn't under the gun to do so. Afterwards he'd come home, open the bathroom window to let the cool air against his hot skin as he showered and shaved. It was a sort of stimulant encouraging his sense of well-being and the early development of a newly found freedom. Following that he'd lash into making an impressive breakfast for Nora and himself with an emphasis on the impressive. Then they'd race to morning Mass laughing together as they went. On weekends he'd head for the Gramercy Park Pastry Shop after his run. It was the croissant-brioche route to the heart that he had followed on sexy romantic weekends when they were first together there. He was finding that as was the case back then just doing this would bring about an aching hard-on, one that he would now have to lose. Unlike before he'd concentrate on thoughts of his writing while warming the pastries in the oven. The first Saturday of this Nora arrived in the kitchen in robe and slippers. "Oh lovely," she said. "I'm only mad for these things."

He grinned as he poured steaming coffee. "*Mad* is it you are?"

Then they both burst into hearty laughter. And for an instant, she forgot.

It wasn't easy for her. During this time, she received calls from a number of magazine editors including those at the lavish *Town and Country* wanting to do more features on her work and her lifestyle. Certainly she wanted to avoid fanning embers of disenchantment with this news. Nor did she want him to be forced to overhear any of the many positive discussions she had by phone with the Winsor de Caine staff over her contractual details and those possible commissioned portraits. Even after Noah went back to work and she returned to full-time painting, pain persisted. She could scarcely contain herself from fearing the day when she would have to pack all her paraphernalia and send it off to Seattle. Would she ever feel certain that he was contained enough to leave? As time passed she longed to be with Conrad, to have him surround her with his love. But then the guilt began to creep back. When she would go to Mass with Noah, she would come away feeling plagued. It was taking her captive. Even at night she would awaken from dreams haunted by the Gardiner Street nuns and their warnings of failure to atone. As the days passed, the more she felt she must disguise these disturbing feelings from Noah. The only lenience came with her calls to Conrad. Calls she would make when Noah wasn't there. Even though he was in such bright spirits over all the work he was doing and the cozy apartment he had rented for them, she was still riddled with fears that she might forever be haunted by the atonement she could never achieve.

THOUGH NOAH NEVER SAID ANYTHING, there were moments when he too was troubled by grave thoughts of reparation. Keep writing, he told himself as he poured through years old notebooks with jottings of short story ideas based on incidents he'd seen and conversations he'd heard. This then was in lieu of any further work on his society novel, for he certainly wasn't ready to face that just at the moment. So then his typewriter became his friend as never before.

Mason portfolio—short stories
September 1969

"I don't ever remember it this cold here," Norma said when Bill parked their deVille at a lookout perch on the Finger Lake hills. "Well, you didn't remember any such uncomfortable intrusions in those days," he grumped and pouted. That made all the more of his allergic swollen nose. It was going red raw from the constant tissue rubbing it was getting this day. Then as if to escape the impending gloom, Bill exited the car stuffing his now rheumatic hands into his Orvis duffle coat and walking through the brightness of the frosty spring morning to the look over. "I don't know why he's so somber today," Norma said shifting about in her seat. Their tall son Ray made no reply as he roused in the backseat from his nodding sleep adjusting his

frayed Phillips Exeter sweatshirt, the one his mother had cursed him for wearing up here. Nervously Norma fished through her alligator handbag then gave up as she opened the door to follow after Bill.

"I can't believe all of the wonder and hope and such great promise this place once held for us," he said as he took in the panorama of valley, lake and far across the way the campus.

"What's got you in this mood and on today of all days when we're trying to convince him that our alma mater is the place for him to come?"

"Should we?" he muttered and shrugged.

"Why are you talking like this? And after all you've become."

"And what have I become?" he asked with such disdain and then answered himself. "N-o-t-h-i-n-g!"

"Oh really. That's some joke. You're only one of the top partners at Toray Plastics with the highest salary going."

"And that's enough after all these years?" he snapped with a surprising rage as his voice rose.

"Well it certainly should be. I can't believe you're suddenly letting this fly for the first time. Why at home you're so silent and distant. When I've asked you time and again if everything's all right, you answer with that half smile of yours 'Oh sure.' And that's it."

"Okay! Well now you know it's not."

"And?" she demanded finally finding and pulling a cigarette from her handbag and hastily lighting it.

"Oh," he gasped. "I so want to be away from all that back there. A-w-a-y. Only away."

"Doing what for god sakes?" And she puffed away furiously.

"Oh I don't know," he said shaking his head but then suddenly exploded. "Something artistic. Anything that's worth something."

Norma yanked up the zipper of her L. L. Bean jacket as an icy breeze sliced them. Then already stamping out one she pulled still another cigarette from her bag and stuck it in her mouth. "I just can't believe you," she bellowed again then sucked on the fag making the worst of her hollow cheeks and shrunken lips.

"And I can't believe you." He fired back. "Standing up here on this high hill where we used to come all those many years ago to dream of what we'd become. You--the spark, the dynamite, the muse." And the smile that had momentarily crossed his face escaped leaving his jawline to droop once again.

"So!" she roared back.

"Well for starters you used to abhor smoking, lecturing everyone on campus who did, including myself. And I could see the wisdom of your words and also because I loved you I quite. And I've never taken another cigarette to this day. Look at us, will you! Money and nothing else!" And now his voice had increased to a bellow.

"Well aren't you just great," she pitched right back. "Goody two-shoes has nothing on you. For god sakes grow up!"

"You call this growing up? Courting mammon? I'd call it growing downward by the day," he roared with fury in his eyes. By now other cars had arrived at the lookout and those who had climbed out of their vehicles for the view began backing away from this domestic horror show.

Ray who had been patiently waiting for his parents suddenly burst from the car and roared louder than his father: "Will you two shut your fuckin' mouths and get back into this car. What do you think you're doing, trying out for a revival of Virginia Woolf?" And as he pushed his circular silver rimmed glasses back up his nose then brushed his hands through his thick curly hair, he went on to apologize to all the others who were scurrying back to their cars. He had never seen his parents like this before. All he had known since his days at Phillips-Exeter were the summers of constant silence that grew more maddening with the years. But now since he'd met a brilliant girl from a neighboring boarding school and she had become his girlfriend, parental hatred had taken him over.

Why did I let them drag me up here. No doubt I should have taken the fuckin' bus and made plans to meet Grace. God we were damn lucky to both be accepted at this university. I didn't need any glad-handing help from my parents and their ancient connections. Fuckin' grow up, Ray, he cursed to himself. Oh Grace, after we toured the campus we could have had a whole weekend here at a great motel. Jesus, I can't stop thinking of all those incredible moves we make in bed together.

"Now Ray when we get to the campus, let there be no doubt that you're going to be a science major," his mother firmly pronounced when they were back in the car and driving away from the lookout. His father behind the wheel only cringed.

"Well that's been decided," she continued demanding.

"And just by whom? Your psychic of the year." Then before she could answer, Ray bellowed. "You know something— let me out of this pissin' fuckin' car. I'll make my own way from now on." As he grabbed his knapsack and threw open the door, his father slammed on the brakes pitching the deVille into the ditch. With that Ray leapt out and fled to the road's edge where he thumbed a ride.

Noah would finish this story in just a few days, spend Sunday morning editing it. Retyping he would do at another time, so he could spend Sunday afternoon starting a new one. He was that enterprising again. His plan here was to finish a half-dozen. Maybe even a few more on this disintegrating family. Then he'd look them over and decide which he felt would be good enough to send to *The New Yorker* or *Esquire*.

"I'D LIKE TO GET TOGETHER WITH YOU," a very pleasant sounding young agent named Jerome Montgomery told Noah when he phoned him. "See some of the stuff you've done. Tim tells me you've written a novel as well."

"Several times," Noah laughed.

"Pick out what you consider the best version and bring it along. Have you ever been published in fiction?"

"Only once. In *The New Yorker*."

"Well that's pretty damn good. And I've gone ahead and checked out some of your *FCD* and *Connoisseur* material. You certainly have the flare." Already his upbeat enthusiasm was transferring to Noah. "Listen, come by tomorrow if you can. I'll be here all afternoon."

"Great. Will do. Certainly will do."

A BLUSTERY EARLY OCTOBER EVENING two days later as he headed home from work, he noticed a man younger than himself dressed in jeans, corduroy jacket and a mail-pouch type bag slung over his shoulder coming out of the subway at the Park Avenue and Twenty-Second Street exit and crossing to the east side of the avenue. There was something about him that stopped Noah. And when the man noticed him he stopped as well.

"Noah?"

"Yes. I—I think I know you. Conrad?"

"Yes. I thought it was you." There was a slight tremble in his voice, detectable even with the wind whipping round them.

"Oh my god. Well--" Noah was stunned and wordless.

"Yeah." Conrad struggled to pick up. "I just got in

from Seattle for a couple of days. I'm headed for the Gramercy Park Hotel."

"Well does Nora know?"

"No she doesn't. I was going to surprise her. I have to clear up some photo work I did here for Conde Nast. So--" And there was another awkward pause as the withered brown-once golden leaves that had blustered over from the Gramercy Park trees swept up giving them welcome cause to make busy brushing them away.

"Well I think she's home now." Noah finally said.

"Oh well—I'd better go and check in and—Well this is awkward." Conrad managed and Noah could see the poor guy was hurting like hell. "I'll go then--" And he started off down Park to Twenty-First Street.

"No wait." Noah said firmly as he went and stopped him. "Don't be frightened or upset about this, I'm glad to meet you." And he took his hand and gripped it firmly. "I'm truly thankful that she's found somebody who's good and loves her as much as I think you do. And will."

Noah could see a great relief as his face relaxed and his eyes brightened. "Of course I do love her. And I want you to know that I'll always be there for her."

"I think I can see that and thank god. Because she so needs that. And I mucked it." And a few seconds of silence passed. "Well enough said. I can only wish you the very best, and I sincerely mean that." And with that Noah gave both his arms a tight squeeze, turned and continued down Park toward

Twentieth.

"Wait!" Conrad yelled. And he rushed after him. "I want you to know that even in Seattle we'll always be there for you. If—if you need anything. And I know Nora will always be in contact. She'll always love you Noah. Always. And I can accept that. I wouldn't want it any other way. Because that is Nora. It's what she is."

"It's what she is," he nodded.

The two parted and Noah walked on and then around the park feeling as if his heart had been torn from him. *I fear oh Noah that the price may forever bear a great weight of sadness upon your soul.*

HE FORCED HIMSELF to brighten as he went up the steps to their apartment. Then he told Nora of the chance encounter and she was both shocked and frightened as he could see the color drain from her face.

"Look, don't go like that. It's a good thing. I think you should call him at the hotel now because he'll probably feel he has to wait until tomorrow when I've gone to work to call you. He doesn't want to hurt anybody. He's an innocent. And I think he's a nice guy Nora. I think it will work for you. For both of you. So call."

And she did, but she was trembling from the trepidation. They made plans to meet in the hotel dining room for dinner. His voice had calmed her some, and there was no denying her longing to see him. But she couldn't stay with him.

That was unthinkable with Noah just across the park.

"Well I'll be back in a couple of hours," she said as she prepared to leave.

"Don't think of me. Think of him. You have a right to this life Nora. You're so good."

After she was gone, Noah thought of how easy it would be to slip out to some of the Third Avenue bars. But instead he went over to one of his bookshelves and took down his tattered college copy of Dante's *Inferno*. Flipping through various passages, he shuddered remembering his own journey. That put the brakes on any bar thoughts for that night.

HE KNEW THE TIME WAS GROWING CLOSER. Most of her art supplies and paintings had disappeared along with a lot of her clothes. He could feel the tension building. "Maybe we should talk about it even if it does hurt," he said one evening. He was smiling at her, this young man with those pale brown spirited eyes. This was the man she had once married. She thought then it was as if he had been away for a long time and had come back.

"Yes, we should. I'm worried about you, Noah."

"Why am I acting strange?"

"No. You're not. That's what frightens me. You seem to have it all so much in control."

"Well I try to for both of us."

"Yes, but will you be able to manage that when I'm gone?" In the October twilight coming through the window she looked luminous. His head went light and his heart leapt.

"I'll have to you know."

She smiled at him and shook her head. "Will you sometime go to the cottage?"

"Oh yes. And if—well when the book sells if I make a little money on it, I'd like to go over for six months or so—whatever I can afford so I can finish the society book and start on another. I guess I've lived enough now to do that," he finished cynically.

"I'd say you have. But what will you do with the apartment and the furniture if you go to Ireland?"

"I think I'd probably like to keep it. The lease is still valid for nearly ten more years thanks to Carole's negotiations. So I'd sublet it furnished to some good tenants. Because I'll be back. And I kind of like the place. Some things don't die easily I guess. But I do think it stops there now."

"Oh, you do love all the grand things, Noah. And right enough, you should."

"No. *Loved*-- past tense is the word now. That's one good thing that came out of that horrible accident. A personality change that I do think will remain intact. All that stuff, that *fizzin'* richness as you would say was an obsession." He shook his head and frowned.

"Well hold on here. Don't be beating yourself up about that, Noah. Because then I should be doing the same. I'm not flawless. And you know that. I can see it and understand it now. I never knew until I met you how much I needed someone—and someone all to myself. I was half-mad that way, and I guess I still am. I disrupted your life being like that. That was wrong because you aren't like that."

And Conrad is, he thought but guarded himself from saying it.

"Well it's more normal than my obsession was. That's for sure."

"Oh Noah, I guess obsession is the defining word for us."

"Well we're working our way through it. And I do have to tell you how very much I want to help make it right for you in every way. One thing, we'll have to do is the divorce."

"I guess but let me do as much as I can on that because it's going to be too challenging for you in the midst of all this."

"Oh there'll be a lot of challenges. You can be sure. But I'll get along knowing I'm doing them for you. And you have to remember after that, we'll have to go through the annulment. It has to be, to set things right for you. To keep you in good true stead with the Church--and yourself."

"U-m-m—to set things right." How could they ever be quite right for any of us, she wondered in the silence.

"I mean I'll do anything. I'll say anything. I'll get witnesses even—Tim, Janet, Russell. They'll back us. The only thing I ask when it's all over is that we stay in touch. That will be the most important thing. The saving grace."

"You already know the answer to that."

"Yeah. I just wanted to hear it."

"I LOVE THIS MANUSCRIPT," Jerome Montgomery enthused when he called Noah. It was nine o'clock at night. "I just finished it, and I had to call you." He paused for a moment. "It's a brilliant novel. Gentle, poetic and real. So evocative of upstate. And it builds through such quiet intensity. In some ways it reminds me of the work of James Agee. And at other times Larry McMurtry. I think it's very important. And in my mind I can think of several top editors who would pretty much kill to get their hands on it."

"Can I call you right back. There's someone I must tell."

"Well sure anytime."

Noah hung up the phone, looked at Nora and his face was flushed. He felt as if his skin was ablaze.

"What is it, Noah?"

"If words could buy the universe, I guess I'd own it right now."

She slapped her hands over her mouth, and her eyes lit up. "He liked it? He liked it!"

Noah shook his head. "Uh-huh. No. Not right." He paused as he jumped in the air. "He *loved* it. And—more important, he said he knows several important editors who would kill to get their hands on it. So I doubt it will end up like the Doubleday fiasco."

"Oh god that's so great." And she sighed letting the relief pass over her.

"How about that? And after all this time."

"A-h-h." And she smiled.

Then he knew she was thinking his thought. What if this had happened years ago?

"NOAH, I'M GOING TO BE LEAVING TOMORROW," she said as they sat at the dining table having tea on another wind swept October twilight. The trees in the park were bare now exposing their black scrawny arms to the bleak sky.

"I thought so," he said as he slowly set his teacup into the old blue Wedgewood saucer that meant absolutely nothing now. Then he sat back in the chair thinking of her walking out the door and never, ever coming back. Tomorrow what was left of his heart would be gone. Tomorrow he would have to begin again.

"Yes," she went on toying with her teacup and not making eye contact. "I've cleared up everything with the gallery here. They know I'll be working with galleries out there, but I've worked it so I still have a solid contract with them here."

"Well, that's pretty fantastic."

"There's one thing I want to clear up though," she said as she got up and went into the bedroom. She returned immediately with a small pale blue cloth pouch.

"No," he said firmly. "No. I won't have it."

"But I don't deserve them anymore," she said as she sat

and emptied all the glittering contents into her now ring-less hand.

Then he put his hand over them and with his other hand under hers squeezed them together. "There from my soul to yours. You can't give them back."

He released her hand and the jewelry fell to the table. Then she took a hold of his still ringed hand with both of hers. And they were both silent for a while. Finally he spoke. "I suppose it's ridiculously redundant to say I wish things hadn't--" But he began to choke on the words.

"I know."

"Tragic. Really tragic," he managed.

Then much to Nora's surprise he started laughing.

"What are you laughing at?"

"Well nanny was right after all. Remember the first time she saw me she inspected me as if I were *The Creature From The Black Lagoon*? Well I did become exactly that."

"Oh ya bleedin' eejit ya."

As they roared laughing one more time, Noah marveled at the milky Irish rosiness that had returned to her tender cheeks. God he so wanted to kiss them. He would always remember her this way. In the silence that followed it was obvious that each was remembering something but decided not to speak it. It was Yeats' words that came to Noah's mind. And now he understood exactly what they meant. *Murmur, a little sadly, how love fled. And paced upon the mountains overhead. And hid his face among a crowd of stars.*

AFTER THAT they went to their separate beds. Nora's flight would be early, and there was no more to be said. But as it was when they were first lovers and often could read each other's thoughts, they were both sleepless rooting through the past. Nora was remembering their happy times from Aran to Queens to Yearnington to Gramercy Park. God it wasn't helping. Noah let his mind drift back to the long ago snowy weekend of passion they had spent in Boston. It seemed as if he could recall every detail.

When it became too much for her, when she began wondering desperately if someday they would all find forgiveness in their souls, Nora got up and in her pale blue nightshirt wandered around the apartment. Since they had left open the drapes of the wide living room windows the city lights cast an eerie glow faintly fading the place as if it were already in the past, as if she might be drifting through it in some distant dream. There were the rooms of love and bitterness, gentleness, lavishness, joyousness and drunkenness, heaven and hell. A crazy quilt pattern of life.

Suddenly she could hear his breathing bringing her back to the present. She knew then that his thoughts must have finally allowed him to drift to sleep. She stood beside his writing desk next to where he had kept the cot and she watched him. He was at ease. Sleeping so effortlessly now, just as it was when they were first together. He was coping and after having gone so far away. Incredible. Incredible that he was even alive.

But to be advancing like this. Dear god, she prayed nothing would impede it.

Then he stirred and stirred some more. Still she watched, watched until he was aware of her presence.

"I love you, Nora. I'll never love anyone else," he whispered into the room as sleepily he sat up.

She went over and sat on the edge of the rollaway. She put her head against his naked chest and they held each other savoring the exchange of their body heat. "Noah, I love you, too. And that's forever."

"I know."

There they held each other till dawn.

"LET ME GO to the airport with you."

"I wouldn't think that would be wise."

"Probably not. But I want to. I've taken the day off."

"All right."

The taxi seemed to be there in minutes. Too soon they were holding each other and kissing and trying to block the tears while all the time the word *cherish* consumed him. Then he was reminded of another time when she had first arrived here. Only things were different then.

When the flight was called, she reached up and smoothed his little errant tuft of hair as she had countless times over the years. Then she smiled at him and her deep blue eyes shown with her love. She turned and didn't look back. She went up the steps, long glistening auburn hair bouncing on her shoulders and was on the plane.

The door closed.

The plane pulled out.

It was gone.

HE TOOK A BUS back to the city. It would take
longer that way. Then he walked and walked in a trance. He
had no idea where. He just knew his feet were moving. His mind
had shut down the sounds of the city, and his vision was a blur.
By dusk and by pure miracle he snapped from his hypnotic spell
and realized Gramercy Park. As fatigued as he was he wanted
to go back to recapture whatever was left. Already the
apartment had surrendered to the hollow echo of the loss as if it
had been stripped. Noah walked about hearing his footsteps as
he looked for the remains. They were there. The fading smell of
her paints. The few framed photographs of the two of them on
the bookshelves. She most likely had left those purposely. But
then there were bits of her clothing and underwear that had at
some point been mixed in a bureau with his and never sorted
out. Never would be sorted out. There was a compass that he
had given her that time when they were in Boston so she
wouldn't get lost when he was away on assignment and so
worried about her. In the bathroom was a jar of Nivea cream she
always used after a day's work when her hands became so red
and dry from paint removal. It was there that he recaptured her
scent. Unlike any he had ever known, it was so delicate and
seemed faintly born of a few rarely perfumed wild flowers from

the west of Ireland—the vanilla-clove of the marsh orchid and the sweetness of the honeysuckle. That brought back the memory of his tongue touching her skin with the hint of salt from the Irish waters that seemed embedded and always fired him. Go to bed where you both used to sleep, curl up and let these thoughts cradle you, his mind seemed to take over and speak. They'll carry you through to tomorrow. But maybe that was her voice. Maybe she was still here.

EPILOGUE

NOVEMBER

And darkness prevailed.

During the early mornings, while he was exercising, while he was preparing breakfast, he would pretend Nora was still asleep. During free evenings and on the weekends, he would make certain he had enough short story material to carry him into his fictional world. If there was any question that he didn't, he would immerse himself in Wilton assignments or go to the movies, go to the theater, always go to Mass and of course talk to Nora in Seattle. He found he could stave off anything that way.

Then there was Tim who faithfully called as much as Nora. Sometimes they would go out to eat and he'd say something to the effect—I suppose it wouldn't do me any good to try to set you up. Noah would glower back. "With what?" And Tim would smile ruefully and say. "Yeah I guess you're right. *Veritas.* I'm beginning to see it that way myself now." "You're not serious," Noah would laugh. Then Tim would shake his head affirmatively and hold the frowning look until he burst into laughter. "Nah. I'm not serious."

But there were times when Noah was taken by surprise. Out of the blue something would happen that could send him plummeting if he didn't fight the battle. One such happening was a charity event at the Café Carlyle where Bobby Short and piano held court with all those Gershwin ballads that cut to the quick. At a number of the tables sat young couples holding hands and occasionally surreptitiously kissing. That would have been enough. But at the end of the evening, Short, who was always incorporating bits of musical history into his evenings, spoke of a song sung during the Depression by the street singer Arthur Tracy—*Street of Dreams*. That sent Noah's mind racing back to the evening he and Nora had taken his mother to The Rainbow Room where a vocalist's rendition had so saddened her. Now Short's moving evocation suddenly crystallized everything. *Gold, silver and gold, all you can hold is waiting in the moonbeams. Poor, no one is poor long as love is sure—* He left soon after that, crossed to Fifth Avenue and welcomed the sharp winter wind that blustered out of Central Park. But it didn't prevent Short's words from following him as he walked down the cobbled street along the park wall. *Dreams broken in two may be made like new on the street of dreams.*

IN SLEEP words began haunting his dreams and because they were only fragments in Italian he tossed about the bed streaming sweat as he searched for their meaning. After a week of this, his mind finally released more words until he realized a terza rima stanza. And then a voice was speaking them. It was the olden profound voice of the professor who had accompanied him through Dante's hell.

Nessum maggior dolore
Che recordarsi del tempo felice
Ne la meseria e cio sa l tuo dottore

It had to be that of the Dante. Then as he forced himself to awaken, the English translation came to him.

There is no greater sorrow
Than to remember happy times
When you're in misery.

"HELLO. PROFESSOR MARCHETTI PLEASE"

"My name is Hilda. Could you tell me who's calling him?" a weak, weathered voice asked.

"Yes, I'm Noah Mason calling from New York City. I was a student of his back in the Fifties, and I've been so very remiss not having called him sooner."

"Well I'm afraid you're a little late in correcting that remission Mr. Mason. You see Dr. Marchetti passed on a few months ago."

"Oh no. Had he been ill?"

"No. Not a day in his life as far as I knew of. You know

he got his doctorate in literature and philosophy some years ago. After that he retired, but he was always returning as a guest lecturer here. Oh he loved his students and they loved him. Started calling him Dr. Dante of recent times. He was always taking off to all sorts of destinations if he thought any of them were having troubles."

"Really?"

"Yes he was down your way to help one of them. Why he just got back and a night or two later he went to sleep one night and never woke up. I think it was in late August."

"In August?" And Noah held himself from gasping.

"Yes. So sad. He was such a fine caring man. Why he moved me up here to the Ithaca hills from my apartment in town. Gave me a room of my own so we could sort of look after each other. Now I find he had left me this whole place. Mr. Mason, few are so caring of others."

"Right. Few so caring." Dr. Dante. *Dear god grant him eternal peace.*

LATE IN THE MONTH just before Thanksgiving, he asked Oliver and the powers that be if he might take a week's leave to go to Donegal to see their cottage. They not only granted it because they were still so delighted with his work and his progress, they insisted on paying him and suggested he could do a major piece on picturesque Ireland for *Connoisseur* if he wanted to take an extra week. "People are interested in buying places in unique areas of Europe these days." So fine, it would give him even more time with his cottage.

And it was beautiful, just sitting out there on the rocky green promontory of the Gweedore River with the sea straight onwards—a little white cottage with nothing but the howling wind that swept round it. He felt the surge of excitement. His spirit groaned, and he could imagine the radiance of Nora's face had she been there to share it with him.

Mhathair and Hughie were both eagerly awaiting their visit—or as it turned out his visit. *Mhathair* still looked like a child with graying hair. "*Wahl, wahl, wahl,* it would be you at long last," she marveled rubbing her hands together and squinting through her glasses. Then she kissed him and expressed extreme delight, like a mother welcoming home a child after a long separation. "I thought you'd be coming, and then I thought you'd never be coming. And you with the house built." She clasped her hands again and stood back beside her house to look at him, letting wonder flood her face.

Behind her, puffing contentedly on his pipe, was her eldest son Hughie. "Welcome." He beamed. "But where is Nora?"

"Oh she had to stay behind. She had so much work."

They were sad about this. Truly sad.

"Ah well now, if it were to be so it would be," *Mhathair* said and Noah wondered if she might not be wise enough to suspect. Then she led them into her cozy warm kitchen that smelled of tea and fresh breads baking in the range. "*Sui isteach,*" she said and Noah remembered it as the invitation to sit. "You'll have the hunger on you now. You'll take the tea and the bit of bread and the cheese in your hand."

Afterwards he went down to his cottage, looking at it as if it might evaporate. Even though the floor was still bare cement, the place was cheery. Hughie had been able to arrange a little furniture, a gas-cylinder stove, a small fridge, a three-quarter bed, some hefty blankets. There was a fireplace, broad and loaded with turf. From the windows, he could see the little land for the gardens, the river, the sea, the breakers. He had made the connection at long last. This cohered to life and he cohered to it. It brought him back in contact with what he had lost and it almost completed the sheer circle of Eden.

He walked out of the house and down the land. His land. That felt good. Then he looked back up at the little white house.

Yes, we will build a cottage in Ireland
Beside the sea.
Fine and proud and whitewashed be.
And it will stand strong, this cottage beside the sea.
Strong to take all gales, this lee.
And stand it will till judgement's due.
Love's covenant that we both drew.

The pleasure of the first night's sleep in the Donegal air was beyond anything he had remembered. He didn't awaken until nearly ten the next morning. And there was this delicious sense of peace. The windows were curtain-less, and the sun along with a brisk caressing breeze streamed across his naked body as he arose. Oh this cottage was the right thing. Even if it had been just for that one night and this moment of awakening, it had been worth it.

He went about lighting the turf fire, then heated the water on the gas stove and washed himself. After that he made tea and had the bread *Mhathair* had given him. He took his time about dressing, first warming his bare skin in front of the fire, relishing every moment of it.

Within a few days a lovely lightness came over him. That, along with an acute awareness of the beauty of the place, one he could never have sensed completely in his drugging days, lent him greater assurance. Mid-afternoons, he would sit on the bank of the Gweedore below his house and watch the easy flow of the rainbow water as it wove around switchback bends to the sea. It teemed with fish even at this time of the year. All this beauty he'd someday be coming away to. His blood raced. Even with the shortening of days, there was scarcely any darkness in his spirit now. But he'd be fooling himself if he said there was no melancholy. And that had to be guarded closely because as it crept in it was less apparent, more dangerous.

No more dangerous than the afternoon he walked the lonely vastness of the velvety Carrickfinn strand, the one he could view from his land. It was where he and Nora had strolled struggling to keep hold of the dreams they had long before given birth to on Aran. And this he realized now had been their last chance grasp at happiness.

Purpling mist came tumbling off the capitulating waves of encroaching winter and he was certain it carried the whisper of Nora's voice. The unbearable loneliness of the moment was nothing but devastating and gave birth to a great fear. God what would he do to stop himself? For as much as he fought it he imagined her figure in the distance and his heart stopped. Were there angels of the sea that could bring her to him and usher in another fine day? No, they would have to be the dark angels and he'd already been there and wanted nothing to do with them. He turned his back on the strand and rushed up the bank and over a dune.

DECEMBER

And the parties were in abundance. So was the drinking. But still he managed and all the more so with phone calls and letters from Nora. It was wonderful to sense her happiness. She and Conrad were getting on so well, especially with, barring his headaches, the lessening of his war traumas. Both had great amounts of work befalling them already. Somehow this buoyed his daytime mood. Then at night in dreams she often came to him. At first she was there at her easel issuing reassuring words as she painted. But then something happened. On latter nights, they would fall into a passionate embrace and soon they were in the throes of lovemaking. Oh god what heaven. The blue of her eyes, the scent of her skin and her moans of ecstasy set his whole being aloft. His own gasps would finally awaken him to the realization of a fantastic wet dream. This was hardly repentance he would think and then worry of it the next day at Mass. But it was not long before a soothing comfort came over him. Maybe there was a greater force out there lifting a small amount of that weight of the sadness.

Over the holidays and on the verge of a new decade, he visited his mother in Yearington. It was yet another test.

"I did have it pretty rough all right," he said as they sat in the living room.

"Is it going to work out for you now?"

"Yes mama. I think it is."

"Well that's good." And she smiled a little. "And Nora?"

"Well--" he sighed and glanced away to where the window was, to where a severe storm had lessened to a soft fall of flurries that tumbled ever so gently brushing the pane as darkness grew round. There were memories here, but not of past Yearington days. No, the softness of the flurries stroking the window with just enough light to be seen were the flurries that fell across the windows of Boston on a fall night in what seemed centuries ago. Soft. But not cold. They fired his blood and sent him racing back.

"You don't have to say anything Noah. Unless it would help."

"Thanks, mama." He didn't need to tell her. She already

sensed the whole story. And he was grateful that she knew and that he didn't have to speak it. But her depression over the heartbreak was unbearable. It gave reason to the fact that for the first time in memory she hadn't decorated the house for the holidays.

"It doesn't go away."

"What?"

"Nothing goes away. You think sometime it might. With the passing of time maybe. But it doesn't you know. Not even with death." She had gone severe, and he worried that he had been the cause.

"It was an awful shock to me. You and Nora. It would have been worse for your father. He would have thought it was another family tragedy that had to be." Even her face was yellowing in the dimming.

"Please mama, don't. I'll be all right. I don't want you to go this way because of me."

"It's not just because of you, Noah. In recent days, this bitter winter has made me remember and face the truth." Now the look in her eyes wounded him deeply. It would not be long before he would stand grief-stricken in a darkened room before her casket.

"What is it mama?"

"I guess it's time you knew. I could never bring myself to tell you before. I'd even hidden it over from myself so many times. But you can't do that."

"Mama, only tell me if you want to. Don't hurt

yourself."

"No, I think it would be better this way. Better for both of us."

She sat silently as the darkness continued to encircle them. Only the dim light from atop one of his grandmother's hall tables kept the room from pitch. "When your father and I got married, I was pregnant," she finally said in a whisper that scarcely sounded like her. "No one knew, except him. At three months I didn't show anything. That's when we went off to New York. Well no sooner did we arrive than the stock market crashed. Disney had already gone back to California, and we were stuck with the little money we had, along with the few dollars your father got for being a relief projectionist at some movie theaters. Most of it went to pay the cost of the boarding house."

"Why wouldn't you come back here?"

"Your father was too proud. And I didn't want us to. I loved him for his dreams. I wanted to go to California myself. We kept thinking at first that things would get better, that he'd get more work and that we'd still be able to go. I guess we were waiting for the gravy train. But it never came. Things went wrong with my pregnancy, and I ended up in some dump of a hospital for a while. That bled us to death. Money—Oh god. Well I came out. But it wasn't for long. The next thing I knew I was in some dirty looking emergency room giving birth. She was a month premature. She was a beautiful baby. That took more money. We shouldn't have paid it. What could they do?

But we did. Your father wouldn't have it any other way. And still there was no work to speak of. Your father was getting more anxious—well I suppose the word was *crazy* by the day. It was sad to see him changing all through those times. To see the hope slip away without being able to do anything about it."

"Without doing anything about it," Noah edited her phrase to fit himself. "Mama, what happened?" he asked with resignation.

"Well then it really went wrong for us. She got a bad dose of the croup that winter. We tried to nurse her ourselves with the help of a visiting nurse's aide. We couldn't afford a doctor. By then we had little of nothing. Even the head of our boarding house was ready to dump us in the street. Then after ten months of holding on fighting one bronchial bug after the other—she got pneumonia and died." She was silent again as was Noah. Finally in the faintest of whispers she spoke. "Just-- like that."

"Just like that," he repeated and shivered.

Both sat in the silence watching the flurries brush the window. After a while, when she could, she began again. "Didn't even have a picture of her. Couldn't afford a camera. We named her---Margaret. This is the first time I've said her name to another, since we stood by her grave in Queens that day. She was an angel."

"My god, mama." Now he knew why she cried that day they passed by the Queens cemetery in a taxi. And he thought of how people kept people's names hidden, like Tim's Diane and

Carole's son Peter. Names that at times in some small or big way kept breaking your heart. He thought of Murphs now and how he had already tried to bury her name below his thoughts. God he could never tell his mother of her, of how she was in a sense her step daughter. That would devastate her. That would forever remain his secret.

"Your father couldn't live with himself after that," she started again. "Well I was just as bad. We both loved her so much. But he kept saying it was his failed dreams that did it. Worse I kept going in and out of hospitals with bad bouts of bronchitis that following winter. Finally when everything was gone, we crawled back here in 1932 and lived between my folks and his mother's sister in humiliation until the movie house paid him enough to get us a loan for this place. At first it was such a relief that we thought of it as a blessing and I got pregnant again and that's when you were born. Oh the pride and joy we felt," she sighed. "But little by little, memories of those old days and their left-over dreams came wandering back to us in this dreary town, and as time passed your father took more and more to the booze. That's when we began drifting apart--until we were never together again. Well you must have sensed it. We lived apart in this same house."

Noah laughed solemnly to himself. Then they sat in silence for a long time. And through it all, he could feel the brush of snow in the darkness. No longer did it kindle his blood. Instead it stilled his spirit and weighed on his soul. Then his mother's hand was on his shoulder, and she kissed him on the head. "Now you know," she whispered before she climbed the stairs to her room, stairs she'd helped his disenchanted father climb so many times in his drunken stupors.

Noah wondered if his mother had any sherry or maybe a drop of whisky to ward off the gloom. He went out to the kitchen, turned on the light and started to open the cabinet. But before he looked in, he closed it again. Go face it, he told himself. It was late. Very late. And Noah went out onto the veranda to watch the snow as it slipped past the street lamp of his youth. Then he went out into the depth on the silent lawn where he could see errant storm clouds let brief flashes of moon escape. There he let the flurries brush over him, brush away at his face until the tears froze. *Gold, silver and gold, all you can hold is waiting in the moonbeams.*

JANUARY

And it was snowing in Queens the day he found Margaret Mason's crumbling mound of a tiny gravestone. The lettering was scarcely there, just as her life had been. But Noah could feel life as his fingers stroked the faint remains. There was a definite prickling. Then he knelt down to place a kiss and a bouquet of dusty mauve roses in front of it. That same day he ordered a fine pale mauve marker to be engraved with the words of the original stone. *March 11, 1930—December 30, 1930.* Then he added: *To my angel—from your brother Noah.*

A few days later he spoke with the Wilton personnel department and got the names and phone numbers of the relatives of Murph's foster mother in the Cleveland area where the casket had been shipped. At least at some point he could go there with flowers as he did for Margaret.

"Couldn't afford a proper burial for her in a cemetery here," the man who said he was Murph's step-uncle though he had never even met her told Noah on the phone.

"Well what did you do?" Noah asked.

"Kinda had to get her c-r-e-e-mated. It was a lot cheaper that way." When words failed Noah, the man went on. "Sold the casket. Got some money out of that ta pay the bill--Well we had to get rid of her somehow. But we took the ashes out to Lake Erie on a sunny day and threw em in. Said some prayers, we did. Oh we're god fearin' people out here alright."

"God fearin' people out here alright," Noah muttered after he hung up the phone. He walked over to the window and looked out at the snowy park in moonlight. "Lake Erie! What an ending." God if I'd known I could at least have brought the ashes back here and taken them up to Bloomingdale's on a windy night. "God! *If, if, if!* If I'd only done something to begin with she might still be here." He shook his head. "And I'm accusing those people of wrongdoing."

On a mid-month Wednesday, an upturn did come. The phone rang about 10 p.m., just after he'd returned from covering what had now become another boring social event. It was Jerome Montgomery. "I hesitate in bothering you at such a late hour. But I think you'll forgive me. I just got the call. Atheneum is buying *Pictures In The Rain*."

Noah sat down on the edge of his wing chair.

"Noah? Hello? Noah, can you hear me?"

"Yes. Yes, I can. I'm just a little breathless."

Jerome Montgomery laughed. "Enjoy the feeling. I sure am. It's great discovering new talent. And get ready for more. They really loved it, Noah. And it went through several editors along with the company chief Simon Bessie. We're still working out the advance. But it looks like it's going to be very healthy. Especially for a first novel. And I'm pretty sure there'll be no more *mishaps* this time."

"I think I feel like I might be going to laugh. And I don't know why."

"Well go ahead and enjoy it. You certainly earned it."

After Noah hung up he did laugh until the tears came.

That evening he called Nora in Seattle.

"We sold it, Nora."

"I knew it. I knew it." She was jubilant. "And you know something, Noah. This is only the beginning."

"Yes, I think you're right. I think I'll get there this time. It's a nice beginning for a new decade."

"Yes, it really is a new decade for you. I can hear and feel how happy you are. And that is so good."

"And you?"

"Things are grand, Noah. Truly beautiful now."

"That makes me happier than even this. We'll talk soon."

"Yes. And very soon."

Afterwards as he prepared for bed he thought yes and I'll see you sooner than that. Then he smiled. "Well I can't help my dreams can I?"

FEBRUARY

And the days were happy as he thought of his novel being published. This had given him the courage he needed to move to Ireland, and as he slaved away at Wilton he was saving as he had never saved.

He thought several times of telling his mother his plans. But given she had faded so in spirit, he hadn't the heart. Even the news of his novel, which she took with great pride, hadn't lifted her from her slump. Often he wondered if the thought of her drifting downwards would stop him from going even though the plan was for only six months at the most. So he decided he would go to see her, spend a little time and decide then. But as it was the situation would never have to be faced. During the early morning hours of February 15, Esther Mason died in her sleep of a heart attack. A brother-in-law found her after she hadn't responded to phone calls.

She had left a note written some weeks before stating she knew her health was failing rapidly and that she wanted

Noah to look after himself. *Once my funeral expenses are paid, take whatever money's left that you get out of this house and put it toward helping you get what you want in this world. That's something your father and I never did.*

The night after the funeral, he lay in his bed listening to the shrill train whistle cut down through the forest and across the valley. Over the years what that sound must have meant to his parents as they thought of all the trains roaring westward without them. The whistle—a constant remembrance of their botched dreams and the tragedy of their mistakes.

Finally he got up and paced the moon-washed rooms, lost in his thoughts. As he grew more anxious, he became less aware of his moves. Rummaging through the past, he plundered the medicine cabinet. Accidentally or maybe not, his hand slipped sending containers of pills cascading into the sink, making him aware. In his hand he held a container of his mother's Valium. He looked at it for a second, opened it, saw the blue pills. They were the strong ones, he thought. 10mgs. Generic—diazepam. Blue—the color of Nora's eyes. He turned, quickly dumped them down the toilet. Nora. She was saving him even now.

He made two more visits to Yearnington that month, ridding the house of its belongings. On one visit he went down to the Ritz—the movie house that was his childhood. In the wash of moonlight cast over the now desolate Main Street, it was apparitional. The Ritz—where his father had spent most of his life. Noah could still see him there in the booth like a butterfly in a jar with holes punched in the top to let in just enough air. His only freedom had been in the glass window that overlooked a silver screen of ever changing images.

MARCH

And the real estate agent sold the house on a cash-no-mortgage deal. Several weeks later at the end of the month, Noah went up for the closing. An exuberant young couple from Buffalo with a hefty baby boy had purchased it as a second house. The emphasis was on happy here, and what a difference that would make to the place.

The day before he left Yearington, he went to the woods behind the house. It was filled with memories of winter storms and spring thaws and the times when he would act out scenes with the real film actors his imagination conjured to life. He didn't go very far, just to one of the small waterfalls. He couldn't see it in the morning mist. But he could hear its rush. There were words in it. Words whispered that he couldn't make out. He leaned against the trunk of an ancient oak tree and listened for a very long time. Finally he understood them. They had been spoken here before, and they had never disappeared. *"I love being alone in the world with you."*

APRIL

And yet another test.

"Don't worry," he said gently when he detected the anxiety in her voice. "It's just a piece of paper. It won't change our feelings. We care too much to hurt one another."

But of course in reality it was a different matter. He never knew what pain there could be in putting his signature to a piece of paper. Now the marriage was truly over. Fortunately an upward move came the next day when Jerome Montgomery called to say Atheneum had agreed on a ten-thousand dollar advance. He went on to say that he loved the batch of short stories he had sent him and that he wanted to market them through the likes of *Esquire* and *The New Yorker*.

A few days later he thought of speeding the process of moving to Ireland, of even finding a used car dealer near Shannon. Ablaze with new fiction ideas, he thought of broaching the subject with Oliver but then hesitated. It would certainly be a major disappointment to him. And even with the thrill of writing day in, day out in Ireland with no interruptions, he held back on his decision. His temporary visa still hadn't arrived and even with his salary increase and new advance money, he wanted to be certain everything was in line so nothing would impede him. Not that he wanted the lavish still he did want to give his heart and soul to writing.

But it was then that the weirdest thing happened. One day at Wilton in the middle of a *Connoisseur* conference, he was called to the phone.

"Noah Mason. This is Kevin Doherty from Doherty, Feinstein and Marshall."

Oh shit, probably still owe some interest money to that fizzin' furniture shop or at the least they're scheming to rob me of more. "I'm sorry if I owe anything, I thought it was all paid up. But I'll take care of it right away."

"Oh we're not calling about anything like that, Mr. Mason," said Kevin Doherty. "What we're really about is Carole Dawson's will. We need you to come into our office as soon as possible so we can discuss details. We're at Fifty-ninth and Park. Could you possibly come in tomorrow around eleven?"

Well of course he could. But oh my god, if what he thought they were going to say even vaguely came true he didn't want to hear it. What once he would have taken as a providential bolt of lightning for the advancement of his career, now would produce a never healing wound. It was all coming true like the worst kind of horror story. This was the greatest test of all.

FIVE HUNDRED THOUSAND DOLLARS a year with a strong cautionary clause that he live away from the madness of the social world. Well it had already corrupted and destroyed without the five hundred thousand. So the two lawyers didn't have to drone on enhancing the wound.

"Are you all right, Mr. Mason?" one of them asked. "Oh yes," he snapped out of it. "Well as we're saying that's only for the first year. There'll be equal amounts coming for five more. Of course we really have no way of controlling the way you live. But I think Carole was right in that she knew she could trust you."

"Well she was right. I don't want this money for myself, other than the barest minimum so that I can continue my work."

"Oh but there's more here than I think you could ever have imagined. There's a codicil to this will."

"What?" he puzzled.

"Well—it looks as if you've inherited *Quintessence*, the Dawson Newport estate."

"What?!" He was instantly stunned as if he had been desensitized by a bolt of lightning. "

"Are you all right?"

"I think I'd better leave," he answered shakily.

"But you've gone all pale. Why I expected you to be joyous. Jumping around this office like Jett Rink when his oil well came in in *Giant*."

Noah's faint chuckle was accompanied by a distant smile. "It came in. A *l-o-n-g* time ago."

Still not understanding one of the lawyers went on to encourage: "Why the place is in superb condition we've been assured. Carole kept everything that way. And there's money set aside here to pay her staff and the upkeep for years to come.

So you won't even have to worry about that."

"Can I ask you one question?" Noah finally said when some of his strength returned. "When was this will written?"

"The original will was written in December 1967. But the codicil was added in May of 1968 when Carole demanded John sign *Quintessence* over to her in return for her silence about his transgressions."

"Oh my god, I don't even know how to begin to deal with all of this." Then instantly the thought came to him. I'd have given my soul for that place once. Now I'd give it away in a heartbeat for the return of my soul.

"She had a superb financial advisor," one of the lawyers told him. "Honest and true blue. She made certain of that. He wouldn't steal a penny from a baby. And that's a rarity today. She strongly advises in her will that you meet with him. Especially with the inheritance and estate taxes and the insurance upkeep on the artwork millions you'll be faced with. Although she's left considerable amounts aside toward those as well."

Noah still stunned went to visit him a few days later. Otto a rather elderly man had a very wrinkled forehead that sharply contrasted with silver eyes as bright as stars and he resided in this tiny frugal office in one of upper Fifth Avenues landmark preserved Italian Renaissance buildings. "When I'm gone, give him a chance, Carole told me. It was rather bizarre in that this was just a few days before that horrible car crash. She went on to say that you'd been through a lot. But never give up on him, she insisted." Noah liked this man because he reminded him of his Ithaca professor now doctor. He was telling him what he should hear—stories of how inheritances can often spawn more evil than they're worth and how easily they can slip into the hands of the scoundrels of this earth.

"Oh I agree," insisted Noah. "And now I guess I've got more to worry about than I ever thought possible. I planned to take a fairly lengthy leave of absence so I could go off to my cottage in Ireland and write my heart out. But I guess this changes everything."

"Well it shouldn't and certainly Carole wouldn't want you to let it. You know Doherty, Feinstein and Marshall is one of the best and I must say honorable firms in the country to deal with such matters. I can work with them, and we'll very carefully and cautiously deal with matters as they come along. Certainly with your approval. You will be reachable over there won't you?"

Noah laughed. "Well—I guess I will be now. I suppose what concerns me the most is *Quintessence.*"

"Oh we're not going to start thinking about that today. It will be well looked after. The legal guys will make certain of that. And if and when you decide to sell it, it will be done in the right way. I know that's what Carole would have wanted, and all of us had the greatest respect for her. We'll do her proud on all fronts, including those many charities."

"Well that's what she would have wanted more than anything."

"*AH* SUPPOSE *AH* KNEW this day was coming. In previous times—not so long ago—*ah* would have been vindictive as hell. But you know as sad as *ah* am *ah* can only feel happy for you now, Noah. But *ah* must say though *awha* publications will survive, they'll never be as good as when you were a part of them."

"Oh you never know. There could be another me around somewhere. But I haven't said a permanent goodbye. I said six months."

With that Oliver smiled with delight as they went ahead and ordered lunch at the Yale Club. You know *ah* am wild with envy. *Ah* so wanted to be what you're becoming."

"Well Oliver, you could always --"

"No! *Ah* could not. Never ever could *ah* become as fine a writer as you. Probably not if *ah'd* set that course years ago. Though *ah* do harbor regrets. And *ah* also harbor them over the personal loss of you. *Youah* one of the very few closest people *ah* know."

"Oh come now, you do have a son."

"Do *ah*? *Ah* wouldn't think so, not anymore as *ah* told you. His bitterness is set in stone. So Noah, *ah* do so wish you would stay in touch. And---you know what *ah'm* going to say. Whenever, if ever as long as *ah'm* here--"

"I know Oliver."

WITHIN A FEW DAYS OF ALL THIS, he met a serious young couple who stopped him of a misty late April morning at the gate entrance to Gramercy Park. Both were doctors who wondered of the possibility of living in the area and gaining entrance. Oh my god, they seemed so much in love— and they were kind and they were gentle. This was his answer to sublet furnished and leave.

Whenever he wasn't working he sorted through belongings, setting the things of his and Nora's aside that he would take with him, and putting the rest into a single closet that he would lock away to remain behind. One day as he went along, he discovered a painting of Nora's behind one of his extravagant chiffoniers. He pulled it out and was stunned. It was his portrait. God, did I really look like that once? He walked into the bathroom and looked into the mirror. Well whatever you do you won't get that back again, he thought. She really did love you. *Loved the pilgrim soul in you*, Nora's voice whispered through the apartment. She had left it there as that reminder.

"OH I GUESS WE'RE DOING PRETTY WELL right now. Considering. She's out of therapy and she seems to have gathered a lot of strength," Russell told Noah that warm day just at the end of April as they lunched at Lutece. He had come to New York to check out some discoveries his casting director had made. "So I guess she's all right." Although his dark eyes struggled to spark some hope, his coal black hair was already flecked with white and his lanky but stalwart frame had hunched.

"Are you sure?" Noah asked.

"Yes. Well I do miss her. And of course the children." Then he shook his head. "When I was young, when we were first married just before Ithaca, I thought having her and then to have our children was going to be the best of everything. Oh god, you don't know."

"Yes, I think I do."

"But I wanted success so badly, after it started happening in those productions at the end of the Ithaca years. Especially when those producers came up from New York."

"Well you have it now. Do you think when your movie comes out next month it's really going to be up for an Oscar, cause that's what they're promising in the press here."

"Oh you never know. But it would be almost heaven if it did. Almost--"

"And that would be enough?"

"Who knows?" he shrugged. "But now I can't live without this business." Then he sighed, took a few deep swallows of his white wine. "So I guess that's it. Signed, sealed and delivered."

MAY

And the warm days of new beginnings rushed. Though still spring, summer was already on the park. Flowers in full bloom, tree buds bursting, robins and jays conversing.

Tomorrow he would leave. Would it be a beginning? He hoped he had the sense to use it wisely.

"I think you will. I never stop praying for that."

"I know. I feel that."

"What of the book if you're over there?"

"Oh we've already gone through most of the editing. They'll send me the page proofs. That'll be that. I hope."

"Well listen, Noah. Take it easy. I know how sometimes you don't"

"Oh I've been there. But I guess I still need to remember that all right."

"I'll be thinking of you all day tomorrow."

"Just tomorrow?"

"No. Every day. Always. Sure you already know."

THE NEXT MORNING, he went to the Emigrant Savings Bank headquarters on East Forty-Second Street opened accounts and transferred the monies from his advance along with his accrued salaries from Wilton. Then he arranged for them to accept all the payments from Carole Dawson's estate into a savings. After that, he went to the Fifth Avenue headquarters of First National City where he transferred all the remaining money accrued from Nora's paintings into her private savings account. After that he closed their joint account. The reason for this was to enable him to make frequent deposits into her account that she would be unable to return to him. And since he owed her his life, this was one of the most important moves he would ever make.

HE WAS ALL PACKED so he had plenty of time, and he decided to walk on from the bank to the Metropolitan. Monet revisited. *La Debacle.* He stood and studied it for a long time. Yes it was there in the severity of the winter's end what he had seen the first time with Nora. There shimmering through the frost were the first pale hints of spring. The victor.

SHORTLY BEFORE HE BOARDED the plane that night, Tim called out breathlessly. "Hey pal, I thought I'd never make it. The traffic was a bitch."

"God, I didn't expect you to be here."

"What miss this big happening?"

"Sure hope it is."

"Only be optimistic, pal. Just think, next year at this time you'll be famous. Atheneum-Knopf no less. And you'll be backing that up with new manuscripts. A veritable legend in your own time."

"Oh *yeah*, sure." And he burst into laughter. "But you, you'll he owning the agency by then."

"Maybe so," he chuckled. But then for an instant he went sober. "Maybe so" he nodded, then tossed off the thought. "Well it's something anyway."

"Something! Yeah. But why are you so pensive?"

"Oh--the road I never took-- Gloomy I guess. I've just been off the merry-go-round for a while. Seemed so little there. But I'll get back on it again. On target with the times. If this nervous market ever settles down and my stocks bounce back, that is." He shrugged his shoulders and laughed it off. "But you through all this are following what you are, not just chasing after another marketing statistic and satisfying the animal urges that complement it."

"You know all those times I was trying to convince you there was someone else out there for you. Now I see. We really are of a kind. One-timers. Love comes in—it's instantaneous, passionate beyond the beyonds and soul binding. There is no second time around."

"Nope. Right on, buddy." And he grinned.

The flight was called.

"Look Noah, how am I going to stay in touch?" In all the years he had known him, he could never remember a time that he had called him Noah. It was always pal or buddy. "Do they have phones in such remote areas? It's going to be up to you, you know."

"Oh you know I'll find a way. Not just for you."

"Oh yeah. Not just for me. God buddy, how you could be so damned honorable."

"It's not just valour, you know. Well, it is and it isn't."

"I know. I know." And there was a silence between them. Then there was the old quick colligate bear hug. "Hey I better get out of here before you miss your flight. Good luck, pal. I'll see you here next year for your glorious return." And he started to leave.

"But wait. Don't go so fast. I never did the reiteration I wanted to. You remember I told you in St. Vincent's how you'd been down there with me. Well, you helped drag me out. So I owe you more than you'll ever know."

"Not so. You took care of that long ago."

Noah was puzzled. "What?"

"You remember that rainy night on the street in Ithaca beside that flooded Cascadilla Creek? I wouldn't be here now. No way—if it hadn't been for you."

And before Noah could come to his senses, he was gone.

THEN HE WAS on the plane. Alone in a row of empty seats. He closed his eyes and kept them closed as the plane began to move out and up for takeoff. When it did, he shifted over to the window seat and watched the lights streaming on across the maze of streets that spread for miles and then became the more perfect streets of the suburbs and the countryside. All were laden with dreams. And that was good if you could reign them in and keep that control. Where should he have done this—on the cliffs of Aran gazing into the deepest blue he would ever know, or that time in his Queens apartment when they first exploded in incredible orgasm together or the night in Boston when all the loveliness of the world was theirs and they were adrift among the heavens? Well any man who wasn't a fool would have stopped there, gone into a holding pattern and let life take care of itself. But he didn't, he sped onwards, trying to fast track it to where?

And what was left? Money. That meant nothing to him now. Oh it would offer him a reprieve of sorts as he doled it to people and places really needing it. Success maybe. But that was only important if it produced something of value. No, he had faith and little else.

Oh there were the words of course. Yes there were the words. Lovely words from Nora on a continuing basis. Words that seemed to fall from heaven and touch his heart with her grace. And then there were his words. They were really all he had left. Hold on tight. They'll have to carry you.

He was so tired he skipped the tray of food, curled up on the three seats and fell deeply asleep. And he and Nora were on Kilmurvey Strand on Aran strolling hand in hand along the rolling seascape making plans, and they were young and joyous once again. He could hear the words of all their tomorrows. Words. Write the words. Get them down. If you get them down, they'll be forever set. The reality will return. But he was struggling and the struggle was awakening him and he was vaguely aware of whispering in the dark. *"Dear god, forgive them, care for them. They aren't the transgressors, I am. I put us where we are. Oh god, forgive, forgive."* Then he felt himself shaken. "Sir, are you all right?" "Oh!" he jumped up. "You were talking so loudly in your sleep." "I'm sorry. I'm so sorry," he said realizing where he was. When he settled back down, it was as if he were traveling to a distant planet. Away from all that had been. Then he reached over to the nighttime window shade the stewardess must have lowered as he slept. He lifted it and was startled. The sky was ablaze with streaking red rays. Nearly blinded he looked back into the plane and as his sight began to return it brought him a vision of Nora smiling as she sat in the seat beside him. It was so incredibly real that he reached over to touch her hand. But then the light dimmed and by degrees the image faded away. When he looked back out the window, dark clouds had rushed the sun erasing its prospects. And he was alone again. Alone except for the heavy sound of that voice. *I fear O Noah that the great weight of sadness will forever be with you growing stronger by the day no matter how much atonement you force yourself to endure.*

www.ingramcontent.com/pod-product-compliance
Lightning Source LLC
Chambersburg PA
CBHW070621260626
47161CB00007B/2526